Underground ENGLAND

TRAVELS BENEATH OUR CITIES AND COUNTRYSIDE

STEPHEN SMITH

Little, Brown

LITTLE, BROWN

First published in Great Britain in 2009 by Little, Brown

A CIP catalogue record for this book
is available from the British Library.

ISBN 978-1-4087-0056-3

Typeset in Sabon by M Rules
Printed and bound in Great Britain by
Clays Ltd, St Ives plc

Papers used by Little, Brown are natural, renewable and
recyclable products sourced from well-managed forests and certified in
accordance with the rules of the Forest Stewardship Council.

Mixed Sources
Product group from well-managed
forests and other controlled sources
www.fsc.org   Cert no. SGS-COC-004081
© 1996 Forest Stewardship Council
FSC

Little, Brown
An imprint of
Little, Brown Book Group
100 Victoria Embankment
London EC4Y 0DY

An Hachette UK Company
www.hachette.co.uk

www.littlebrown.co.uk

Underground ENGLAND

TRAVELS BENEATH OUR CITIES AND COUNTRYSIDE

To June and George Sutton

CONTENTS

ACKNOWLEDGEMENTS

With many thanks to Kirsteen Astor, Gerda Barlow, Peter Barron, Richard Beswick, Dr Ian Cubbin, Lesley Delves, English Heritage, Penny Gallon, Harvington Hall, Siobhan Hughes, Adrien Joly, Meirion Jones, Cat Ledger, Matt Leiper, Mike Levett, Malling Abbey, Zaiba Malik, Natasha Mardikar, West Mercia Police, Robbie Morgan, Sue Phillpott, Megan Price, Stephen Rankin, Dr Keith Ray, Vivien Redman, Paul Smith (Nottingham), Roger Smith, John Taylor and Mark Weir, Phil Thirkell, Friends of the Williamson Tunnels. In memory of Scott Smedley.

'I believe there never was a boy yet who saw a hole in the ground, or a cave in a hill, or much more an underground passage, but longed incontinently to be into it and discover whither it led.'

J. Meade Falkner, *Moonfleet*

FOREWORD

ET IN SUBTERRANEA EGO

There is another country, a hidden England, a happy valley. Those who sigh for a prelapsarian Albion would be astonished – not to say restored – by the idyllic delights that go unnoticed under our very noses. There are secret swathes of this land untouched by modernity, with crystal streams, and groves of stalagmites to rival any stand of oak. Here the pipistrelle, rather than the curlew, tolls the knell of parting day. I can lead you to caves as decorated as the finest church, like the troglodyte transepts explored by Axel and the Professor in Jules Verne's *Journey to the Centre of the Earth*: 'A succession of arches appeared before us like the aisles of a Gothic cathedral; here the architects of the Middle Ages might have studied all the forms of that religious architecture which developed from the pointed arch.' We can enter hallowed hillsides, bestride storied hummocks, that preserve the slumbers of Englishmen as old as antiquity. There are secret passages in the grounds of convents that are almost unchanged since nuns flitted through them to illicit medieval assignations – or so the story goes. In steepling piles near the Welsh Marches, where recusant families sheltered priests from the agents of Queen Bess, you can almost smell the commingled incense and fear. There are English cities under water, drowned towns, which could be the models for the lost Arthurian citadel of Lyonesse.

If this all seems a little rose-tinted, even reactionary, for your taste, have no fear. The secret shires are a marvellously mutable backdrop to England-as-she-should-be, whether your reveries are nostalgic or your fancy is for something more republican, even revolutionary. It is down in the underground that we uncover the compromising secrets of royalty, as well as the subterranean Sandringhams, the bunkered Balmorals, where the Windsors and the rest of the Establishment would have sat out a nuclear blast in splendid insulation.

Under the soot-streaked streets of one of our great northern entrepôts we may roam the spellbinding labyrinth built for the private delectation of a reclusive nineteenth-century millionaire. Are you weary of shopping, our national sport? Well then, perhaps you'd like the distraction of an upmarket menswear boutique in a Midlands city where a secret door leads to a deep and sinuous cave? Is there a soul so dull that it doesn't thrill to the thought of the tunnels hewn from the living chalk of Buckinghamshire, where a select few of the English ruling class indulged in dark and decadent rites two hundred and fifty years ago? You may walk these sulphurous passages to this day: every Eden contains within it the seed of corruption, even our subterranean one.

Like any enchanted kingdom, any perfumed walled garden, this other England is retiring, strangely diffident, a reward for the patient and the diligent. But though it may hide from us in plain view, it offers many a clue as to its identity and whereabouts. In the blood-warm waters that have risen immemorially from below the West Country, I glimpse through a skein of steam a lion – a lion and yes, a unicorn. Looked at one way, these magnificent beasts are merely figures in relief on the honeyed stone of the municipal architecture of Bath, visible from the rooftop spa pool where I lie like a torpid croc. But they are nothing if not heraldic, and what they herald is surely the semi-mythical land of which I speak. 'I lay back on the warm marble, breathing in the vapour. I thought of Emperor Justinian's vast, underground cistern in Old Stamboul,' writes Alexia Brue in *Cathedrals of the Flesh*, her soapy tour of the bathhouses of the world.

Ah yes: Old Stamboul . . . Part of the allure of these baths, for me and I'm sure for others, is that here we're recreating an ancient recreation – the Romans did this, the first invaders of England. The subterranean spring is the river of time, in flux between the present and the not so distant past; in turn, this tub is an infinity pool. I wear a bracelet, and this admits me to any part of the multi-storey grot of Thermae Spa, from the sauna to the plunge-pools underground. Any incidental expenses that I might incur – a mineral water at the wet bar, an extra towelling robe – are swiped and registered on this bangle. I can run up a tab on my tag; my wrist is good for it. Depending on your point of view, this gewgaw is either a status symbol or yet another marker of our surveillance culture. For myself, I prefer to think of it as a charm, an 'Open Sesame!' device, part of the charismatic trinketry of an ageless England.

I feel the same way about Doug Bower's plank. To the naked eye, this is no more than a length of four-by-two, showing some signs of foxing, to be sure, and bandaged here and there with gaffer tape, but otherwise sound – remarkably sound, in fact, for all the miles it has clocked up. And yet Doug and his lumber-yard cast-off made headlines around the world, eliciting wonder about an uncanny phenomenon descending from another world – or perhaps springing up from underneath this one. In 2008 the government declassified its files on UFOs, which revealed that the MoD's Little Green Men unit went to Middle Wallop, Hampshire, in the 1980s to placate a farmer who was indignant about crop circles in his fields, blaming them on army manoeuvres. The papers released to the National Archives at

Kew recorded: 'Lt Col. took a Major and Air Accident officer to the scene to investigate and found "an exactly circular hole in the wheat [which had] been laid flat in a clockwise twist 40ft in diameter *as if a plank had been put with one end at the centre and swept round in a complete circle.*"' [my italics].

It was like the moment in *Our Man in Havana* when the field officer who is running Wormold, the vacuum-cleaner salesman, realises that the sketches he has been receiving of Soviet missiles in Cuba bear an uncanny resemblance to the hoses and nozzles, the accoutrements and appurtenances, of the cleaning cupboard. Just as in Greene's entertainment, the mortifyingly prosaic explanation was not the one that Whitehall was ready to hear. So the MoD duly sent in a chopper, swept the tousled cornfield, carried out aerial reconnaissance, dunked its photographs in a developer. 'These were passed to DS8 and the Defence Intelligence Staff (DI55) for scrutiny,' the official minutes go unbelievably on. '[The circles] remain a mystery [but] from a purely defence viewpoint I don't think there is anything in the report to worry us . . . I lean to some kind of natural phenomena such as mini-tornadoes bouncing off the ground.'

If it wasn't 'mini-tornadoes' it was over-zealous war games; if it wasn't the urgent ciphering of an alien master race, it was a seismic disturbance. The last explanation was the closest to the truth: it was a subterranean happening. It was underground art – to be specific, the work of Bower, a mischief-making picture-framer from Southampton. He and his wife had taken a passage to Australia in their early married life, and the strange aboriginal markings upon the rufous earth that met their eyes had stayed with Doug, a handy artist in his spare time. Plotting with his best mate Dave in the snug of a pub near Winchester, Doug resolved that the wheatfields of Wessex would be his canvas.

And so the pair of them went out in the dead of night, slipping on masks as if en route to a harlequinade, and launched themselves like pole-vaulters – on the ends of specially whittled hazelnut boughs, the better to cover their tracks – into a clump of cereals. For years, it was a private joke between Doug and Dave, while the rest of the world speculated ever more fancifully about the occult agrarian designs. Doug was filled with contempt for the gullibility of the *soi-disant* experts – and their cupidity in making money from the media for their wild surmisings – but also excited about the effect he was having. The mysterious cuneiform of his arable patterns spelled out an enormous and elaborate V-sign – and it was also a great 'public art' project, anticipating the gable-end graffiti of Banksy by twenty years or more.

'You were like Dennis the Menace,' I tell this marble-eyed octogenarian.

'Just William,' he corrects me in his Hampshire burr. Of course. Not the inner-city tough in the hornet knitwear, but William, the always-boy of the endless English summer.

It is May Day, an auspicious date in the calendar of old England. There is a brilliant blue sky and we are in a flinty field under the bluff of Cheesefoot Head, an ancient Roman fort on the South Downs, in order to see Doug do his stuff. Just William is deceptively wardrobed as an old countryman, in twill trousers and ox-blood brogues. But as he places his trusty plank on the herbage and begins to rotate it, his wiry frame seems inhabited by an even more archaic presence. With one foot keeping the board flat, he moves it around on a rein, describing a still-compact circle after all these years. With his ramrod back and his ride-a-cock-horse gait, Bower might be a mummer or chevalier, and his terpsichorean tramplings a rain dance or worm-charming. Even his name evokes a poetic landscape; and as for the hairs that sprout from his ears, they put one in mind, perhaps, of a long-vanished hedgerow grass – 'Old Man's Lughole', maybe, or 'Knave's Lobe'? He is a figure of English folklore, and his ploughshare a sword: Excalibur!

Like crop circles, the hidden Arcadia of which I speak in this book can appear so remarkable, so otherworldly, that it too seems extraterrestrial; and, of course, it *isn't* terrestrial, but rather a realm beneath the familiar one. It often breaks cover – when an archaeologist's trowel deckles on a Roman flagstone, or a hobbyist's metal-detector pingingly strikes gold. There are yet more wayposts to this buried demesne, from the rocky niches once occupied by hermits, to the extraordinary brace of flint-and-slate huts in the churchyard of St Thomas à Becket in Warblington near Chichester, where sextons once kept watch by night for grave-robbers.

This hinterland isn't always winsome, it isn't always salubrious, and yet once you encounter it, it's difficult to wrench yourself away. A plot to tunnel under a shopping precinct in Manchester and dig up underneath a cash machine was only foiled by chance when builders broke into the forty-foot hidden passage in 2007. The criminals were within fifteen feet of their prize. Detectives found that their excavation was rigged with electric lights and wooden scaffolding and that the would-be robbers had extracted tons of spoil from below a car park without being rumbled. According to one report, 'The design and level of secrecy were on a par with wartime tunnels dug by British prisoners in Germany, notably in the "wooden horse" escape in 1943 and the Great Escape in 1944, both from Stalag Luft III camp.' One of the workmen who inadvertently thwarted the ruse expressed no fears about the tunnel collapsing on him when he stumbled into it. 'They had made a really good job of the supports and even the police were impressed with the workmanship.'

In 2007 the nation was agog at the story of the canoeist John Darwin, who admitted faking his own death in order to cash in on life policies. The *News of the World* devoted its front page to the discovery of the 'tunnel of love' that the fugitive had installed in a terraced house at Hartlepool, so that he could sneak through a 'coffin-shaped door' to the marital home next door. 'When family or friends called on "widow" Anne, "dead" John could use the hidden passage to nip into his three-bed bolt-hole in the adjoining terrace.' Darwin had even laid a concrete floor and a carpet across the threshold, so that he 'would not creak floorboards as he flitted between No. 3 and No. 4.' His victims were insurance companies.

To happier matters, and the remorseless downward drive of property. I'm not talking about falling house prices – not much happiness there – but rather the subterranean tendency in home improvement. When the housing market is in a hole, the answer is: keep digging. If it's too dicey to move, if planning regulations put a crimp in loft conversions and granny flats, the solution is to refit the basement, or even quarry out a new sunken storey altogether. While the builders have been heading south, the graph of demand for cellar makeovers has been travelling in the opposite direction. The uptake for this kind of 'downsizing' has tripled in a couple of years in England's bigger conurbations, while the average dimensions of these condo-grottoes have expanded from 400 square feet to 700. 'People are now digging under their gardens and drives as well as underneath their entire ground floor,' according to one housing insider – better say, undersider. Of course, campaigners against development have been known to take to the subsoil, too, most notably when eco-activists led by snaggle-haired Swampy quarried out a warren of tunnels in front of the bulldozers digging out the Newbury bypass in 1996.

We can't resist the tug of the subterranean, any more than we can the insistent pull of gravity. The Tate Modern gallery has never seen crowds like it had in 2007–8 for *Shibboleth* by the Colombian artist Doris Salcedo. This consisted of a crack running through the concrete floor of the former turbine hall. Despite many posted warnings, it was all the gallery staff could do to keep their many visitors from probing this fault-line – some dipped a questing toe into it, while others could not resist lowering their phizogs at full stretch into the void. We yearn to peep into the cave, to find the cavern under the menswear racks, to do the graveyard shift in the stony hides of Warblington.

It's time to light out now for this terra incognita, this half foreign land beneath our feet. And you'll come with me, I hope. Even if I wanted to put you off, it would be useless, I like to think. Just about the most counter-productive thing you can say to another living soul is, 'Don't look down!'

Stephen Smith
2009
Somewhere under England

1

EXTREMOPHILES

'Are you Kurtz?' said the man.

'No,' I said, 'I'm not Kurtz.' I'm not Kurtz but *you* could be, I thought. Here, in this end-of-the-world place, indulging in your unspeakable, your *unnatural* practices. He was sitting in the abandoned schoolroom, wearing a blue woolly hat. He introduced me to 'some Dutch friends' who guffawed. At this simple declaration of their nationality, the Netherlanders laughed to see such fun.

Now, though, I'm beginning to think that the man in the knitted headgear was right all along. I'm beginning to think that I might be Kurtz, after all, or that I might just as well be. (Did he say 'Kurt', I'm now wondering, rather than 'Kurtz'? Well, it scarcely matters any more). I'm lost, in the howling Conradian meaning of that term. My Heart of Darkness might not be a beaded curtain of humidity, an air-throttling raffiawork of palms and creepers, a hooting mangrove – but it's a savage and primitive place, all the same. I've fallen among a remote people who are in thrall to rain gods, to fire and fire-water.

I've treated with them at their trading post, their river station, long into the unforgivable night. Now they've led me far from the light of day, beyond the ken of civilised men, to the terrible immensity of a monstrous conundrum: do I press on with them, do I thread my aching body through an inhuman, practically indiscernible, needle's eye of a grot? Or must I go back the way I came, into the groping cavern, through the Stygian stream, only to face the sheer sides of the pitilessly drumming waterfall?

I'll take another tot of cockle-warming Ribena from Andy's battered Thermos, his storied hip flask, and I'll think it over. No point rushing into anything. After all, it's not as if I'm going anywhere in a hurry, I reflect, as the cordial works its sweet alchemy on these old bones of mine. The Letterbox? I think. How bad can it be? As bad as it sounds – or, on the other hand, worse, unutterably worse?

We come into this life through a tunnel, the birth canal, and for the most part we end up underground, at the other end of it all – in this ever-changing world of ours, these are surely thoughts to hug to ourselves. Outside of a hospital bed, the most realistic way to simulate these drastic experiences is to go caving; though cavers themselves, who tend to be philosophical, in the sense that they don't like to think about anything very much, or at least they pretend that they don't, would scoff at this idea.

And we in turn scoff at them, don't we, us non-cavers? Let's see if we have this right: you want to spend your time under a hillside miles from anywhere, sidewinding through claustrophobically narrow crevices in the cold and wet and dark, and the most you can look forward to is coming out knackered and covered in mud when it's all over? You might get up to some staggering things down there – as a matter of fact, we'll bet you do – but it's not as if anyone's going to see them, is it? Let's face it, you can barely see them yourselves.

Cavers have an extraordinary sangfroid – on second thoughts, that sounds a little exotic, a little continental. It's more of a leg-pulling, bloody-minded stoicism, combined with a certain defensiveness, towards the media at least, which borders on wariness – and often crosses the border altogether, in truth, though cavers are hardly alone in that. In Gloucester, at the annual expo of the great below-doors, 'Hidden Earth', there are men in detachable trousers and T-shirts with slogans like 'Time to Cave, Said Zebedee' and 'If You Die, We Split Your Kit'. One of the country's leading spelunkers is describing – *defending* – a film he produced for the BBC. 'We're not making the film for us. We're making it for a bunch of people in London,' he says, London being a kind of Sodom to cavers, London with its sheer size and urbanness, as antithetic and unsympathetic to their chosen country pursuit as it is to the Beaufort Hunt.

There is laughter at the producer's mention of 'health-and-safety guidelines'. It seems that TV bosses overruled his idea to make the presenters 'dig their way out' of a cave system. He goes on to say that it was 'not my choice of script', a reference to a provocative line of commentary about 'the possibility of being buried alive'.

A delegate from a northern cave system takes the floor. He's now entirely bald but is recognisably the same man who appears, with tufts of hair around his ears, on videos about the northern cave system which are on sale at Hidden Earth. He has been an outspoken critic of the caving film in on-line chat rooms, going so far as to call it 'dishonest'. Confronted by the film-maker himself, the man from the north backtracks quite a lot, but still manages several swipes at the dire state of television. We hear about *Beneath the Pennines*, a documentary made about caving in the 1960s and 70s. The man from the floor rates it for its no doubt expansive truthfulness, and the caver-producer chips in from the podium, 'That's what got me into caving in the first place.'

This isn't a book for cavers. It's a book for us, for everyone else, the non-cavers; though the cavers are very welcome, too. Before I went caving, I was searching for a book about caving. I read what cavers read – in so far as they are ever caught reading anything at all. The problem was, the books that I could find were all written by cavers, those strange and forbidding, if courageous and therefore rather enviable, people in overalls and hard hats. I enjoyed the books I read. They were full of incident and drama. I read about the great, the legendary cavers, I gathered from the diagrams that cave systems radiate out like cracks in glass. There are galleries at the end of brutally difficult systems in Yorkshire that have been explored by fewer people than have walked on the moon. The cataract that tumbles into Gaping Gill on the dales drops further than Niagara Falls. I began to absorb the meaning of the verb 'to cave'; as in 'I caved last Wednesday' or, simply, 'Are you caving?' But none of these books seemed to transport me, a non-caver, into the cave alongside the writer. I'm sure it was no reflection on the books, or the authors, themselves.

All right, you think, I'll ask the cavers face to face. 'Why do you do it, then?' you say. They can't tell you. Anglers appreciate the peace and quiet of the riverbank, as well as the visceral if one-sided contest. Boy racers get off on speed. But cavers are at a loss to put the allure of their pastime into words, so much so that you begin to think it must be a sworn secret of this subterranean sodality. So you put aside all your preconceptions and aversions to wriggle where they wriggle, squirm where they squirm. Yes, and eat where they eat, bunk where they bunk.

Somewhere in the moon-rimed dales, in a pub where time is never called, I'm drinking with one of the leading, the elite, cavers. Keith has a crew-cut, an earstud. 'You have to be *cave*-fit,' says this lean fifty-something. Keith's son-in-law plays five-a-side and also does something with dogs, perhaps he hunts – 'But when he caved, he was knackered.'

Cavers have their own specialities, their quiddities. Sue, tiny Sue, explains how it's possible to walk up a waterfall underground, unaided and in wellies. The answer is there's no sun underground, so no treacherous algae can grow under foot. Sue can only be five feet tall, at most. She can walk – *amble* – through the kind of constriction that the chaps have to climb over ('traverse'). She tells me she's as wide as her Tim is deep. The thankfully chunky Tim is also tall and speccy: I like him on sight. To make or reinforce a point in conversation, he raps Sue on her head.

This is not a place for girly girls, nor for men who know what to do with them. So Sue can shapeshift through rock; another woman is good in water. Cavers are like superheroes, like the X-Men, each with their own recherché powers.

In this lonely spot, there is only the pub by the beck, a humpback bridge, three or four houses and an old school, the cavers' clubhouse. I scribble my notes on my bunk in the schoolhouse, by the light of my new Maglite, which I have surprised myself by adapting into 'lamp mode' – maybe I'm developing X-Men powers of my own. All the fittings and fixtures are cave-related: there are pictures cut or torn out of cave mags on the walls; signs and notices about cave events. The only reading matter is a caving journal (*Descent*). I didn't expect a bound set of *Cahiers du Cinéma*, but I mean to say. Four bunks have been claimed in here so far, including mine. My roomies include a buxom, chirpy blonde of sixteen – and her dad, Andy, ex-services, who's sleeping shotgun.

Later, we're all asleep and the lights are out when the door is booted open, and a gristly ex-services type whom I'd seen in the pub vaults with a single bound into a top bunk. He's another elite caver. Presently, there's the noise of running water. 'Jason, what the fuck are you doing?' says the man in the bunk beneath the newcomer. 'Have you pissed yourself?!'

Jason is long gone by the time I finally come to – at the not very outdoorsy hour of 9 a.m.

It's raining hard, and there's a lively brook under foot in Long Churn. That's the name of the cave, or 'pot', that we're attempting this morning, though it also does pretty well as a description of the thoroughgoing experience itself; it's nigh on onomatopoeic. The darkling limestone channel, which the elements have corkscrewed out of the hillside over the centuries, twists and turns before us. Within a few paces, the water is in over the top of my boots, drenching through two pairs of socks. In another moment, it's waist deep. Now my boilersuit, even my pert bodystocking, are saturated.

Long Churn is part of the Alum Pot cave system. The Alum Pot itself, sometimes known as 'Hell's Mouth', is a yawning opening on the fellside from which a beck drops as a waterfall for two hundred feet, cascading another hundred to a deep pool. Alum Pot lies in a natural bowl where rainfall swiftly accumulates. When it's pouring, like today, water rises rapidly in Long Churn, racing inside the hillside to the pot – it's even more rapid if the moors are already teeming after sustained bad weather.

My *Selected Caves of Britain and Ireland*, the Baedeker of the buried world, tells me that there is not one Long Churn, in fact, but two: the lower pipe, first tamed in 1848 by 'J. Birkbeck and party', commences at an altitude of 351 metres and descends to a depth of 107 metres over a length of 366. It's described as 'a fine though heavily used cave'. However, we are winding through the upper bore, to begin with: it may be gained at exactly the same height, but it's longer – 762 metres – and boasts the eccentric feature of a depth of '+18 metres', according to my handbook. Alum Pot is frequented by beginners and school parties but also by serious cavers. In this respect, it's a bit like the North Circular or Marble Arch: it is shot, or forded, by the most white-knuckled novice and by the adroit veteran alike. It's not free from peril. 'It is quite possible and in fact easy to die a horrible death by straying off route,' wrote the great fellsman Alfred Wainwright in a book of walks in limestone country. 'The dangers of Alum Pot are manifestly obvious. Other deathtraps, unseen, occur in the black interiors of the caves.'

Our group of half a dozen is led by a taciturn outward-bound specialist from Wales. Last night in the pub, I took his brooding silence for quiet authority, but in the passage of Long Churn, my doubts grow about his communication skills. I yearn for words of encouragement, for a morale boost – oh, all right then, for praise. Of course, it's probably the sign of a good guide to say less rather than more. It's noisy enough down here as it is: maybe that's why he's cheese-paring with his remarks. The water thunders in, as if on to the movie set of a scuttling ship or breached U-boat. These conditions are described by more than one seasoned caver as 'sporting'.

Geoff, an older man, who's wearing thick bins and some sort of hood or balaclava under his helmet ('bonnet'), tells me that a group such as ours poses problems: some people inevitably stand around while the others catch up. 'That's how you get cold.' Plunging body temperature is one of the biggest hazards to the caver, he says. Once or twice, as we are flattening ourselves against slippery inclines, he gives me a lift – it's no more than a manly, two-handed push on the buttocks; there's nothing over-familiar about it – and there's him giving me fifteen years or more.

Our party includes a young teacher from the North East. 'She's very driven,' says her boyfriend. You wouldn't necessarily say the same thing about him. He's out of shape: I can't tell you how he gladdens this old heart of mine. His blue bonnet, admittedly not really his size, makes him look like a man in a fancy-dress policeman's helmet. As he'd floundered windedly up the hill towards the mouth of the cave at the start of the day, I'd felt waves of gratitude for this Keystone Cop – I wasn't the least fit, I wasn't the one with the longest face.

We plummet into chilling pools; we wade through fast-flowing streams; we haul ourselves up streaming rockfaces; we shuffle forward on our hands and knees, our arses, ultimately our elbows, beneath a swooning roof. It's probably a good thing that I don't know what's coming next – that I literally can't see it, face down as I increasingly am – because all at once the headroom is so limited that we're obliged to hit the deck. I'm spreadeagled – no, I'm butterflied, I'm a spit-roast prawn.

At full stretch, and sometimes less, my fingers are brushing the wriggling heels of the person in front of me. My bonnet clangs on the sinking ceiling and I effortfully – with an effort of *will* – twist my neck until my jangling jughead clears the choke point. 'Beneath – in the great, mythic hollows of the earth itself – lies a separate world, timeless and in large part still unknown where one travels in darkness through mazelike tunnels, down cliffs, in icy streams, and through passages so narrow that there comes a point where there is not room to breathe and the panic of death begins,' says the writer James Salter.

As I proceed, in increments of inches – as I *cave* – I try to apply a piece of advice that I was given by Keith, the earringed elite caver. I think of him telling me to relax – 'It makes you smaller' – and then exhaling in an exaggerated way in front of me in the pub, collapsing like a faulty airbag. Unlike Keith, I have no idea what I'm doing, which ought to be a cause for concern. On the other hand, whatever it is, it's too preoccupying and exhausting to leave any nervous energy for fear, for 'the panic of death'. The only sound I can hear is my own stentorian breathing. 'Underground noises always sound weird and solitude heightens the impression,' the caving journalist James Lovelock has written. 'The oddest thing that happened to me once was in a long, narrow crawl with two companions. We all stopped to rest and as we lay still there was a deep, rhythmic booming sound to be heard like the rhythm of a water ram in a stream. In a few minutes it dawned on us what it was – we were listening to the sounds of our own hearts and the passage was acting like a stethoscope. The friend behind me commented drily: "It proves we are bloody well alive at any rate."'

Exhilaratingly, Long Churn opens up around us again. I know the relief that the crawl is over, at least for now, mixed with the satisfaction that I've somehow done it – as opposed to bottled or botched it. And what unanticipated diversions await. We negotiate an extraordinary passage which is serpentine – but from head to toe instead of horizontally. There's Dr Bannister's Handbasin, which has the unhappy ring of Victorian gynaecology about it, but proves to be a five-metre cataract of water hammering into a pool the depth of a standing man.

Amidst the exertion, amidst the racket of the battering water, the otherworldly aspect of the cave stealthily insinuates itself. The constant action of acidic rainwater on limestone carves scallops into the rock: the bigger the bivalves, the slower the flow. The crown of the cowrie points in the direction that the water's going: this is the kind of lore that can be a life-saver to a backwoodsman – an *under*woodsman – in the confusion of a dark and flooding cave system. The cave is 'decorated', in the jargon. The roof sparkles with pyrites, fool's gold: in reality, it's millions of swanky bacteria hanging out together at their glittering parties. Elsewhere, the prospecting fingers of the mountain stream have grubbed nuggets of limestone from the hillside.

A cave is like the bottom of a deep ocean, perpetually dark, constantly cold, reliably wet. There is little or nothing in the way of food, and yet caves sustain their own arcane and otherworldly ecosystems: creatures that can survive without organic material, subsisting on the chemicals and minerals they glean from their forbidding surroundings; mud-dwelling bugs that inexplicably get by without oxygen. Sue isn't entirely right: there *are* algae, as well as mosses, lichen, moulds, and these in turn sustain tiny crustacea such as *Asellus*, which dines off water fungus at the edge of limestone pools. He has to be quick about it, or else he winds up as lunch for *Niphargus*, a blind and semi-transparent crustacean. Spiders, worms, slugs, snails and flies share this hidden habitat. Many of its denizens have adapted to its gruelling conditions: in the absence of light, eyes have dwindled or else disappeared altogether, while feelers, probes and probosces have flourished in compensation. 'Perhaps, here in caves, is a wonderful process of life comparable to that of the "primeval slime" from which evolution as we know it today began,' as Donald Robinson and Anthony Greenbank muse in their *Caving and Potholing*. Scientists have recently discovered flourishing microbial ecosystems thousands of feet under the soil, some so deeply embedded that they are warmed by the hot magma of the planetary core. The creatures that inhabit these fastnesses, making do without oxygen and light, are known as 'extremophiles'. That's what the elite cavers are, I think, extremophiles.

The wetter it gets in Long Churn, the better the teacher's boyfriend likes it, the better he's faring. 'I'm a swimmer so I don't mind this,' he says. In turn, I tire, slip back. I'm holding on halfway up a wet wall, a sore and sorry starfish.

Older Geoff says to me, 'First time caving?' I feel him administer a bolstering goosing.

'Yes.'

'And the last?'

'Well, we'll see,' I manage. But perhaps my lack of gusto is all too apparent. It's an uncanny replay of an almost identical conversation that I once had with another old fart from Subterranea Britannica, a group of underground enthusiasts, after a run out to a demobbed radar post in Lincolnshire.

It's two and half hours before we emerge at last on to the stair-rodding fellside. When I empty my boots, it takes quite a long time for the water to run out. Taking my cue from the others, I'm soon in my birthday suit beneath the tipping Yorkshire sky: exiting my saturated bodystocking, it's less like stripping off, more like upending a catch on to the deck of a trawler. I wouldn't be surprised if a salmon flapped from my fishnets.

I'm shaken that I failed to negotiate one or two of the modest climbs without help. I'm weary and I ache, and I'm not sure I'm in a hurry to go through more, perhaps worse, the following day. It was one of the hardest things I've ever done. But I'm very pleased that I did it, pleased that I got round Long Churn; pleased to have caved it.

In the secret heart of every speleologist, he knows that the excruciating underground effort is climaxed, reified, by the safe return to terra firma, and the blissful prospect of going on about it all for a long time in the warm. The delightful expression, 'It's home for tea and medals', which we heard more than once in Long Churn, speaks to the truth of this, albeit from the safe distance of irony. In the seminal *The Eightfold Way of Caving*, John Gillett takes the reader briskly through the prosaic if necessary preliminaries – the choosing of kit; the cave selection; the other bit, the caving – before arriving at last at his true Tao: 'The cavers who can change into dry clothes the most quickly are the first to enter the sixth stage and can bag the best places in the pub. The sixth or refreshment stage is rarely short.'

In our case, it's a troglodyte-friendly Yorkshire buttery, rather than a pub, in which we enter Gillett's blissful state. Tim, the big bloke, who had kindly lent me my now-beached long coms, reads aloud in an arch voice from the personal ads in the *Guardian*. The café has a box set of Dave Pelzer's misery memoirs: a trilogy of them, in a little card holder. I remember a similar set of D. H. Lawrence that I had as a youth; they were a lot less dog-eared than the Pelzers.

The teacher's boyfriend tells me that she went out with a caver before him, a *proper* caver, a cave diver: the best of the best, the elitist of the elite. 'Yes, she lost her last boyfriend,' he adds. For a dopey moment, I imagine that this poor bloke is still wandering around out there somewhere. But he got trapped in an underground pool. 'She was his time-out,' says the new boyfriend. This is the person you call before you go caving. You tell your time-out that you'll be entering such and such a cave system and what time you expect to be leaving it; if your time-out doesn't hear from you by the appointed hour, it falls to them to raise the alarm.

At the old schoolhouse that night, there's a reckless fireworks display in driving wind and rain. The fun is coordinated by Tim and by a short but sturdy lad – he may be the ideal build for caving, I think to myself – who is wearing shorts. At this saturnalia of bonfire and gunpowder, fireworks are *definitely* returned to after they've been lit: well before one would want to certify them extinguished, they're picked up again and tossed on to the fire, snatched by the ragged lasso of the flames. The lad in the shorts lets off a rocket from the launchpad of his arms. I hear Geoff being asked by a young friend, 'Have you caved this week?'

In the pub, Geoff's missus is eking out a glass of red. 'This will last me forty minutes,' she says. It's hard to know why this is such an appalling thing to hear. Still, she makes my day when she says, 'Geoff didn't report you going white.' I'd voiced my concern that I might have been underperforming, letting the side down. But Geoff had marked her card on which of the novices were faring badly, who had been looking pasty, and I wasn't listed among the casualties. She tells me about the 'pothole widows', the wives left at home when the men are caving; and the paradoxical fact that, of their circle of friends, two or three of the men are already widowers, confounding the actuarial tables by surviving their spouses. 'The wives died of neglect,' she clarifies. Decades of sourness and disappointment in that, one feels.

She goes on to allude, all too fleetingly, to Geoff's ideas about 'a parallel universe' – and to his discovering one, if you please, right here in the wilderness of the north country, barely a barm cake's throw from Settle. As well as being a caver, Geoff is a digger. He and his mates like nothing better than going into a pot right to the sump – that is, as far as they can go – and then shovelling out centuries' worth of dreck and gloop in the hope of making a breakthrough into another, unknown chamber or even cave system.

Well, Geoff's been digging for years 'and found absolutely nothing', in the unsparing tyke tones of his bride and helpmeet. But not long ago, he and his friends came across a passage – literally unearthed it – the like of which none of them had seen before. Geoff and co. couldn't get over finding this übergrot, this platonic version of the cave. His wife is on the point of outlining Geoff's belief in a parallel universe, and what this has to do with the discovery of his 'perfectly geometrical tunnel', when she elects to go on instead about how another group of diggers came across the hole, and started poking around in it themselves. From the moment this incursion was discovered, Geoff was not his usual self. He went right off the incredible new tunnel, never went near it again, never even brought the subject up. Mrs G. puzzled over her husband's behaviour, she says, until at last it came to her: 'It was like his virgin had been violated.'

Most of the cavers are in the other bar, the one that has fruit machines in it, but not Geoff or his wife. Tim and Sue are in the group. I'm fascinated by the courtship rituals of the cavers, their love dance. Winched once to the bottom of the great nave of Gaping Gill in Yorkshire, beneath an endless rood-screen of rock that flew past my bucketing bosun's chair, I was smitten by the astonishing sight of overalled lovelies playing rubbers of badminton in the void. By the pale glow of my mobile phone light, the lantern I had shrewdly stowed on my person for the trip, the girls were striking with their cork-blackened faces, their damp yet fetching pigtails, the awful one-size-fits-all dowdiness of their cavewear. One of them clinched a set with a smash worthy of Joan Hunter Dunne. The girls were thrilling, like the women of the French Resistance. Leaving the cavern had a little of the atmosphere of Dunkirk, come to that: we were wet, exhausted, waiting to be lifted off the shingly beach at the bottom of the gill. A Thermos of hot Ribena was passed down the line like a packet of ciggies. I basked unentitled in the camaraderie of the queue as my Joan told me that she had first caved after her boyfriend, a stalwart of the Bradford club, asked her if she'd like to come along. 'I loved it!' she told me.

In the pub on the dales, one of the gang is a warehouseman by day, a young, goofy lad who has an alpine hat with integral ear muffs. He folds and refolds it in his lap. He sleeps free of charge on a bench in the bar, in the unimaginable hour when the punters have finally left (thought to be six o'clock). This is in order to save the heartbreakingly nominal fee levied at the schoolhouse.

Keith the elite caver is here; he's on the BMWs. 'It's Bailey's, Malibu and whisky. You can have a taste,' he says. He boxes me in near a slot machine so that our knees touch. Keith of Derby, and his life of stag-dos in the new fleshpots of Europe – Prague and Riga and Barcelona. Like the lad with the deerstalker who kips down in the snug, Keith seems to have an aversion to sheets, preferring to spend nights going round and round on fairground rides on his away-days with the boys, rather than booking a hotel and lumbering himself with the unnecessary ballast of a room for the night.

I ask Keith about Jason, his fellow elitist, the man who sprang into bed last night from a standing jump. Keith sheds light on Jason's midnight micturation. 'He were just pouring water on the bloke in the bottom bunk,' Keith clarifies. It seems that Jason, like the teacher's former boyfriend, is a cave diver. 'Possibly the best in the world,' adds Keith thoughtfully. A few years back, Jason rescued a group of British squaddies after they got into difficulties in a distant cavern. He himself has known near-misses. Once he was diving with a 'scooter', a hand-held motor, and re-breathing – an impossibly advanced and dangerous feat of oxygen-recycling. 'He hit a rock and cut his arm open to the bone. Insisted on putting the stitches in himself.' Jason doesn't carry a knife when he goes cave diving, Keith explains, because it takes two hands to use one: one to hold the knife and the other to hold the rope, or whatever it is that has to be cut.

Keith tells me about a cave diver who became entangled under water and died. He had oxygen on him – ten minutes of it. So, said Keith, he would have known, must have counted down, that he only had ten minutes to live . . . and then nine, and so on. 'Jason has a pair of secateurs,' says Keith. 'Keeps 'em strapped to him.'

In the morning, I've made up my mind. I'm leaving after breakfast. The cavers have been marvellously hospitable and friendly. But I won't be caving today. I'm sitting in the youth-club-style lounge with little Sue, or at least she's there at the same time as me, and she looks up from her caving mag and says, 'Are you excited about going underground again?'

'Well, I *am* very excited, yes,' I hear myself say, 'but the thing is, it won't be today. I've got to get back to London.' A truth bookended by two lies. But then I think, Going underground? Of course – that's what I'm here for! OK, I could legitimately claim to have popped my caving cherry now, but to spurn a tailormade opportunity seems perverse, with nothing else in the diary.

In the club's equatorial drying-room, my kit is warm but still wet – sopping, wallowing wet. I've done myself no favours by leaving my tackle piled – *balled* – on the floor. Tim's pantyhose is, I fear, unconscionable. Rummaging through my trunk, I snag a nail on the leg of my thermals – last worn in action, I think, at a media-hostile environment course, and before that as long ago as Bosnia, a real hostile environment. They will have to do.

In Old Lings, I surprise myself with a new agility and elasticity, an unheralded access of superpowers. The passages of this cave are tight and U-shaped, so that instead of grimly fording them, you have the alternative of straddling the divide and moving along the walls as if on a fly's Velcro-like soles. Even when a handhold *doesn't* hold and I feel myself swaying backwards, away from the wall, about to drop into the water – even then something affixes me to the rock – the nook where a foot is slithering? – and I stay on: all this without the kind of contact from Geoff that, in the workplace, would see him frogmarched to HR (but which I shall always be grateful to him for). All the same, there comes a moment when I have no choice but to stretch across a boiling pool. Shimmering under the water are columns of limestone, sunken piers on which the caver may tread in reasonable confidence. One such reef is just visible four or five feet in front of me and this is my goal. I swing my leg out to reach a foothold – it's there! It's all going terribly well, in fact, until the moment when I have to follow through with the rest of my body. I push off with my trailing foot – and drop chest-deep into the pool. Andy, the old soldier and protective dad from the bunkhouse, chortles to see such sport. I'm an Inuit in an ice hole.

Nor is it an unalloyed boon to have the wringing walrus pelt of my boilersuit clinging to me from this early hour, because Old Lings is merely a warm-up (you could have fooled me). The main event is the freak of geology – the contortionist's conundrum, the human hole-in-one – of the Letterbox.

'How big is the Letterbox?' I ask someone.

'Well, have you heard of the Cheese Press? That's eleven inches wide.'

'Yes?'

'This is tighter.'

Eleven inches! That's the kind of clearance I like to give myself when I'm flossing my teeth. And I've got to pass through a cleft in a rock that's tighter than that. That's when I finally get there, mark you: the Letterbox is separated from us by a frothing waterfall and the uterine unknowability of another stooping cave in a different part of the Alum Pot system.

Andy is guiding today, along with Stuart, and they opt to send us over the twenty-foot cascade on the end of a bit of rope. I bump down the side of this stony showerbath. Stuart yells something about a ledge a metre below the drop, and using this for a foothold. But then he says, 'Let the rope take the weight of your body! Push out!'

I suit the action to the words: in another moment, the

indifferent Newtonian universe slams me back against the hard, slick rock. I'm underneath the overhang now, and beginning to wonder if I might end up hooked and dangling there like the less winsome novelties in the fossiling waters of Old Mother Shipton's cave – when all at once I've bottomed in the surging shower stall.

I'm nonplussed to find that my teeth are chattering: actually working independently of me. Materialising through a skein of waterfall spray is the immensely reassuring sight of Andy holding out a nip of Ribena in a battered mug, like a mind-reading manservant of Middle Earth. His Thermos appears to be sheathed in brown paper, or lashed Jiffy bags. 'It's bomb-proof,' he says. He doles out rations of Mars bar, as well as tots of blackcurrant grog, our short commons of confectionery. It must be a tradition in the services to take a flask when caving, judging by the memoirs of the distinguished old campaigner and potholer Arthur Gemmell. His own trusty canteen went with him to Gaping Gill, and many other tight spots besides:

> I was the proud possessor of a remarkable Thermos flask which had been my stalwart companion on many expeditions and which had safely endured the ordeal of being dragged a quarter of a mile over a rough stony floor wrapped in an old shirt inside a haversack, tied to my foot. Though battered, dented and rusty, it never failed to keep its contents warm and intact, and I would not have parted with it for its weight in gold. Perhaps the saddest day of my life was that one, five years later, when it finally gave up the ghost on being subjected to the savage treatment of my batman who, lacking other utensils, poured boiling water into it to mash the tea.

Stuart warns us that the cave that opens at the foot of the falls is noteworthy for the way the roof closes in. Sure enough, it soon becomes necessary to hobble through it in a scuttling Richard III mince, your top half almost at right-angles to your pistoning thighs; after that, it's only accessible on your hands and knees. Andy lends me his knee-pads, which help a lot, though I still scrape my shins up pretty good. He also takes the balaclava from under his bonnet, making me a priceless gift of the sweat-soaked article. 'I could see you were shivering,' he says. Too true, mate, but is this the cold? Or rather, is it *only* the cold?

I have a healthy respect for the pillarbox of rock that lies ahead. From the novels of Martin Amis, we have an unforgettable simile for impotence: putting an oyster into a parking meter. With the clunky carapace of my hard-hat and all-in-one, not to mention the flailing claws of my gauntleted arms, I imagine myself as another piece of star-crossed seafood, mounting an equally doomed assault on another unavailing slot. This is going to be like stuffing a lobster through the Letterbox, I think.

I'm assured by the older hands that I'll get through it, though one man is only willing to commit himself to saying that I *might* come out the other side. I don't want to funk it outright, but nor do I wish to get stuck in it. Now that I'm in the cave, with the means of entry to it still fresh in my mind, I have no overwhelming desire to retrace my hunched steps to the pool at the bottom of the waterfall – and make my way out of it up the slippery sides of the rock on the rungs of a dainty rope ladder (Plan B, according to Stuart and Andy). From what I gather, the Letterbox is almost the last test that lies ahead – so all things considered, it's better to get through it, if at all possible.

We are sitting by a vision of the Styx: a smallish stream, to be sure, but in the dark, and seemingly far from the everyday world. We are trying to keep warm, waiting to be called forward by the guides to essay the unforgiving trouser-press of a fissure. 'Sometimes it is better to avoid using names,' says Gillett in a chapter entitled 'The Unknown'. 'For many years I sidled down the "Crab Walk" in Giant's Hole, Derbyshire, without any bother. Then one day someone asked me if I had had any problems in passing "The Vice" . . . On my next trip, I managed to become stuck in it! Unnamed, I had no slot in my memory for it; named, it became an obstacle to be overcome well before I entered the cave.'

Now it's my turn. I have to snake towards a kind of antechamber from where the Letterbox itself is accessed. This room, never mind the ultimate objective itself, looks impossible at first – a cramped space almost filled to its low cornice with rocks, it's like an air pocket, a tiny bubble left behind after a landslip. Stuart is coiled up somehow in a corner of it.

The first challenge is to move into this little cell at all. It feels as though my shoulders are jammed. At Stuart's instruction, I move my top half until I gain a little breathing space, a little play on my upper arms, and swing my legs round until my feet are over a niche, a mousehole, in the stone floor: this turns out to be the Letterbox itself. As it's explained to me by the marvellously patient and encouraging Stuart, the knack is to go in feet first, but without bending your knees. 'Imagine you're going down a slide in a kiddies' playground,' he says. 'Keep your arms up over your head, that'll reduce the span of your shoulders, and slide through on your bum.'

Well, the first bit seems to go OK: I manoeuvre my boots into the hole and drop my legs in after them, bracing them stiffly as though they're splinted. 'Well done, mate,' grunts Stuart.

I sink down into the slot – I'm thrilled. I'm out of the tight chamber, or half out, anyway. I'm getting – *earning* – rare compliments from my guides. I won't have to go back through anything, do anything again, I won't have to climb out of the pot with the waterfall discharging into it.

Then I get stuck. My chest is piniored by an outcrop – a spar, a spur, a snag – of rock.

It would be going too far to say that it all disappears, evaporates, in that moment – the bulking, louring limestone, the fatigue, the cold and wet and dark. But you find that you become intimately acquainted with the interiority of caving. It's not about the space, or the lack of it, *out there*; it's about you, and how much of it *you* take up (or others take up around you) – as in a lift or an aircraft. It's also about the way caving, even a beginner's experience, turns you in on your own resources – of confidence, of cool, of pluck. As Gillett writes, 'The caver has two unknowns to contend with, the caves and himself.' Wedged in the foot or less of the Letterbox, I don't feel any panic or distress; I have complete faith in my guides. I have a job to do and my lot will be much the better all round – as will everybody else's – if I get it done. Somehow.

I breathe out, I duck and feint, I move to my right, I lift my arms higher to release the pressure on my chest – and all at once, I'm a cork fizzing out of a bottle.

We exit the cave through the fug, the jet stream, of our own milling exhalation, and flop on to the dales still breathing hard. Why do cavers do it? For moments like this, for when it's all over. Yes, they love the caving – the crawling and the climbing. They love to *cave* – of course they do. They enjoy every stage of Gillett's eightfold way, every house of his Tao. But it's also about the unique exhilaration that comes from having outfaced not only the possibility of death but also Salter's 'panic of death'. Cavers would scoff at this, too, but you have only to substitute the unlicensed wilderness of their chosen milieu for, let us say, a 'caveworld theme park' expunged of all risk, health-and-safetied to a vanilla threatlessness, to know that it would be no place for an extremophile.

'We kicked the arse out of it,' someone says. It emerges that yesterday's circuit of Long Churn, euphemistically described as 'sporting' on account of the swollen stream, had been 'touch and go' because of the poor weather. We almost didn't cave it at all. It's barely a month later, in the Christmas holidays, that a man of thirty-three and a twenty-eight-year-old woman, both experienced cavers, are trapped by rising water in Long Churn, and drowned.

2

AN ENGLISHMAN'S HOME
IS HIS CAVE

I think that perhaps you and I are not so very different – born in the twentieth century, into industrial or post-industrial societies – am I right? People that we know, people we're related to, they don't live in caves. That's what I thought when I started digging about in them. I found there was no end of things you could do in caves. You could *cave* in one, for a start, as we've seen, but a cave wasn't only for recreation. You could also hide yourself, or secrete your stash of booty. You could practise satanic rituals away from scandalised eyes, or turn your cloistered crevice into a sanctuary where the guttering flame of the one true faith could be tended.

A hundred feet beneath a branch of Ladbroke's in Royston, on a snowy Easter weekend, I entered a cave that might have come from the pages of *The Da Vinci Code*. Heretical Knights Templar are thought to have quarried out this chalky pit as their secret chapel after a change in the religious weather left them out in the cold. It was uncovered centuries after the last of their courtly order had died out, by workmen installing a new bench in the Butter Market in 1742. Somewhat improbably, the knights ran a market stall at Royston from 1199 to 1254 on their return from the Crusades. One theory is that these mailed traders, these Middle EastEnders, dug out the bell-shaped cave as a kind of early lock-up. But extraordinary carvings around the chamber – Christian saints and depictions of Calvary, as well as archaic pagan motifs including human heads, hands gripping hearts, a raunchy Sheela-na-Gig – have persuaded some scholars that the out-of-favour chevaliers attended to their forbidden devotions below the bookie's, in the dank recesses of the Hertfordshire commuter belt.

You could go to a cave for the most basic stuff of life. Where better to draw water than from a stream tricklingly filtered through untouched limestone? At the same time, an earth, a remote and germ-free environment, made an ideal laboratory. In 1782 a plumber called William Watts patented lead shot after a recurring dream in which he dug a hole beside his house in Bristol into the Redcliffe Caves below. Suiting the action to the nagging reverie, Watts was able to drop lumps of lead a distance of 120 feet, from the top of his roof to the limestone floor of the cavern, and so fashion musket-ready rounds. This great boon to the small-bore industry was recognised in a Grade II listing for Watt's shot-tower; that is, until 1968, when the burghers of Bristol elected to widen the road it stood on and took a potshot at it themselves with a wrecking ball.

You can even make cheese in a cave. One purveyor of these stalactite Stiltons, these troglodyte truckles, whom I consulted in Wookey Hole promised, or perhaps warned, 'They taste of cave' – and he wasn't wrong.

But people didn't live in caves . . . Oh, sure, they *lived* in caves, of course they did. Once upon a time, they lived in caves, all right. The cave was man's earliest abode, his starter home; perhaps a folk memory of this is at the root of the expression 'digs', meaning a rudimentary place to stay, with only the barest basics found. As with so many other architectural trends, the English were at the forefront of cave habitation. Archaeologists have discovered natural caves that were inhabited during the last ice age. At Pin Hole, Derbyshire, they confirmed a long unbroken sequence of occupation. Other settled caves include Creswell Crags in the same county, where engravings of birds and an ibex are twelve thousand years old; Kent's Cavern in Torquay; and Oldbury in Kent. Prehistoric people set up home inside a high chalk ridge a mile south of Salisbury. There is evidence of more than a hundred subterranean living-quarters, each broadly circular in shape, some of them as much as fifteen feet deep and twelve feet across. There were portholes in the walls of these chalky rooms, just large enough to crawl through, so that they formed corridors of underground cabins. In the remote Himalayas, people still retreat into such earthen accommodation when the weather is at its bleakest, which suggests that our forefathers wintered in the Wiltshire gullies. Bones found in the caves indicate that when times were hard, our ancestors were not averse to dining off each other – perhaps when times weren't so hard, too. These rock-hopping cannibals may well have inspired folk legends of ogres, and were perhaps what H. G. Wells had in mind when he depicted the Morlocks of his *Time Machine*.

In order to lead their sheltered lives, hermits resorted to caves at Dale in Derbyshire, Bridgnorth in Shropshire and Pontefract, Yorkshire, among other places. Westminster Abbey only stands where it does today because St Peter appeared to an anchorite called Wulsi at his rude and rocky abode in Evesham and told this blameless soul that he wanted Edward the Confessor to erect a great church at Thorney, two leagues from the city of London. 'Pass it on,' said the doorman of the Pearly Gates, or words to that effect. In 1346 Lord Thomas Berkeley paid for a hermit, John Sparks, to sit in a cave in Bristol and pray for him. This practice was a feature of the Bristol scene for another three hundred years or more. The hermits retreated into their limestone cells for seven years; thereafter they were entitled to claim a pension for the rest of their lives.

But this is all ancient history. My countrymen might have a
formidable track record of reposing underground, but people
haven't lived in caves for centuries, have they? We're also told
that an Englishman's home is his castle, and yet very few house-
hunters come across drawbridges and turreted battlements in
vendors' HIPs.

How wrong can you be? It turns out that people – yes, even
the English – lived in caves well into the modern, the industrial,
era. As late as the nineteenth century, entire cave communities
thrived in the Midlands, in Staffordshire and Worcestershire. The
largest settlement was Dunsley Rock, near Stourbridge, known
to its inmates as Gibraltar. More than forty of them had their
post directed to seventeen separate holes in the ground, while
other nooks did service as cattle sheds and pigsties.
Anthropologist Robert Garner asked one woman of Gibraltar
how many others shared her cave. 'Nine of we,' was the
charmingly colloquial reply. The woman's rent was three shillings
a week. Writing up his field notes for *The Reliquary* magazine in
1865, Garner observed, 'We were satisfied with what we had
seen of the troglodytes, without feeling any strong desire to
become a member of any class of them ourselves.'

Another subterranean village was at Buxton in Derbyshire,
where workers in the lime-burning industry made their thrifty if
not wholly covetable homes among the spoil heaps. A French
geologist called Faujas de Saint-Fond (1741–1819) described
how he happened upon these not-so-des reses. 'I looked in vain
for the habitations of so many labourers and their numerous
families without being able to see so much as one cottage when
at length I discerned that the whole tribe, like so many moles,
had formed their residences underground. This comparison is
strictly just: not one of them lived in a house.' Another
eyewitness, writing in 1813, took the spectacle of the 'Lime
Houses' even harder. 'Wretched and disgusting are these caves in
the extreme, and but for having their entrances closed by a door

might be more easily taken for the dens of wolves or bears than the abodes of humanised beings.' These slums were still occupied well into the latter part of the century. A local folklorist, Nellie Kirkham, wrote in 1947 that a man who was then aged seventy had grown up in the Lime Houses.

Nottingham can claim to be the most cave-riddled city in England. When a Welsh monk called Asser wrote *The Life of King Alfred* in the ninth century, he called Nottingham *Tigguocobaucc* in his Taff tongue, meaning 'the house of caves'. It became Snodenegeham – from the Anglo-Saxon *snodenge*, or caves, and *ham*, a house – and it was but a short etymological scramble from this to its present name. Two great sandstone outcrops, familiar today as Castle Rock and the Lace Market district, furnished many people with their cave dwellings. In the Middle Ages, people suffering from contagious diseases were incarcerated in Castle Rock in rock cells known as 'Bugge-holes', after a local textile merchant, Hugh Bugge.

There's an old cave under Marks & Spencer in the city centre, not sealed until 1974. Rather thrillingly, another can be entered from the men's department of Paul Smith's. You sashay through the striped shirts and socks, with their equally gaudy price tags, until you reach a door in the wall. Christian, an assistant with asymmetrical hair, will do the honours with the keypad entry device, ringing up the digits with his digits; and before you know it, you're descending a white stairway, passing the staff lockers and negotiating another, older, door which opens on to a descending flight of thirty brick steps. You find yourself at last in a round chamber with a central column or prop like the arch of an undercroft or the bobbin of a great loom.

The soft Bunter sandstone is pockmarked where it has been chiselled, jemmied, worked. There are low stone thralls, or benches, running around the cave: 'It is possible that this was designed as a venue for a novel underground drink', according to Tony Waltham of the East Midlands Geological Society.

Certainly, the cave was used as a wine cellar in the days when
Paul Smith's, or Willoughby House, to give it its grander name,
was in private hands. The house was built in the eighteenth
century and 'possesses a magnificent set of caves contemporary
with the house', notes Dr Charles Deering in his *History of
Nottingham*. The set is completed by a matching brace, one on
either side of the master chamber. They are identical to it, only
smaller. The subterranean space beneath the outfitters is 40 feet
long by 46 feet wide and 17 feet 6 inches deep. A crouch-making
sandstone defile leads to a patch of wasteland behind the
benighted Broadmarsh Shopping Centre.

In Nottingham, I lunched beneath the petrified foam
upholstery of a cave roof. I was in a cave pub, eating cave grub –
the microwaved magma of a jacket potato. It looked like an
exploding pouf; it looked exactly like the ceiling. I was with my
friend Penny Gallon, who once worked at the city's museum and
is an enthusiast of the subterranean. Penny is great company, an
attractive woman in her thirties with reddish-blonde hair. She
grew up in Mansfield. Her father was a lecturer in ceramics but
despite or perhaps because of this delicate vocation, he was tough
on Penny and her brother, as she saw it. He took them, or sent
them, caving. And when he decided to dig out the sandstone
underneath the family home to create a bigger basement, this
heavy work was deputed to his children. 'I think we got paid a
shilling a bucket, which we not only had to fill but carry outside,
across the road, and empty into a quarry,' said Penny. 'My Mum
got pissed off with all the sand being trampled into her carpet.
And it never got to be much more than a rammell store – that's
a local word, meaning rubbish.'

Penny gave me a postcard of houses in Mansfield like the one
she had dutifully undermined. She told me about a repository of
relics created by a mad subterranean type, a nineteenth-century
Nottinghamshire gentleman called R. S. Wilson. At his home in
Tuxford – 'the Hell at Tuxford', as it became known – Wilson dug

a pit into which he cast familiars and voodoo dolls, gargoyles and ships' figureheads, to represent all of society's ills, 'until a long catalogue of unrepentant sinners had been collected'. Penny produced a list of 'the imps of Satan', as unmasked by Wilson. They included King Alcohol; the Tobacco Devil; the Hypocrite; the Time-Server; Superstition; Priestcraft; the Religious Lawyer; the Man who can Tell where he was Conceived to the Square Inch; Two Faces under One Hat; the Woman with the Proud Look and the Lying Tongue; the Young Man whose Heart and Understanding are Void; Joe Brady; Skin-the-Goat; the Jingo Party; and President Kruger, the one-time leader of the Transvaal.

Wilson wouldn't have been out of place in The Trip to Jerusalem, though he would have balked at the booze, of course. Quarried out of Castle Rock in the early 1600s, the pub has the mad moraines of a diabolical pit. Or perhaps I should say the distended lobes of the poor old Elephant Man, with whom it shares a certain gothic Victorian grotesqueness. Its noted conversation-piece is the Haunted Galleon, a grimy model of a clipper, the gift of a sailor, mounted in a filthy display case. Pub lore has it that whosoever attempted to clean the exhibit would meet a horrible end. The last couple of people who presumed to violate this taboo reportedly suffered freakish and unnatural deaths; it must have been a long time ago, by the look of it.

Stuart the barman poked about behind his counter to find me an early photograph of the pub. He produced an entire see-through wallet of them, in fact, flicking them out with a lissom snap of the wrist as if he was showing off a deck of credit cards. Penny persuaded Stuart to show us the pub cellars, the cave vaults. According to Jeremy Errand's *Secret Passages and Hiding Places* (1974), 'A passage is supposed to lead into Mortimer's Hole . . . from a blocked-up entrance to an ancient inn . . . the Trip To Jerusalem . . . Many inns claim secret passages merely as advertisement, but the likelihood at the "Trip" is less flimsy than most.' Mortimer's Hole has been described by one historian as 'the best known and most romantic' of Nottingham's many apertures and tunnels, and by another quite simply as 'Britain's most famous secret passage'. Roger Mortimer was regent of England following the murder of Edward II in 1327, in which regicide he played an instrumental role. In 1330, he was holding a parliament at Nottingham Castle when Edward III stole up on him by means of a secret tunnel, known ever after as Mortimer's Hole. The tunnel was more than a hundred yards long: it ran through the sandstone hill like the legend in a stick of rock. Despite the cries of Mortimer's lover, Queen Isabella, the pretender was taken to London and hanged at Tyburn.

'That's cask and this is keg,' said the now cruciform Stuart, pointing out his barrels as a flight attendant might the doors of his aircraft. My eye fell on a folder, as dusty as the Haunted Galleon itself. The words 'Food Hygiene Rules' were just discernible on the cover. 'That's the old one,' said Stuart, following my gaze. There were insects on the wing in the cellars, and strips of fly-paper like curing beef jerky. As we followed Stuart in single file, Penny turned to me and smiled conspiratorially, *girlishly*. It was the done thing in Nottingham to go drinking in a cave, a tradition dating back to Daniel Defoe's day:

> The town of Nottingham is situated upon the steep ascent of a sandy rock; which is consequently remarkable, for that it is so soft that they easily work into it for making vaults and cellars, and yet so firm as to support the roofs of those cellars two or three under one another; the stairs into which, are all cut out of the solid, though crumbling rock; and we must not fail to have it be remembered that the bountiful inhabitants generally keep these cellars well stocked with excellent ALE; nor are they uncommunicative in bestowing it among their friends, as some in our company experienced to a degree not fit to be made matter of history.

Penny and I didn't find a hidden entrance to Mortimer's Hole, but Stuart showed us a part of the vaults which had once been a prison cell, or so he said. He ducked under a wavy cornice – it was like the settled head on a pint of stout – and waited for us to catch him up. 'Now then,' said Stuart, '*this* was where they had the cock-fighting.'

Caves under Brewhouse Yard, around the corner from the pub, were lived in as late as the 1970s: here was evidence of the habitation of English caves from practically the day before yesterday. The yard was developed after James I sold the land 'to two men from London' in 1621. It became a notorious quarter of the city. It was lawless, not only in the sense that decent folk feared to venture among its drunks, prostitutes and cutpurses, but also in that it was beyond or exempt from the law; it was its own Hobbesian republic. A notorious nineteenth-century murderer, Charlie Peace, made his home among the caves, as did a sinister society known as the Family of Love.

These days, Phil the janitor saw order at Brewhouse Yard, in tie and crested V-neck. Penny and I toured the recreated subterranean kitchens and utility rooms of the old houses, a wall of brick cheek by jowl with stone the colour and texture of confectioner's honeycomb. There were dressers, stoves, a machine for fitting metal tops to bottles. One cave was mocked up to look like a Second World War bomb shelter. Penny pointed out an unremarkable white door tucked in a corner – a broom cupboard, to my untutored eye – and asked if I'd like to see where Nottingham's cave people used to draw their water. Naturally, I said yes. I followed Penny down a metal ladder to a well. It had a rounded brick mouth, in the approved children's book style, and there was even a limpid pool, a foot or two deep, at the bottom of it.

There was one more troglodyte treat in store under Nottingham. Phil procured a key to admit us to a cave, out of bounds to the public, where scientists had allegedly experimented with 'cosmic rays'. 'If you go in here, you'll come out a glowing green colour,' warned Penny. The story was that physicists associated with Nottingham University had dabbled with Dan Dare technology during the Second World War, when their fellow citizens were taking cover against more conventional weapons in another fold of the sandstone hillside. I tiptoed across the threshold.

If I was hoping for walls running with ectoplasm; for the stock of a monstrous, aged weapon, like the barnacled butt of a harpoon gun; even for a dazed and undemobbed figure in a soiled lab coat offering to X-ray my sorry Boche private parts to kingdom come – if I was hoping for something like that, then the reality was, at first sight, a little less busy. The old atomic-ray chamber had been converted into a storeroom, so there were long, low benches of the sort that children might sit on, a sprung bedstead not needed in one of the wartime austerity displays elsewhere, and a mock-up Anderson shelter. But then Penny pointed out deep clefts scored into one face of the cave. 'They're completely unlike any other marks.' Below them, a bench was dusted with freshly fallen sandstone, as if the desperate alchemy of wartime was still transmogrifying in this forgotten, unacknowledged silo. I noticed that evening as I was leaving Nottingham that my scalp was gritty; as shingly, in fact, as if I'd spent the day on the beach.

As it was becoming clear to me, the English have been among the last people in Europe to relinquish the shelter of the cave. We're familiar with the idea of 'two up, two down', but it wasn't so long ago that it was *all* down. We like to think of ourselves as sophisticated, with our mezzanines and our piazzas, our decking and kitchen 'islands'. But put us in a corner and primal considerations will out. We want a patch of warmth, we want a roof over our heads, and we aren't too fussed if there happens to be a sooty skidmark on it. My God, we're cavemen! The red sandstone knoll of Kinver Edge in Staffordshire, for example, is a great work of scrimshaw – rooms have been chiselled and

gouged out of it, as well as passages and stairways – and it was
throngingly inhabited within living memory. There could be no
surer sign that the cave is close to an Englishman's heart than the
fact that one of the Kinver Edge grottoes was turned into a tea
room; the sign 'Teas' was clearly legible there.

My travels brought me into contact with people living not far
from Kinver Edge – in the very middle of Middle England – for
whom subsisting in hollowed rock is not the stuff of fur-clad
figures of legend but as unremarkable as setting up home in a
semi. As if I'd stumbled upon the Valley of the Lost, as if I'd
hitched a lift in Barney Rubble's stone limo and pogoed alongside
him all the way into Bedrock, I found myself in Wolverley, a
village where my fellow countrymen live in caves to this day.

Long before the housing market in the rest of the country
turned rocky, that's how it was in Wolverley – and that's just the
way the folks there liked it, too. In July 2007, I went to the
village to meet a man named Charles Morris who had recently
become the proud owner of a cave. The cave had been on the
market, though not as a cave, or not *just* as a cave: it had been
up for sale as a three-roomed house. There was a glossy handbill
of particulars, a photograph in an estate agent's window, an
asking price of £25,000. Rock House was said to command
panoramic views over the Severn Valley. You could make an
appointment to view it. It didn't come with all mod cons,
however: there wasn't a phone there, for a start, nor any
electricity or running water, come to that.

So what did Charles Morris want with it? He already had a
place of his own in Wolverley: 'Mar-Tiny' (like the aperitif),
named after Mr Morris and his late wife – 'Mar-' for Marjorie
and 'Tiny' because this had been the nickname of the imposing
Charles since his schooldays. Not only that, but Mar-Tiny was
right next door to Rock House: bungalow and cave were only
yards apart. When I wondered what had persuaded Charles to
invest in his craggy lair, he came back drily with 'So no one else

does.' A widower in his late seventies, he wasn't keen on the idea of people moving in on top of him, with all sorts of ideas for developing the cave, so he bought it so as to keep it exactly as it was – empty – for the sake of a little peace and quiet. Sure enough, all was still in Wolverley . . .

Overhung with creepers and swags of holly, the cave house was set in a red-brown rockface. A weathered blue door and a pair of windows, leaded but no longer fully glazed, could be made out in the rugged façade. Rock House was as creased as old leather. It could have belonged to the old woman in the nursery rhyme who reared countless children in a shoe. The missing panes of glass were like the eyelets for the laces. Squinting through one of them, I could make out a dim but sizeable room, extending perhaps thirty feet back into the cliff face and capped by a low ceiling. This stony living-room was bereft of any furniture or amenity apart from a clinkered fireplace.

But Rock House had been lived in until the 1950s, Charles assured me. 'Mrs Thompson had it. I used to be in the gun club with her son Bert. He's dead now, of course.'

'You've lived in Wolverley a long time then, Charles.'

'All my life,' he said.

Rock House wasn't on its own: it wasn't an odd shoe, but part of a little line, a row of hobnailed boots. An adjacent cave, behind another house, had been turned into a utility room, or was it a junkyard? It was full of old newspapers, white goods that no longer looked quite as pristine as they once did, and two large buckets of evil-looking fluid. But then proactive cave husbandry was a feature of life in Wolverley, according to a woman I met in the village. 'Living in caves is nothing to us round here, you know,' she confirmed.

'Isn't it?'

'Oh no.' There was a house in the village, she said, that was almost all cave: the white façade was exactly that, a façade. Another property had a cave for a bathroom.

I discovered that the parish church stood on a hill that was made of the same hide-like stone as Rock House, and at the foot of the hill were more caves. They were behind metal railings, but otherwise open to the elements. They were the rock-cut habitations occupied in the nineteenth century by labourers working at the village blacksmith's, which was also established in a cave.

Backing on to the hillside was a white cottage with an attractive bottle-glass bow window. I wondered if it was one of the cave conversions that the woman had mentioned; I wondered how much of it was cottage, and how much hillside. There was a trim man in leisure shirt and jeans going in and out of the cottage, shuttling between it and a car parked on the driveway. From somewhere came the thrum of a generator. The man, whose name was Edward, told me that the cottage had not long ago been flooded. The damage was done by the river, which was dawdling through Wolverley innocuously enough that morning but had lately burst its banks. Edward and his family had cleared everything from the ground floor and moved out for the duration. He was trying to dry the place out, which accounted for the generator.

He kindly gave me a tour of his dehumidifying home. A dog-leg staircase was on the right of the cottage as you entered, on the side set against the hillside. As I climbed it, I admired the wall. Like the exterior of the cottage, the wall was whitewashed. It was bearing up well, considering its recent watery immersion. For all that, there was something curious about it, something stirringly amiss in its igloo-bright compactness. On second thoughts, there was nothing amiss about it at all – rather, something thoroughly archaic. That uneven surface, those curious striations – as if channelling some long-buried folk memory, I suddenly knew where I was. I was snug within the antediluvian shelter of my forefathers. I was gathered into the stony bosom of my ancestral hall. I was inside a cave.

3

WORMHOLES

More fool me for doubting that the English literally dwelt in marble halls, when there was plenty of evidence, in Wolverley and elsewhere, that that's exactly what we did. And I do mean 'we'. My grandmother lived in a cave. Does that surprise you? It surprises me. If I find it unlikely, goodness knows what she'd make of it, put like that. She'd turn in her cave.

Because my paternal grandparent – Nana, to distinguish her from our other granny ('Granny') – was no knuckle-dragging Neanderthal, given to entertaining her grandchildren in the whistling fissure of a hillside. On the contrary, she was a respectable, church-going woman who would no sooner contemplate living in a cave than on the moon. And yet when I think of her old place, it's always with memories of the scullery, the back kitchen, the dark potato-reeking room to which Nana frequently repaired in search of veg, dry goods or other victuals. You might find yourself in there on an errand, or when intending to spring out and catch a family member unawares. It was a hidey-hole in a house that was full of them, an unlit chamber in a building which, now I think of it, had an inky and cavernous quality to it overall; though I found it a happy place, I enjoyed exploring it and wasn't scared to be on my own in one of its gloomy crannies. If ever a child was calculated to develop a curiosity for dark and hidden places, then it would be while amusing himself somewhere like Nana's house, with its shadowy landings, its bedrooms with locks that were apt to stick (one imprisoned my then knee-high sister for hours on end), its tuber-rich black hole.

What was different about the back kitchen, apart from the springy duckboard matting under foot, was its striking irregularity, an unfinished quality about it. I remember the walls as whitewashed, but my sister insists the scullery was tiled. What we're both agreed upon, thirty years or so after the event, is that the room seemed to grow smaller the further you went into it. The ceiling came down to meet you and the walls closed in. It dwindled, it tapered: what architect or builder would have put in a room like that?

Nana's house was in New Brighton, on the north-eastern tip of the Wirral peninsula, a *soi-disant* resort on the Mersey riviera. This unlikely spa was the brainchild of a man named James Atherton, a Liverpool merchant who came over to the Wirral in 1830 and bought up a great swathe of land facing the river at Wallasey. There he built New Brighton, a watering-hole and holiday spot. Why should the southern swanks have all the bathing and the golden sands to themselves? New Brighton became a popular day out and Wakes Week destination among families from Liverpool and the Lancashire mill towns. It acquired a pier in the 1860s and a tower in 1900, the tallest building in the country at the time.

Many of its large houses were turned into inexpensive hotels, including Nana's house. It was a b&b called Seacliff on Victoria Road. The family also owned the place next door, Hazeldene Hotel; one substantial concern, all told. It was very much a going concern, too. Seacliff and Hazeldene were full, or nearly full, during the war, when they became a billet for servicemen as well as resident guests, and the business was still going during my childhood in the 1960s. The big, dark house smelled of cooked breakfasts. My auntie Bessie hit a brass gong for dinner at seven, a ritual observed at Hazeldene like the lowering of a standard in a far-off, fly-blown colony.

Guests tended to be commercial representatives, men who travelled in ladies' clothing, as the old musical-hall joke had it. They were joined by men who actually told musical-hall jokes; the clientele was leavened by theatrical turns who were booked to appear at the Floral Pavilion at the bottom of Victoria Road. I'd like to be able to tell you that we would sometimes hear muffled explosions from the human cannonball's room, or that the ventriloquists would take their dolls in to dinner and order gottles of geer from Bessie. Nana was to all intents and purposes a northern seaside landlady (though she was nothing like the Gorgon figure once familiar from stand-up routines), and for all I know her roof gave shelter to many comedians, as well as musicians, illusionists and contortionists, balloon-folders and fire-eaters and knife-throwers and tightrope-walkers. But these troupers evidently chose to save their acts for paying customers, and passed their leisure hours affecting the mien of actuaries. They were only known to draw upon their experience of the boards when my auntie Ethel, an accomplished pianist in her own right, gave one of her recitals – then, the travelling players could be prevailed upon to join in.

We stayed at Seacliff during school holidays, my brother and sister and me. I helped Bessie to take a good swing at the gong. With less success, I applied a scoop to catering tubs of ice cream: it pinged off the unyielding vanilla like a grappling hook rebounding from a glacier. Bessie and Ethel were accommodated among the guest rooms, as were several more aunts and uncles. But Nana lived entirely underground. She and my grandfather – who preferred to be known as Uncle Stephen, which he felt was less ageing – had rooms in the basement of Seacliff.

People stopped coming to New Brighton in the late sixties. Holiday-makers wanted the sun, and now they could fly off to it. The tower came down and the pier was demolished and Nana's hotel closed to paying guests. A sign that hung on Victoria Road for many years, advertising 'The Wallasey Water Skiing Club', looked more and more bathetically misplaced. The b&bs of Victoria Road had been built on shifting sands. Allowing for poetic licence, this was true: not shifting sands as such, but sandstone. Atherton had commissioned his fine houses on a range of rocky cliffs and dunes.

This geology, with its tractability before pick and shovel, had lent itself admirably to the earliest enterprises of Wallasey people. Long before the Smiths were engaged in the hotel business, another rackety trade was pursued by the community. Not to put too fine a point on it, they were smugglers. Smuggling! Was there a more colourful and romantic use to which to put a cave? It's been claimed that nearly all the inhabitants of the Wirral were bootleggers at one time, though they presented themselves to the outside world as guileless as provincial Sicilians, apparently pursuing the blameless vocations of farmers and fishermen. A Customs report from 1750 noted: 'Smuggling into the coasts around Liverpool . . . is generally from the Isleman [sic] . . . in small boats that never appear on the coast but fall in with the land just in the dusk of the evening, that by their observations they may run in the night time into the place intended for the discharge of their goods where persons are always ready to assist and convey them to a proper place of safety.' A local man wrote: 'Fine time the runners used to have in my young days! Scarcely a house in North Wirral that could not provide a guest with a good stiff glass of brandy or Hollands.' In 1837, a report by a Royal Commission found that 'Chester' (Cheshire) had the greatest incidence of illegal trafficking outside Cornwall. The authors wrote: 'On the Cheshire coast not far from Liverpool, they will rob those who have escaped the perils of the sea and come safe on shore, and mutilate dead bodies for the sake of rings and personal ornaments.' In 1839, the *Pennsylvania* and two other ships were wrecked off the Wirral in a fierce storm, and their cargoes and furnishings were later found divvied up among residents. As if it wasn't enough to prey on the victims of groundings and sinkings, the supposedly dim country cousins, the 'woolly-backs' of the Wirral, weren't above drumming up business in their own cunning fashion, by 'wrecking'. As a contemporary account has it, 'Many a fierce fire has been lighted on the Wirral shore on stormy nights to lure the good ship on to the Burbo or Hoyle Banks, there to beat and strain and throb, until her timbers parted, and her planks were floating in confusion on the stormy waves.'

Disposing of this spumy bounty couldn't have been easier. It was stored underground, in cellars and tunnels, in the soft, buttery substrata of the Wirral. One notorious hiding-place was beneath a pub known as Old Mother Redcap's, after its scarlet-bonneted landlady. It was 'an inn addicted to the contraband', like the Bugle at Newport in J. Meade Falkner's story *Moonfleet*. Its blowsy barmaid was the moll of sailors and smugglers, who came to her with their pay and prize money, which she hid in various nooks and knots of wood about her premises. To foil the efforts of the excise men, the windows of the pub were shuttered and the door was five inches thick. Forcing it merely released a catch on a trapdoor just over the threshold: an unsuspecting inspector would find himself pedalling air nine feet above the uncushioned floor of a cellar. A weather vane on a flagstaff was nothing of the sort; when it was pointing towards the inn, it meant it was safe for the gentlemen to call (when not, not). The pub was still standing as late as the 1970s. It was finally torn down, but the building that subsequently went up proudly assumed its name: the Mother Redcap's sheltered housing unit also inherited the pub's original gnarled gateway.

It was believed that tunnels beneath the pub led to caves in a rocky outcrop known locally as the Red Noses, after the rufous sandstone they were made from. 'Above the "Noses" is a fine stretch of flowery grassland where, on warm summer days, butterflies and moths flit among the clovers and harebells, and rabbits hop about in the long grass,' wrote Wallasey-born author Kenneth Burnley:

> I wonder how many of the folk who walk these pleasant airy heights realise that, a few yards below their feet, extends a labyrinth of caves and tunnels. These are the aptly named 'Wormhole Caves' which, legend has it, extend for miles below New Brighton and Wallasey . . . Originally a natural feature of the coast, man has, over the centuries, used and enlarged these dark caves and tunnels for his own, sometimes illicit purposes.

I was reading Burnley on freebooters and their coverts, but what I was thinking about was Nana and her basement rooms at Seacliff, her underground granny flat. What was her scullery, the irregular, tapering room, but a feature below New Brighton which man had used and enlarged for his own purposes (no more illicit, in Nana's time, than games of hide-and-seek with her grandchildren). That was it, I thought. (It had to be.) The back kitchen was a cave. A previous owner of Seacliff, perhaps as long ago as old Atherton's day, had fancied a little more storage space, perhaps a coal hole, and had scooped out the workable rock – much more biddable than Bessie's vanilla – the spreadable sandstone on which the house stood.

I tried the idea out on my sister. 'It wasn't like a normal room, was it? Do you remember? It was more like a cave—'

'Yes!' said Victoria at once. 'It took a lot of courage to go in there.'

I sounded out my auntie June, another former regular at Seacliff. The back kitchen was a cave, I suggested. 'Oh yes,' June agreed.

Burnley goes on to say: 'If you ever get the opportunity to go down the Wormhole Caves, take it – it's quite an experience!' And that's what I determined to do, to go down the Wormhole Caves of New Brighton.

In physics, a wormhole connects different parts of space, even parallel universes, with one another. The presence of wormholes in the warp and weave of space and time was first suggested in 1916 by the Austrian Ludwig Flamm, and many scientists now accept them as a logical corollary of Einstein's theory of relativity. Anything entering one end of a wormhole instantly appears at the other end, so long as the tunnel can be kept open. It was like a game of Snakes and Ladders: if you could wriggle through a wormhole – a Wormhole Cave – you would be returned to the past. The caves would connect with the hollow under my grandparents' house, I felt, if not literally then *relatively*. They would take me back to the original, the platonic, cave, so to speak; the template for every other underground chamber I've ever had the urge to see.

My family had long since left Seacliff. In contrast to Old Mother Redcap's, the old place was still standing, but the name had gone. I'd been past it once or twice, and it seemed to have become a dance studio. Out of curiosity, I entered Nana's address into an Internet search engine. To my glee, this revealed that a private detective agency was now on the premises, too. I couldn't wait to meet the gumshoes. What part of Seacliff had they taken for themselves? It would make sense if they had set up shop in Nana's basement flat, keeping a low profile. And where better to keep their sophisticated surveillance equipment than out of sight in the old scullery, making use of the famous secrecy of the caves of Wallasey just as earlier cloak-and-dagger types had done. Watch the wall, my darling, while the private dicks go by!

I was going to look for the Wormhole Caves with my friend Gerry. I couldn't have been in better hands: Gerry was an experienced Green Badge guide, who led walking tours of his native Liverpool. He was a retired engineer. He was mad-keen on railways. He was a trim, compact man with piercing blue eyes and a crew cut. There was a bit of the Jeffrey Archer about him – at least, in that novelist's mature, Magwitch phase.

Gerry had visited the Wormhole Caves as a boy. 'I couldn't tell you much about it now. But I remember enjoying myself.' The Wirral was a bit off the beaten track for Gerry nowadays. But he had been doing some research, as he explained when I met him outside James Street Station, Liverpool, in July 2007. There was a lively wind off the river that morning, funnelled up the slope of the street towards the city centre, and Gerry was snuffling into a large Lincoln-green handkerchief. He told me that he had the phone number of a woman who lived in New Brighton. He had tried ringing her that morning, but no luck so far. He gave me a railcard that he'd thoughtfully bought for me. It entitled me to come and go as I pleased all day long by bus, ferry and Merseyrail, the Scouse subway.

Long before motorists could cross the Mersey in a road tunnel, a route was excavated for trains. The original plan was for a 'pneumatic railway', which would use air pressure to move carriages from one bank of the river to the other, audaciously harnessing the technology of blow football for the purposes of subterranean mass transit. The Pneumatic Despatch Company, founded in 1849, had enjoyed limited success in firing parcels 452 yards through a two-foot-wide tunnel at Battersea, and a similar system was used to distribute letters and parcels below the streets of London on the original Post Office railway. But at length the Merseyside engineers settled on a more conventional scheme. Work began in 1879, at George's Dock in Liverpool and at Birkenhead on the far side of the river. The rail tunnel was 19 feet high from the tracks to the roof, and 26 feet across, wide enough to accommodate two lines running side by side. It had the thickness of eight layers of bricks: thirty-eight million of them went into it, in all. To save money, the contractors wanted to excavate the Liverpool end of the line using the shallow cut-and-cover method, but after encountering vocal Liverpudlian resistance from residents and traders, they resorted to deeper, more expensive shafts. All the same, they still managed to undermine the foundations of several buildings in Hamilton Street in the city centre.

Unlike Brunel's men who had dug the Thames Tunnel, the first beneath a river anywhere in the world, the labourers on the Mersey Rail Tunnel basked in the glow of electric light, although gas was preferred at the stations because the supply was more reliable. In view of the risk of flooding, huge sumps, or reservoirs, were dug out at the bases of the main shafts of the tunnel. They could hold 80,000 gallons of water. It was calculated that in the event of a breach, the labourers would have enough time to escape before these reservoirs fatally overtopped. The two gangs of tunnellers, approaching each other beneath the river from opposite banks, met in January 1884, five years after they had set out. The Prince of Wales formally opened the Mersey Rail Tunnel in January 1886 and the first trains ran through it on 1 February. They carried thirty-six thousand passengers that day.

The station on the Liverpool side of the tunnel was quarried out at James Street. From the ticket office at street level, Gerry and I made our descent to the platform, a journey which took us through eighty feet of rock. On the way down, we passed a locked, concertinaed metal gate: beyond it was a passageway. This was a pedestrian subway which rose steeply from the station to the office buildings of Water Street. Every morning, passengers got off the train at James Street and strode 160 yards up the subterranean incline towards their desks, then the subway was padlocked behind them. It was opened once more at teatime, when the wage slaves jogged back down the same slope to catch the train home again. 'It's what we do in Liverpool instead of going to the gym,' said Gerry.

At length, we found ourselves on the platform. It was pleasantly cool and fresh – there was a breeze blowing from the tunnel out of which our train would in due course materialise – and a gurgle of water was coming from beneath the tracks. The platform was wide and coated in rubber. There was no yellow line of the kind you'd find at a London Underground station, to indicate the minimum safe distance that passengers should stand from the track. And the reason for this was immediately apparent: there weren't any passengers. Or at least, there were hardly any. The modest cluster of commuters barely added up to the queue you'd find at a bus shelter. Of course, Liverpool is rather smaller than London, and Gerry and I were travelling mid-morning, but later I would encounter the same light sprinkling of strap-hangers at five o'clock in the evening. (Once when I was getting off at James Street, I was surprised to find a surge of people coming down the stairs towards me – there must have been at least a dozen of them – so surprised in fact, that I stood back to let them pass. Among them was a teenage couple. As the girl reached the platform, she let out a moan, and the boy said sharply, 'Well, it *is* the rush hour!' as they took grandmother's footsteps on to the half-empty platform.)

Where was everyone? I wondered aloud. But Gerry leapt to the defence of hometown honour. 'This is the busiest system in Britain outside London,' he said. He claimed that one hundred thousand commuters travelled on Merseyrail every day. The way was opened to a rapprochement between us when Gerry added that Sunday was the most crowded day on the railway: that was when trippers took to the rails. From this it was possible to conclude both that the railway was as popular as Gerry insisted, *and* that it wasn't the iron horse of the working week that I was familiar with from the capital.

With amity restored, Gerry told me that the gradient on the railway was 1 in 33, 'the steepest on Network Rail's passenger network'. The line opened as a steam-powered concern but was electrified in 1903 'by an up-and-coming American engineer named James Westinghouse', said Gerry the Green Badge guide, lapsing into the argot of the peripatetic pedagogue.

Our service duly pulled in, higher off the ground, it seemed, than its London counterparts. I had the impression of the thing running on outsize wheels; by contrast, you could almost imagine that the London Tube carriages slid along on their static-crackling rails like Scalextric toys.

Bit by bit, the railway under the river expanded into a Merseyside metro. On the Liverpool side, the line was extended from James Street to Central Station in 1892; when underpasses and stairs were built to give the citizens of Liverpool access to the new station from the thoroughfare of Waterloo Place, the basement of the Lyceum Theatre was converted into a waiting-room. James Street and Central are now part of a compact Liverpool 'Tube', known as the Loop. Trains circulate in a clockwise direction through just over a mile of tunnels and call at four stops (the other two are at Lime Street, the city's best-known terminus, and at Moorfields).

This was a journey I'd made more than once in the past, from Liverpool under the river by train, alighting at Wallasey Village to see June and my uncle George, or staying on all the way to New Brighton, to go to Seacliff. In the sudden sunlight of the Wirral shore, I mentioned as much to Gerry, whereupon he made the – to me – outlandish claim that Wallasey was an island until as little as three hundred years ago. A lot of the land that was familiar to me, like the park at Harrison Drive where June and George had walked a succession of dogs, had been dunes until comparatively recently. It was these drifts, said Gerry, that Wallasey had emerged from. 'Sand dunes are called *meols* in Norse, and there's a place called Meols in the Wirral.' It was at the selfsame Meols, just days after our excursion, that builders came across a suspected Viking longboat under a pub car park. The thousand-year-old clinker-built tub was found in ten feet of clay beside the Railway Inn.

The Wirral was colonised by Vikings, according to Gerry, and later the Irish. 'Around here there's lots of Scandinavian names: Ormskirk, Skelmersdale. Same thing with family names.'

'What about Fenby?' I wondered, citing Nana's maiden name.

'Yes, Viking,' said Gerry quickly. He was eager to be iterating what he knew, to be *guiding*. He wasn't swallowing his words, he was gulping them down. 'You can see the Irish heritage in the name of a church round here,' he said, 'it's called St Hilary's.'

With that, Gerry fell back into his seat. His show-and-tell was at an end, at least for the time being. He could be obsessive but this was offset by his native sense of humour. He was a Scouse savant. We drank in the view of the old windmill of Bidston Hill, a Wirral landmark. I told Gerry about once disturbing a wasps' nest up there. I was Robin Hood, adroitly finding a chink in the chain-mail of one of King John's goons; only, my well-judged thrust must have gone right through my adversary, because the next thing I knew it had penetrated a thicket of gorse and punctured the wimple-like hive, too. I was covered in wasps and then in their stings. There was one last prick in it for me: I found myself on the end of a hypodermic of antihistamine, like Uma Thurman in *Pulp Fiction* (though it was adrenalin in her case). I told Gerry and he said drily, 'That was clever.'

We went through Wallasey Village. 'It's very nice, Wallasey Village,' said Gerry. 'Very light.' He claimed that the place was known for its mild winters. I thought about our Christmas holidays in these parts, coming out of the slot-machine arcades on the prom into the tingle of salt in the air, the wet-towel snap of the wind. He could have fooled me, I thought. 'These lands here are very fertile,' he said. 'Wallasey's famous for its cabbages.'

At New Brighton station, I was appalled to discover that I had misplaced the travel pass that Gerry had given me. It might have been a small gesture on his part, but something about the fact that he hadn't needed to make it, and that I hadn't been expecting it, had made it strangely touching. I couldn't have been more mortified if Gerry had made me a model of Seacliff out of matches and I had absently snapped off a length of guttering to use as a toothpick. I also had an instinct that my folly would discombobulate Gerry, the creature of routine. Sure enough, I noticed that he was going through his own pockets – he was tearing at his clothes, in fact, like a man stricken by marching ants. It seemed that Gerry had become concerned that he, too, had lost his travel warrant.

'Are you all right, Gerry?' He was subjecting himself and his accessories to a vigorous and uncompromising frisking. Gerry had a natty 'man bag', I now noticed, a Ted Baker job, which featured a handy slot for his brolly, or at least that's what he used it for. It seemed as though everything was going to be all right, after all. He held up his pass. 'Here it is!' He was beaming with relief. He was going to be OK. Phew!

He had another go at getting hold of his contact in Wallasey, and this time she answered the phone. She told him to try an address in a road that ran parallel to Victoria Road. It was the next road down the hill, in fact, towards the coruscating river. Gerry and I found ourselves in front of a substantial white-washed villa. In the south of England, you might expect such a residence to border the bracingly exclusive Wentworth greens; here it overlooked the scally-haunted links where my dad and brother used to play pitch and putt.

Gerry rang the doorbell. 'Let me do the talking,' he said. He was drawing on his experience as a tour guide, his people skill-set. I suppose I should have been entertained, or offended, that he took no cognisance of my own experience in this field, as a reporter who has effected an entrée from the odd doorstep in his time. On second thoughts, perhaps Gerry was simply taking me as he found me, and judged that our cause wasn't likely to prosper if it depended on my bedside manner. The door was answered by a young Polish woman called Katia. Gerry asked her about the caves and Katia haltingly confirmed that we had come to the right place.

This was cheering news. It was glad, confident morning under a periwinkle sky, I was back in New Brighton where I'd spent so many happy days, and fortune was favouring our cause. It reminded me of accompanying my grandfather Uncle Stephen to the shops and looking on attentively – absorbing what I would later recognise as a life lesson – as he flirted with the shopgirls with a view to a bargain.

'Can we see the cave?' pressed Gerry deftly.

Katia said 'It's OK' with an indifference that I found enchanting at that moment, and we followed her through a gate and down some steps to the back garden.

Thick, lustrous grass garnished a hexagonal helipad of a lawn. On closer inspection, this proved to be a turf terrace that had been laid over a brick amphitheatre or circus. I admired a nesting pair of stone eagles; had they been a pound or two lighter, you could imagine Roman legions marching behind them. Clearly, these sumptuous surroundings were all so much mounting for the priceless gems that were the caves, the fixing that held these black pearls. The proud owner had invested time, trouble and hard cash in showing off his priceless treasures to best advantage. Gerry and I swiftly established that there was not one but two entrances to the Wormholes, one higher than the other. The upper entrance was behind a padlocked metal wicket, not unlike the barrier we'd encountered over the mouth of the subway at the James Street Merseyrail station. Beyond this grille, the eye made out builders' clutter: tubes of sealant, a putty-festooned radio. Winsome pottery gargoyles were mounted on the walls. The lower entry-way to the caves was similarly unavailing: it was boarded up with wooden railway sleepers, in front of which an iron trestle table had been upended, the whole amounting to a formidable barricade. 'The family is away,' shrugged Katia.

Gerry and I enjoyed splendid uninterrupted views of Liverpool bay. We quaffed like hummingbirds from the intoxicating ambrosia of rosebeds. We were buggered, and we knew it. The householder, a pharmacist, had gone on holiday with his wife and children. Katia had no knowledge of a key to the caves, and would quite rightly have had no intention of admitting strangers like us, even if she did. The tranquillity of the squint-making noon was disturbed only by the buzzing of a mower. Over the wall at the rear of the property, a gardener could be seen toiling on a far fairway. There was a gate in the wall, giving on to the golf course by way of a path down a rocky outcrop. 'Those are the Red Noses,' said Gerry. Of course, I thought. Well, thanks for telling me, I also thought. Maybe there were other entrances to the caves beyond the freehold of the villa; surely I would find an opening among the Red Noses – a nostril, forsooth? Gerry sat on the rocks as I scrambled down them. I flung myself into a coppice. Was this Kenneth Burnley's 'flowery grassland', with butterflies and moths flitting among the clovers and harebells, and rabbits hopping about in the long grass? No, not entirely. I jinked past beer cans, a pair of knickers: I was in the al fresco romper room of the Wirral's excluded scholars. I danced across the cold coals of an old fire – but not even this initiation rite granted me open sesame to the caves.

Now I frogmarched poor Gerry down the pitch-and-putt course. He tried to alert me to the likelihood that we had committed several infractions of the local by-laws, but I wanted to collar the municipal ghillie and find out what he knew of the Wormholes. I explained our quest to him, whereupon he immediately gave up his workaday burden and followed us. You'll forgive a messianic tone, I think, when I tell you that this man simply turned off the ignition on the mower and left it exactly where it was. He abandoned his prosaic but necessary calling to take up the uncertain cause of underground exploration.

'Do you know where the Wormhole Caves are?' I asked the honest fellow. In that moment, leader became follower; and follower, leader: unerringly, the young gardener took Gerry and me right back to the gate in the wall of the whitewashed villa. I could hardly blame him for returning us to square one, but what was to be done?

*

Later, Gerry and I sat outside the Perch Fish Bar on the prom at New Brighton. He ate freshly fried haddock and chips. 'This is gorgeous, the best I've had in a long time.' He munched beneath a brilliant cerulean heaven. 'This is the best thing you could have done for me, Steve,' he confirmed.

Across the water, on the Liverpool docks, wind towers turned. There was a great petrified landslip of glittering pig iron on the quayside. It looked like one of the brilliant stacks of pennies that had teetered so temptingly in the old Cascade slot machines in the New Brighton arcades: slide another copper in and it might break the logjam, nudge the hoard right into your hands. According to Gerry, an entrepreneur had made a fortune out of this pig-iron chaff by reducing it to walnut-sized pieces that would fit snugly into containers, to be shipped to the Far East and turned into cars and white goods. From time to time, Gerry said, the piles of walnuts caught spectacularly alight. It was the oil on the iron that burned.

At Liverpool aerodrome, known these days as JLA (for John Lennon Airport), some of the late Beatle's best-loved lyrics from his hit 'Imagine' had been co-opted as a blazon: 'Above us only sky'. The baggage handlers, in turn, had cribbed their own motto: 'Imagine no possessions', Gerry joked. Here we were, just around the corner from the old Floral Pavilion theatre, a rotten tomato's throw from the stage where Nana's tenants had earned their rent money. Would I ever settle the matter of the caves at Seacliff? Would I see the Wormholes? Perhaps they would appear when I least expected them, as Einstein said they would – a sudden breach in the cosmos, a rending in the narrative, a sting in the tail. I wouldn't give up hope, I decided. I suggested to Gerry that his gag was taken from his guiding repertoire. He went on eating his fish dinner, with a look of seraphic passivity on his face.

4

ANCIENT WONDERS

Many wonders of the English subterranean have a becoming reticence: they must be coaxed out of hiding before we can appreciate them. Sometimes this happens by chance. Relics and remnants are snagged on the end of a contractor's pick and exposed to the light of day, perhaps for the first time in centuries. Archaeologists live for moments like this. They are the firemen of history. See them on call in their offices and common rooms, this shirtsleeved watch of antiquarians, their boots and hard-hats by the door. Look at them flicking distractedly through *History Today*, giving each other rococo nicknames – it's 'Dr' this and 'Professor' that – and superstitiously waxing and re-waxing that familiar item they all rush for and struggle into the minute there's a shout – yes, where would they be without their Barbours? There's tension in the air because the balloon could go up at any moment, and once archaeologists are on the job, they're racing against the clock to get it done. The very passage of time that cultivates the pearls of history is always threatening to sweep them away again. The same contractors who accidentally dig things up are impatient to see them buried once more, and get their work finished. Me, I was along for the ride, I was on the spot and at the scene, notebook in hand.

On a summer's morning in 2007, we were pitchforked from our beds by the news that a great 'rock serpent' had been discovered in the Midlands. If the details were confirmed, the 'Rotherwas Ribbon', as it was being dubbed, was as much as four thousand years old. Blue-chinned archaeologists were out of the door without kissing their wives, and bouncing to the site in their four-by-fours and Land Rovers. Workers building a road for a trading estate outside Hereford had barked a shovel against a Bronze Age sculpture set in the earth. They'd turned back the topsoil on almost two hundred feet of the sinuous feature, but this was thought to be a fraction of its true length. Nothing like it had been seen in Europe before; its nearest lookalike was a 1330-foot effigy of a snake in the Ohio River valley. But unlike this established US tourist attraction, the Rotherwas Ribbon would never be laid out for the edification of visitors. Digging it out to its entire extent was a non-starter for the boys from the black stuff. As it was, they were prepared to give archaeologists only very limited access to it before construction resumed. I picked up a newspaper: 'This weekend a few hundred people will get a chance to see the stone snake but after that it will be encased in a special membrane of layers of sand and crushed stone to protect it for ever.' Or to cover it up again for ever, to put it another way. There wasn't a moment to lose. I made a few phone calls and within a day or two I was in Hereford, tailing a blue Suzuki SUV driven by Dr Keith Ray. We were on our way to see the Ribbon.

It had put Herefordshire on the map historically, or prehistorically; and it had also put Keith in the spotlight. Keith was the county archaeologist. There was a lot of interest in the find, and it would surely be the most remarkable on his patch during his career. Fate, serendipity, the chance buckling of a navvy's tine beneath an indifferent and heedless empyrean: call it what you will, but the nexus between a £12 million road scheme, a piece of Bronze Age public art, and Keith's tenure of the big chair in Herefordshire archaeology was a happy one. It did not find him wanting. On the contrary, Keith was a man seizing his moment. In the pitching off-roader ahead of me travelled not only Keith but his guests, glamorous colleagues from the world of antiquity.

We were in the flood plain of the River Wye rattling up a flinty track, Watery Lane, towards a wood which rose from a hillside. We came to a halt beside a field. Here, the turf had been peeled back to reveal the red-brown earth. A great pastry-cutter had apparently been at work, punching out squares and crescents in the exposed subsoil, and the whole had been sprinkled with hundreds-and-thousands of stone and gravel. It was a deceptively hot afternoon: hazy, and without the merest zephyr to stir the firs that overlooked the excavation. Keith debouched from the Suzuki followed by Julian, an eminent don, and archaeology writer Chris. Keith busied himself at the tailgate of the vehicle, tucking his trousers into his socks and pulling on his boots. He stowed his tie inside the breast of his shirt. He might have pegged or clipped his very beard out of the way if he could, you felt, such was the single-minded meticulousness of the man. As he was settling a cricket hat on his head, Keith shot me a look. In another moment, he had looked away again but I knew what he was thinking: 'Shall I advise *him* to wear a hat? He's a bit thin on top, after all. But it might embarrass him. And anyway, I haven't got another one.'

We stepped out on to the foreshore of the salt flat of the revealed Bronze Age site, Keith in his kit, Julian (leather jacket, jeans, specs), curly-haired Chris and myself.

Chris indicated a modest incline, an earthwork. 'Is that a ramp?' he said.

'It might be,' said Keith.

'Ah, ah, ah!' said Julian.

The four of us examined a little pit: it was half full of rainwater, the surface just covering a ledge. This had become the site's water feature. The chaps had dubbed it 'the jacuzzi'. It was in fact the sump beneath an old post, a post which had at some stage been set on fire. Fire was a big deal to the people who had passed this way long before us. It was the key to the extraordinary artwork that the chain gang had so recently happened upon, as Keith was about to explain. He said, 'I want you to look at the definition of the structure.' Sunken into the reddish dirt was a distinct route, or pathway. This was the coiling progress of the rock serpent, or a stretch of it, at least. It was ten metres across at its widest and it was thought to start somewhere beneath the firs. At first it was assumed to be a track, said Keith. 'If it was a track, it was a very funny track because it sloped from side to side and undulated down the hill.'

'Well, West Kennet Avenue is what leaps to mind in that respect,' said Julian, naming a distinctive early installation in Wiltshire.

The Ribbon hadn't been laid upon a flat surface, but one that had been designed to twist and turn as it descended the gentle slope of the hill behind us. Keith thought it continued beneath the neighbouring meadow, towards the Wye. He pointed out that we were at the confluence of three rivers.

'Yes!' said Chris.

'Ah!' said Julian.

'I'd like to do full-five geophysics in the field there', said Keith, citing the latest non-invasive archaeological technique.

'Does the shape somehow mirror the sky, the clouds, I wonder?' wondered Chris.

We all thought about this for a bit and then Keith said, 'What's extraordinary about this is what it was made of – stone, which had been deliberately shattered by being heated up and dropped in cold water. I think these people were shattering stones to create a mass of smaller pieces which could be laid on a surface . . . Is it representing something, a material form?'

The Bronze Agers had come up with an innovation in the kitchen known as 'pot store technology'. It meant that if you were short of a decent set of pans, you could heat up stones in the fire instead, get a skin bag, fill it with water and pop the stones in to jolly dinner along. At Rotherwas, it seemed, someone had finished his boil-in-the-bag supper, stared at the gritty leftovers, and invented crazy-paving.

As if he was quizzing this unknown seer, this true trail-blazer, Julian said, 'Why are you paving with burnt material?'

'What if you are *evoking* burning?' said Keith.

'It's more than that, because you're evoking fire *and* water,' said Julian.

'Mm, mm, mm,' said Chris. 'So it's not a serpent, it's a river of fire?'

Keith considered. 'Well, it has to do with transformation. Both water and fire are to do with transformation.' There was evidence that huge structures had been burnt down with great stores of grain inside them. 'This was more than just conspicuous consumption.'

'It wasn't just a fire then?' I didn't dare say.

Contractors' vehicles in the middle distance were a reminder that we only had the blink of an eye, in geological time, to enjoy the serpent. It must have been hard for frustrated antiquarians not to say 'I told you so' to the builders. They had warned against putting the road through here from the outset. After all, a Roman farmstead had been found in the copse and there was the Iron Age fort of Dinedor higher up, on the top of the hill, so this was already established as a locale positively rattling with history. The Romans in their time had dug out a ditch beside the Ribbon itself, echoing its waving lines. At one time, it must have stood out in the flood plain as vividly as any chalk homunculus carved into grassy downs.

Keith had been measured in his comments to the papers. Although he'd have liked nothing more than to see this monument completely unearthed and preserved, he was quoted as saying, he accepted that the county could not afford tens of millions of pounds to divert the road. 'It really is remarkable and, as far we can tell, unique in Europe,' he said on the record. 'It does have international significance and that's why we are taking steps to give it the protection it deserves. But realistically it's not possible to move the road to avoid the feature completely and we have to strike a balance. These are very crowded islands with a rich history.'

The surface of the Ribbon was very fragile. Relief road or no relief road, it would have to be covered up one way or another for its own good, according to the county council. A CD-ROM about it would be coming out, a spokesman added soothingly. But there was so little time to work out what it meant.

They understood this, the charabancs of the curious who followed us out to the Ribbon that hot afternoon, game old girls running up the contractors' bunds, straining past each other for a better view. 'Could it have been something to do with cremation?' said one in a striped Breton jersey. A little girl thought that the old-timers had wanted to leave posterity a clue about how they lived. The sightseers at the Ribbon were accompanied by guides from the Worcestershire Archaeology Service, from the neighbouring county – this thing was so big that old rivalries, old scores, had to be set aside – and an OAP in slacks put one of these experts in a fix by arguing forcibly that Cromwell's men must have had a hand in it.

'Look at Swampy,' muttered Keith, 'telling all his mates where to come . . .' We followed his gaze to the thronged berm. Surely Keith didn't mean the young man who was talking into his mobile? This figure wore a pony-tail, it was true, under a beanie hat, but otherwise he was rigged out in pristine pastels, conformist casualwear, like everyone else. Keith didn't seriously think that this blank-faced twenty-something was coordinating an occupation of the Ribbon by eco-warriors? I decided that he didn't. Or if he did, it was only for a moment, an aberration brought on by the stresses and strains that were the occupational hazards of today's public sector archaeologist. I could imagine Keith spending the summer showing his distinguished friends over his find. And yet, as his public statements had made admirably clear, his professional duty to the council lay in seeing that nothing got in the way of the JCB's maw. By the time you read this, its work will be done, and the Rotherwas Ribbon returned to its long invisibility.

I felt that my travels would be incomplete without a sojourn among the buried treasures of the West Country. In particular, I was anxious to see a reputed tomb, an ancient feature that dominated its surroundings the way the Rotherwas Ribbon once did.

But first to Stonehenge, or rather, the Stonehenge Riverside Project. It was a wonderfully warm and sunny late summer afternoon. On the edge of a field, the visitor facility for the SRP was operating out of a Portakabin standing on a patch of straw. In the field itself, young men who had removed their shirts toiled in a trench that was swagged with tape like a crime scene. Another group of fully clothed young people, perhaps site visitors like me, stood around looking into the hole, watching the first group.

In the Portakabin I met my guide, Megan Price of Oxford University. Before we toured the shadeless field, Megan said, 'I think I'd better get my parasol.' This turned out to be an accessory straight out of the outrageous children's story *Little Black Sambo*. For all that, it was a charming, a witty, article – suggesting a tea-cosy, only rather more boho than that. It was a bricolage of yellows and magentas; I'm not sure that there weren't tassels. Mindful of the sun myself, I lathered up with lotion. I offered some to the tremendously game and fun Megan. She declined at first, but then she caught a whiff of my rich unguent and declared, 'I love the smell!' So I arched my bottle of cream over Megan's palm – 'Say when!' – and poured a luxuriant gloop on to her flesh. (This all sounds a good deal more torrid than it in fact was.)

We went out into the hot afternoon, to the hole where the shirtless students dug. They had quarried it out to a depth of three feet or so, to reveal dazzling chalk and flint. Megan pointed out a 'feature', a large lump of off-white mineral lying against this brilliant backdrop. 'It's something old and we can't quite work out what it is,' she said, but perhaps it was part of a 'portal' to the henge. 'We're back in deep time here,' she added.

Stonehenge is the showy centrepiece, the big dipper, of the Henge Heritage Park, or perhaps Hengeworld, as it may yet become. Many people rightly regard a perambulation around these forbidding stones as a highlight of their tour of the British Isles, and go away satisfied. But these visitors are missing other intriguing, if not quite so spectacular, attractions only a short distance away (admittedly, it must have felt a lot further to the ancients, whose lifestyle centred on lugging dense obelisks across the Wiltshire savannah). In the same way that every scandal since Richard Nixon's time in the White House has attracted the suffix –gate, it seemed that Stonehenge had franchised its name out to every mound of earth or pile of stones for miles around. You couldn't move in the West Country for ancient places that had 'henge' appended to them. There was Woodhenge, for instance, an intricate series of concentric rings staked out with wooden posts; there was the village of Avebury Henge; and Britain's largest henge, at Durrington Walls. To the layman, the term 'henge' had a vague but undeniable numinousness. It was practically onomatopoeic: it tolled like a low chant heard in the distance, like the reverberation of something striking a great rock. Somewhat disappointingly, it means 'enclosure'. (On the other hand, you can see that 'Stone Enclosure' wouldn't really do as the title of

England's world-famous prehistoric monument; it's not the sort of name that would have the Druids up in the wee small hours, pointing their Dormobiles west.)

With Megan's help, I was going to see these great but overlooked wonders for myself. This was architecture that had dominated the early landscape and was still unequivocally present in it even now. But time and the elements had inevitably taken their toll, and much of the story had to be divined, by the archaeological equivalent of holding a twitching sprig of hazel over a buried watercourse. The past survived in fragments: what was most immediately unmissable had perhaps passed away, and apparently unprepossessing witnesses were left behind to tell the tale: holes in the ground and the impressions made by the long-ago imposition of great weight.

Megan and I began at the 2500-year-old Durrington Walls, within the Stonehenge World Heritage Site. The enclosing of the henge – its very hengeness – was achieved by a great 520-metre circle of chalky ridges or bluffs, and by a ditch which was more than six metres deep when it was first hacked out. As Megan told it, she and I were within the hollow of a vast shallow bowl created by Neolithic man. The experts believed that there had been some two dozen different earthworks going on at roughly the same time; there was little evidence of matter falling down between these various berms, as would have been the case if there had been long lapses between projects.

We watched cars on the A345, which ran through the middle of the henge. I said, 'Didn't people use to think that the Neolithics were a bit thick compared to, say, the Romans?'

'Oh, sod the Romans!' said Megan gaily. There was a settlement at Durrington even before the walls went up, it seemed. It had been a large village, perhaps home to the creators of Stonehenge itself (the village was occupied at the same time as the famous monument was being built, around 2300 BC). The houses were arranged in a wide circle around a central space.

This piazza was in turn occupied by a timber circle and a small number of other buildings. It was speculated that these were shrines, cult houses, or perhaps the fashionable homes of pre-Neolithic swanks and nobs. By good fortune, the floors of at least three of the houses had been preserved beneath the external bank of the henge; they were small and square with plaster flooring, and efforts were under way to coax them fully into the light of day. Incredibly, their wooden walls had survived – albeit as post-holes, like the one I'd seen at Rotherwas – and hollows in the ground marked where their Flintstone furniture once stood.

When the Durrington Walls were erected, there were four entrances to the henge. For some reason, the north and south portals were blocked off some four thousand years ago. The south entrance appears to have led to Woodhenge, and the trench that Megan and I were looking into had been sunk with a view to finding this pathway. The experts believed that Durrington was all about ritual. 'Mind you,' Megan confided, 'when archaeologists don't really know what went on somewhere, they put it down to ritual.'

She invited me to imagine a roadway, thirty metres wide, leading from where we were standing, over the A road and down to the Wiltshire Avon, which was winding bluely through the trees below us. She said that this ancient route not only connected Durrington to the river but was so aligned that it faced the midwinter solstice.

'That was very important. We've found middens of bones, representing hundreds of years of animals being consumed here. Mostly pigs, farrowed in spring, fattened, then slaughtered and eaten, to mark the solstice. It was pure conspicuous consumption.'

'No humans, then?'

'No. Eating people is wrong,' said Megan.

Indeed, there was little evidence of human bones dating from the Neolithic period. Their cremated remains were committed to the waters of the Avon instead, or so the director of the dig apparently believed. He thought that the ramparts, Durrington itself, represented a way of honouring the dead. I wondered whether any archaeologist, historian or other explorer of this deep time had ever proposed the view that some clutch or other of our ancestors had *dissed* the dead, or were merely nonchalant about them.

Other archaeological finds indicated that when the Bronze Agers came on to the scene, they too had shown respect to their remote elders. A sure sign that they had bent a shaggy knee to the Neolithics was that they had elected to be interred near the various henges which their predecessors had established. These structures were as baffling to them, presumably, as they still are to us, since the Bronze Age folk were separated from the Neolithics by the same boggling order of time as we from them.

Megan and I crossed a country lane, Fargo Road. On our left was Woodhenge. The closest resemblance this bore to anything I'd seen before was to the parlour entertainment Solitaire, in which pegs or balls are installed in slots on a circular base. Was it a board game of the gods? Never mind 'deep time', Woodhenge appeared to hail from deep space. Indeed, its handmade wooden pieces in their concentric, not to say eccentric, configuration were first discovered from the heavens. It was 1925, a warm day like today, and Squadron Leader Gilbert Stuart Martin Insall VC was tootling overhead in his Sopwith Snipe. This decorated airman, honoured for his gallantry in the Great War, took the old crate down to buzz the fields. There were primordial disc barrows down there, he noted, more or less ploughed to obliteration; but the flyer's gimlet eye was caught by one hardy hummock in particular. He could make out a number of white spots within this disc. He was struck by its similarity to Stonehenge, just two miles away to the west, and resolved to make a closer study.

The days lengthened into June, the barrow grew greener, but this only made its curious markings stand out all the clearer from the rarefied vantage of Insall's string-bag. The disc was in fact oval in shape, he saw, and one day on an early-bird sortie he noted that its axis was approximately in line with the midsummer sunrise. Insall's cockpit photographs confirmed that there were pits in the chalk. An archaeologist called Maud Cunningham and her husband then embarked on a three-year excavation which found that Woodhenge was very similar to its more celebrated stone neighbour, and if anything even more illustrious. It was made up of an outer ditch and bank 250 feet in diameter. Within the henge, dozens of holes, the ones Insall had seen from the skies, marked out circular patterns. The holes had once held timber shafts but these had long since turned to dust. These days, sawn-off concrete pillars stood in their place, giving an impression of what Woodhenge might have looked like. Unlike Stonehenge, the site lacked the focal point of an altar stone. But Megan told me that the skeleton of a three-year-old child had been exhumed from the chalk about a metre and a half from the centre of Woodhenge, its skull cleft open in what was unmistakably a premeditated assault.

It was mid-afternoon and the sweated student labour engaged on the various digs was enjoying a well-deserved ice-cream break. A young woman sat down in the hole that she had been hollowing out and all but disappeared: you could only see her head and shoulders and her dwindling lolly. Megan said, 'They all camp at a pub, six miles up the road. The poor director's wife caters for 150 students every night.' Unusually for under-graduates, these apprentice archaeologists were tidy, if the efficacy of their earthworks, the shortage of their spoor, were anything to go by. Typically, a neat square incision was made in the earth; the topsoil, removed like skin, was folded back from the cut; and the striking subcutaneous layers exposed: the chalk, the dully lustrous flints. 'I wasn't especially enamoured of flints when I first came to this site but they do grow on you,' Megan assured me. She mimed striking a long match against a box, or perhaps whittling a King Edward with a peeler. 'It's lovely to watch them being knapped. They make such a good sound.'

In the field around Woodhenge, Maud Cunningham's dig was being re-examined with the benefit of modern technology. There was a whole new raft of knowledge being applied to archaeology, and a matching range of slangy nicknames. There was Keith's favourite, Geophysics, abbreviated to 'Geophys' – a Land Rover went by with the legend 'Geophys Crew' stickered over its windshield – and another occult process which apparently harnessed the power of magnetism.

At the site of the Cuckoo Stone, a four-by-four was backed up to the edge of the pit and a camera rose on a telescopic arm until it was twenty metres overhead. This was in order to take 'aerial' pictures of the boulder. The Cuckoo Stone was glacial and had once been effortfully jemmied out of a hole in the ground by the ancients. Like the pi symbols of Stonehenge, the Cuckoo had been a standing stone, until the moment in its long history when it crashed to earth; and like them, it was a dirty great hunk of sarsen. 'Sarsen' means a sleeping knight; the word first appeared in the seventeenth century, perhaps as a corruption of 'Saracen'. When would this drowsing nobleman throw off his languor and explain his business, when would he give an account of himself? The Cuckoo Stone was a tabula rasa. Megan couldn't even tell me how it came by its name. Some authorities held that it was in some way connected to the Stonehenge Cursus, a prototype dragstrip more than a mile in length and up to 150 metres across, which is enclosed within one long continuous bank and runs alongside Stonehenge itself. The Cursus (Latin for 'circuit') was once thought to have been an early racecourse, but it's now believed to have been a processional route, perhaps linking the dead with the living; or alternatively, keeping them apart from each other. 'The Cuckoo Stone is aligned with the Cursus, you see,' said Megan. 'We like that word "aligned" in archaeology.'

A pair of students were using a laser to take images of the

rock. We were told not to look at this laser, myself and a pair of apparently deaf biddies who were out walking their dogs and had strayed within range of the laser's red eye. We were warned not to look at it, but of course we did. Or *I* did. The biddies probably didn't hear, which was all the luckier for them.

Had the stone always stood by itself or was it once part of a cluster, a Neolithic rockery? Recent aerial photographs had revealed more crop-marks – ancient scars in the earth which become visible from the air as crops ripen, like the ones seen by Squadron Leader Insall VC from behind the joystick of his Sopwith – and these indicated that there had indeed been other features around the stone. Somewhere, there was a Cuckoo Stone-shaped hole in the ground whence this landmark had sprung: very satisfyingly, this was known as the 'solution hole'. Less satisfyingly, the archaeologists hadn't found it yet.

5

SILBURY HILL

The jouncing people-carrier, the agreeable if unremarkable view – and then all at once, it's in front of you, an attention-grabber at the side of the road, a colossal piece of street furniture in the shape of a hazard-warning equilateral. This is crushing archaeological time expressed as trigonometry. Old Egypt hands could be forgiven for thinking that the terrible shark's fin I'm talking about is the sort of thing that rears up at you so thrillingly in the windscreen of a tourist minibus on the outskirts of Cairo, but they would be wrong. Or only half-right. As unlikely as it may seem, the staggering impact of a Cheops can also be claimed for a pile of chalk off the A4.

I don't deny that I was primed before arrival to compare Silbury Hill with one of the acknowledged wonders of antiquity. Silbury has been called Europe's answer to the pyramids, and with good cause. Its profile immediately recalls the tombs of the Nile delta; some of the many tons of calcium carbonate that went into it were quarried at about the same time as those pharaonic ziggurats were going up, some 4400 years ago; and perhaps most resonantly of all, no one knows how or why the architects of

Silbury pulled it off. But none of this exhaustive research brought it home to me as forcefully as the experience of simply cornering a Wiltshire bend and coming face to face with the great tepee of my own woad-striped tribe.

The idea that our distant kin are credited with building something so otherworldly is what immediately connects Silbury in the imagination with the outsize Toblerone chunks that were cast like manna on to the edge of the Egyptian desert. It's hardly surprising that people have sought phantasmagorical back-stories for the hill. It's said to have been a clod of mud which Satan scraped from his spade while he was digging a trench at Wansdyke, part of a massive sixth-century earthwork that stretches from Andover to Portishead in Somerset. Alternatively, the hill might have fallen from his diabolical boot as he flew over North Wessex. Denizens of chat rooms hold that it's a landing-beacon for UFOs, plangently pinging into the ionosphere on a frequency that only aliens and small dogs can pick up. Yet others have maintained that the mound is the mausoleum of a long-lost King of England, Zel or Sil by name (hence 'Sil-bury'). A version of the myth noted by John Aubrey in 1670 had it that the King was buried there on horseback while the hill was raised around him in the time it took for a pot to come to the boil ('while a posset of milk was seething'.) In the nineteenth century, R. C. Hoare added the shimmering gloss that Zel had been laid to rest in a golden coffin and that his ghost could sometimes be seen riding on moonlit nights, wearing armour hammered out of the same precious metal. In other variations, the hill's eerie tenants were an unknown warrior wearing a golden breastplate and his gilded steed, or a pair of effigies – 'a horse and rider, the size of life, and of solid gold'.

It's the hill's very inscrutability, its blank look, that has encouraged this speculation, of course, and turned it into a possible portal. When we gape at it, we might be toddlers bidden by the *Play School* presenters of the spheres to 'look through the triangular window'. But some weren't content to sit and stare, insisting instead on stepping through this fifth wall, so to speak, breaching the tightly packed and yet fragile membrane that seemed to separate us from our ancestors. In 1776, strolling Cornish colliers a long way from home were retained by the Duke of Northumberland, who instructed them to tunnel into the hill that was such a feature of his property. A little over a hundred years later, Dean John Merewether led a party which entered the hill by its flank, more or less at right angles to Northumberland's shaft. The reverend would invite friends to join him in the passages that his men had hollowed. Locals also piled in, hopeful of stumbling upon swaddled kingly remains, or better still, a glittering Sil and his matching horse.

The third significant irruption was carried out over successive summers in the late 1960s by Professor Richard Atkinson, one of the last of the gentleman antiquarians. Sucking on a briar even in the confines of his subterranean tunnels, Atkinson was interviewed by Magnus Magnusson on black and white television as the nation was smitten by Silbury fever. 'This was Early Man's equivalent of the spaceshot,' said Atkinson, aligning himself with the other notable scientific programme of the day with the deftness of a lunar orbiter. The professor could perhaps be excused his rhetoric: the hill was the largest Neolithic structure in Europe.

Now, in 2007, one last expedition was afoot, a final journey into the heathen Wiltshire interior, and *Newsnight* had been invited to tag along. Researchers wanted to penetrate further into the hill than anyone had ever been before, both literally and in terms of the fieldwork they hoped to do on its builders: so physically and astrophysically, then. But I say one last expedition because the team also had the paradoxical goal of stopping all the tunnels up, sealing the hill as they left, boarding it up for good. They were filling in the blanks of Silbury in more ways than one. We would be the last journalists, the last outsiders, to be allowed inside before the hill was restored as far as possible to its enigmatic whole.

English Heritage, overseeing the operation, said the rock of ages was showing signs of wear and tear, the old sentinel was doddery and in danger of collapse. The only way of conserving Silbury was to pack it with chalk and return it to its original condition. After all, it wasn't as if the hill had ever been formally opened to the public, unlike its brother obelisks in the Middle East. The riotous stewardship of Dean Merewether, when he said of his hilly theme park 'Come one, come all' as if he was barking trips aboard the *Skylark*, was not necessarily an ideal business model. English Heritage's solution was laudable and thoroughly à la mode, of course, though it also smacked a little of a good idea taken to excess: preserving Silbury for the nation by putting it beyond the reach of hoi polloi.

In the foothills of the louring Wiltshire wigwam, a peripatetic community of archaeologists and surveyors, miners and engineers dwelt in their own tented village – strictly speaking, under the sheltering aluminium of trailer homes and Portakabins. This was where *Newsnight* also made camp. It was the eve of the winter solstice, and the brief interval between the lifting of the morning mist and the onset of the late-lunchtime dusk found every prospect tinged with an ethereal light. I saw that Silbury hadn't weathered, hadn't bedded in or in any way taken on the lived-in lineaments of a natural feature. Even now, no one could say what it was for, but it looked uncompromisingly intended, thoroughly *meant*. No wonder so many fortune-hunters and dream-seekers had been in thrall to this once pristine stack. It was a great white, the Moby-Dick of monuments.

With its blind and yet somehow minatory gaze upon me, I tramped through the rushes beneath it in the company of Dr Amanda Chadburn, who goes by the magicky stamp of Inspector of Ancient Monuments. She told me that the mission to rescue Silbury began when her phone rang in May 2000. 'I got a call on

a Tuesday morning after a bank holiday saying a hole had
opened up in Silbury Hill. I didn't think much of it but I went out
to have a look. To my astonishment, when I reached the top there
was a very, very deep hole – forty feet deep – and it looked for all
the world like a mineshaft, which is exactly what it was.'

This was the blowhole of the barnacled Leviathan. It was the
legacy of the Duke of Northumberland, who had marched his
miners to the top of the hill back in the late eighteenth century.
His lordship was a veteran of the Grand Tour, said Dr Chadburn.
'People were going abroad, they were seeing the wonderful things
in Rome and Egypt. And he came back and perhaps saw his own
green pyramid on his back doorstep. He thought, "Why not
investigate it?"' The overseer of the works was one Colonel
Drax, whose name unimprovably suggests not only a baddie
from a pot-boiler but also an ever so slightly sinister public works
from our own time, viz. a power station. Latter-day
examinations revealed that the hole hadn't been properly
backfilled. Drax had put some timbers over the top but it had
been a botched job: he'd left behind a howling cavity which was
bound to be in need of attention sooner or later, though I suppose
you couldn't really grumble about getting two hundred years' life
out of a cowboy operation.

I went to inspect the damage for myself with Rob Harding, the
site manager, and archaeologist Sarah May. It was a climb of
some forty metres, but we took it in a mazy, circumnavigatory
fashion, following a path that wound itself up the side of the hill:
we were coming round the mountain when we came, you might
have said. Did something in the slumbering scarp speak to me, or
was it only my prior knowledge that it had been hewn out of
chalk by aboriginal Brits that alerted me to a queer foreignness
about the going, a sense transmitted up through the soles of my
boots that this was not as other terrain? I was reminded of
childhood romps through the manmade knolls of Harrison Drive
in New Brighton, a park which had been deposited like so many

scoops of mash when they were reclaiming land from the Mersey estuary, though I had little suspected such a thing in my youth.

Our party breasted the brow of Silbury and pulled up short. In front of us was a hole as big as a swimming pool; not Olympic size, to be sure, but one you'd be happy to find if friends lent you the keys to their villa. Rob and I teetered on the precipice of this crater.

I said, 'You'd have to watch yourself here on a windy day, wouldn't you?'

'Absolutely,' said Rob. The hole had been no bigger than about eight feet across at first, he said.

'But a person could still have disappeared into it quite easily?'

'Oh yes,' agreed Rob. He was lean and keen: a keen beanpole, in fact. Though he himself was clean-shaven, as I was in a position to vouch, a strongman's waxed moustache had been indelibly added to the mugshot on his security pass. He went on, 'There was another collapse this year because of the extremely wet weather.' At first, contractors plugged the orifice with polystyrene: tofu-coloured rafts were choppered into the maw. Off-cuts still lay at the bottom of the hill, like old mattresses. Rob said, 'It was important to protect this site while we were working inside.'

'To keep the rain out, I suppose?'

'To stop the sides collapsing in on the blokes below.' An ancient English monument was in danger of falling in on itself like a sagging Yorkshire pudding, and taking all hands with it. In fact the polystyrene gave robust support without increasing the pressure on the collapsed material within the shaft.

In the brief waxing of the winter sun, the hill cast its angular shadow across the Wiltshire plains. One theory was that it had once served as a kind of concert platform. Some months before my visit, passing motorists had been distracted by the sight of adepts of early music swarming up the slopes with their horns and fifes, their skins and bladders, while listeners were posted to the fields all about. 'We were amazed at what people could hear.

Bone flutes, very, very fine sounds, even at distances of up to a mile,' Sarah May told me. So Silbury might have been at the heart of community singing back in the old days, the symbol and enabler of inclusive interaction; the great tepee was also a big tent, it seemed.

The ancients might have gathered around the hill for a bit of a sing-song but I was disappointed to learn that there had been nothing stronger on the bill: no boy-king in a housecoat of swansdown holding a freshly knapped flint to a virgin's throat. 'We've found no evidence of human sacrifices,' Sarah confirmed. 'There are things that would have shown up, like bone, but we haven't found them.' Her own jacket, I noticed, was secured by toggles got up to look like bone, like wolf's teeth.

What did show up on at Silbury were post-holes near the summit, and tests indicated that they dated from the late Saxon period, practically the day before yesterday in the long life of the hill. This required a reimagining of Silbury's distinctive look: it had very likely been crowned by a voluptuous dome until the time of the Norman Conquest, when this had been summarily lopped off like the top of a boiled egg, and Silbury had been pressed into service as a lookout post or even a fort. This was a triumph of deduction, because at first sight the hill offered scanty pickings to the historian. As Sarah put it, 'This is an extraordinarily clean site in archaeological terms.'

This would have been a cause of regret to others, but not to Sarah. A lively redhead with a Canadian accent acquired in her childhood, she was impatient with those who were preoccupied with what the hill held. 'I'm interested in why we think there should be something *inside* a hill. Why do we always ask that about Silbury when we say of Stonehenge "Why was it built?" That's the real question for me. It's an astounding thing to have built without the technology we have today. Even *with* the technology, we're finding it difficult to fix it.' Her eyes were streaming with the cold.

Sarah had mentioned the Druid-bothered megaliths of Salisbury Plain, which were barely a crystal's throw away from where we were standing, and this led me to ponder aloud about the arcane rites that Silbury itself might still witness. 'Well, I personally have never seen anyone naked round here,' Sarah considered. 'There is a lot of public interest in the site, a lot of spiritual importance for a range of people, but no, I wouldn't use the term "crusty-infested" myself.'

All at once, I knew a hot moment of contrition. Who was I to scoff at New Agers and their practices, after all, when I was nothing but a 'crusty' myself? That's right, I might as well admit it. I was helplessly drawn to the core and kernel of Silbury Hill, down towards the earth's sucking magma . . .

At the base of the hill, the final dig took as its starting point the passage cleared by Prof. Atkinson back in the 60s. 'When we arrived, his old door was still here,' recalled Mark Kirkbride of Skanska Engineering, the contractors. Ah yes, the door! I remembered it from the BBC footage I'd seen of the excavation. A capital 'S' (for Silbury) was embossed on it, in an unexpectedly groovy font – there appeared to have been a bare-faced case of theft involving the stencil used to monogram Superman's six-pack. The film included a respectful shot of Professor Atkinson unlocking the heavy hatch in his own good time and then stepping inside it. Mark went on, 'We couldn't budge the door, so being good engineers we forced it. Then, under a stone by the entrance, we found the key! Atkinson must have just left it there when he locked up for the last time. It hadn't been touched in forty years!'

Just as the archaeologists and the contractors did every morning when they began work, Mark and I ducked under a lintel dated '1968' which the Professor had put up over the mouth of his tunnel. Strip lights led the way into the innards of the hill, picking out an undulating passage. There was a tang of diesel, an olfactory howdy-doodie from work that was going on out of sight ahead of us. Not only was the project piggy-backing on Atkinson, so to speak, but the Professor in his time had also exploited the seam worked by the Revd Merewether. So Mark and I were retracing the steps of both pioneers towards the centre of the hill. The passage was roofed by struts and spars as rusty as the ribs of a shipwreck. Mark indulged me on the matter. 'Yeah, it's just like *Pirates of the Caribbean* in here,' he said.

The great handmade mountain rested on a base covering five acres, it was 167 metres in diameter, and the tunnel that we were in extended to the point directly beneath the apex, where it met Northumberland's old excavation. The horizontal tunnels of Silbury were in a cruciform configuration, with a brace of shorter passages branching off the main drag at right angles. Long before we reached this junction, however, the tunnel sloped down, until we were lower than the foot of the hill itself. We were gambolling through a prehistoric ditch, in fact. This had been dug out to supply chalk during the construction process, or else it was part of a series of pits and trenches which surrounded the hill. They were all part of the puzzle of the place. After heavy rain, Silbury was transformed into a moated redoubt, an island fastness. The archaeologists ruminated that standing water would once have returned a dazzling image of the hill. What might have been the impact, the propaganda value, of seeing that great mammoth's tusk reflected in all its enamelly glory?

'We've walked up a bit now,' said Mark, 'we're at the interface between geology and archaeology.' We had hauled ourselves out of the ditch and were now striding through Silbury proper, through chalky halls of Xanadu. Estimates vary about how long it took to complete this remarkable feat of early engineering. One suggested that seven hundred men would have had to toil for ten years: in excess of six million man hours. Another calculation would have you believe that the whole thing was over and done with in the blink of four million hours, including making good.

English Heritage consulted radiocarbon dating experts but their initial findings only added to the uncertainty. They offered two different timespans for the job: it had either taken 115 years, or between 140 and 435.

Fortunately for those who had done the back-breaking graft, Silbury hadn't gone up all at once. Mark and I were in a stretch of tunnel where the wall was as marbled as beef. The hill's development could be plotted in deposits of different hues. The dense, dark stratum at the foot of the wall represented the prototype hill. A circular mound made of turf and gravels gathered from the nearby River Kennet, and all capped with clay, it stood about five metres high and was erected between 2445 and 2190 BC. Here towards the base of the structure, the research party made some of their most rewarding discoveries. An archaeologist called Gill Campbell produced a piece of turf from a swagbag. The sample was a dark and matted clump, a hank of scalp from a crime scene, a hairpiece that you'd have a hard job returning to the salon. But as I looked closer, I made out whorls, tendrils – remarkably, these were perfectly preserved fronds of moss which had grown four millennia ago on Silbury's original slopes. Removed from the corrupting effect of fresh air and weather, grasses, insects – all kinds of organic remains from the Neolithic period – had been dry-cured inside the hill.

During a second flurry of building, the stack had risen to a height of some twenty-five metres, rather more than half of its final stature, on alternating bands of soil and chalk. Silbury II, to use the pet name coined on site, had then itself been subsumed beneath the chalky *embonpoint* of Silbury III.

At the very heart of the hill, I was spooked by a loud rumble. Was it the thundering hooves of King Zel's twenty-four-carat nag? Was I about to get a visit from the horseman of this particular sleepy hollow? Or was it some of the half-million tons of chalk over my head stirring and shifting, boulders bigger than a man's head going about their unbiddable business of filling in unoccupied spaces? I watched interestedly at the way the weight was making the timbers of the tunnel sag and bow. It was like a goldmine down here, what with a hallmarked ex-monarch rattling around the place – and it was the old prospectors who were to blame for all the disturbance. They had left the dense minerals of Silbury with an irresistible itch to make themselves comfortable. None of these adventurers had filled their tunnels in properly behind them; no, not even Prof. Atkinson. He had rebuked television viewers in Olympian tones ('That's *very* silly!') when they had written in to doubt the wisdom of his great borehole. But he had, after all, left the hill prone to voids, to air pockets, in just the same way as his predecessors.

In one of the smaller side tunnels of the hill, work was going on to correct this. 'We've found arrowheads. We found them up there.' This was Terry Hilton, a miner from the North East, and he was pointing towards the top of a pile of slurry. We were in a chamber at the end of the side tunnel. Terry looked quite at home here, on his haunches in the muck, at the foot of this petrified landslip; and no wonder, because it was like the face of a coalmine. He said that the miners had also turned up antlers – they were as tough as pokers and had served the early builders as tools. Terry, who was making do with a shovel himself, said, 'It's pretty tough going now, so think of those guys four and a half thousand years ago.'

Colin Wilkinson, another Geordie, explained, 'We're filling the void stage by stage, packing it in.' From where we were crouching, you could turn round and look back at the tunnel, at the last overhead beam of it, and then stare into a cavernous space directly above it: this aven was another hollow that would have to be filled in. A small diesel-fired digger, a pint-sized JCB, was bringing chalk to the miners. There was just enough room for it to poke its hinged bucket into the chamber, and tip out the contents at Terry's feet.

'Are you safe in here?' I asked him, thinking of the booming clods above us.

'Yeah, we make it safe. If we come across any bad ground, we rectify it before we go any further. We're covering our own backs.'

If Terry and Colin had a fault, it was that they didn't have snap tins on them, so raising the possibility that I, in turn, wouldn't be able to write about their snap tins; indeed, that I wouldn't even be able to use the term 'snap tin'. How did they account for themselves?

Colin said, 'In a coalmine, you might be gone ten or twelve hours. You can't travel from A to B in two minutes, so you've got to have your cold tea in a bottle, a bite to eat in your snap tin, as you say. But here we're only five minutes away from the site and they've got all that catering down there.'

They were coming out for good soon. In a few more weeks or months, Terry and Colin and the other miners would have done all they could to block up the passages. Skanska would then pipe a sealant of chalky paste into the remaining gaps, to exclude the oxygen which would otherwise break down the ancient deposits and make Silbury unstable again. It was like filling a tooth. The polystyrene plug would be removed from the Duke of Nothumberland's pothole, and this too would be capped with chalk, winched to the crown of the hill on a miniature railtrack.

They hadn't found King Zel, though, and now they never would. The archaeologists had plumbed the hill with lasers, subjected it to all manner of sonic strafings, and yet drawn a blank on burials, royal or otherwise. It seemed that Silbury simply wasn't a grave, and never had been. The idea of a burial chamber had never needed much encouragement, admittedly, but it had taken hold because scholars such as William Stukeley (1687–1765) had argued that whoever built the stone circle at Avebury, a short distance from Silbury, had also designed the hill itself as his own resting-place. Most historians agreed that the hill had to be seen in the context of other landmarks including the Avebury henge and the stone circle across the fields at West

Kennet, which I'd heard about from Julian, the don, at Rotherwas. It had been established that banks of earth at Avebury were constructed using the same methodology as employed in the final phase of Silbury's construction.

At Silbury, they'd also unearthed dozens of sarsen stones. Because sarsens were heavier than chalk, and would have required more work to place in the hill, they very likely had a religious significance. Sarsen stones were found on the beds of rivers including the Kennet, which wound close to Silbury. It was highly likely that the Neolithic people made a connection between the precious Kennet and the sarsens. As mentioned above, they had created the first Silbury out of materials from the riverbed. And associations between the river and the hill dated until as late as the turn of the nineteenth century, when locals were in the habit of collecting water from the river and carrying it to the summit, where they mixed it with sugar and swigged the posset down. Could it be that Silbury was not a tomb but a kind of cenotaph, or a chalky Elysian Field, where the spirits of the dead could be at peace? Well, now at last they would be.

The archaeologists said they had no qualms about their course of action, which was akin to boarding the monument up. Dr Chadburn said, 'We've taken samples, we've made excellent records, we're going to get a fantastic story out of Silbury. We've got as much information as we can out of it . . . But it's certainly the best thing for the hill.'

Terry and Colin weren't wrong about the fine dining to be had on site. They were well looked after. In the kitchen hut, for example, there was a big, a *super* fridge. The remnants of last night's supper – partridge stew – stood on the spotless hob in a Pyrex dish beneath a lid of aluminium foil. Barry Caplin from Derby had come down from the hill for his lunch, as Terry and Colin would also do in time. It was a cold day, Barry was looking forward to some food and a bit of a warm. He wasn't really in the mood for chatter. He was dining off piping-hot beans 'n' bangers, straight from the microwave. Barry was a taciturnist, tipping his beans on to his Flora-ed toast with ease and relish.

I sipped a mug of tea and thought about what Sarah the archaeologist had told me: 'I'm interested in why we think there should be something inside a hill. Why do we always ask that about Silbury when we say of Stonehenge "Why was it built?" That's the real question for me.' I could see her point. Everyone queues to see Tutankhamun, but it's the sarcophagus you remember, not the wizened contents of the winding cloth. And in our own lives, how much more exciting is the thrill of anticipation than the reality. It's not the gift, it's the wrapping. The hill was more than enough to be going on with.

6

SUTTON HOO

When a neighbour finally broke in and found him, the poor old boy was lying in a filthy bed with rainwater dripping on to him. Vermin had the run of the place. Local youths used it for target practice. And this was a 1400-year-old gentleman who'd fought in the war! It's disgusting the way we treat old people in this country. I might have filled out a direct debit to Age Concern there and then, in a field in East Anglia. These things were often worse in the countryside – they didn't have the buses – but two things stayed my hand. The first was that the old timer was a bit of a bugger himself – they often were, of course, but this one could be a right barbarian when roused – and the other was that he was a smear of phosphate in a handful of acidic soil. No, he really wasn't feeling himself, wasn't Raedwald, a warrior King of the Anglo-Saxons. With the best will in the world, there wasn't a lot you could do for him.

The dunes and bunkers of his seventh-century riverside retreat at Sutton Hoo in Suffolk, his visionary golf spa, were cropped by sheep; by Norfolk Horn, to be precise, the breed that most resembled the variety that were grazed here in the old days. But as you walked the course, there was no mistaking that these links also bore the marks of Death's levelling scythe. One minute you're lord and master of all you pillage, with a dream retirement opportunity to look forward to, a chalet-bungalow with an environmentally friendly turf roof *and* no need to part with your old boat – mooring fees just weren't a problem at Sutton Hoo. The next thing you know, the ceiling's leaking, you're pushing up daisies and they in turn are being munched by rabbits. Not by a proud horse, like the one your mate was interred with a few yards away; not by a mighty auroch, the strain of cattle which furnished your drinking horn but did not long survive you. No, by bloody hares. You, a carnivore of the wipe-it's-arse-and-put-it-on-rudimentary-earthenware school, ending up as rabbit food. The last straw was when those squaddies were running amok in the Second World War, letting off their rifles, their grenades and their mortars; driving their bloody tanks up and down all day long and never quite getting the hang of them. And a decorated old soldier like you expected to lie back and take it. It was more than you could endure, and so you didn't.

The deliquesced inmate of Mound 1 at Sutton Hoo had been a fighter, a leader, in life. Even after he was interred in a barrow with his trusty longboat, his posthumous odyssey was far from uneventful, as you see. His is the fearsome countenance that has come down to us as the face of his ancient people, in the shape of his almost biometrically expressive helmet, more mask than headgear, that is now displayed in the British Museum. This biker's bonnet surely qualifies him for the title of England's first Hell's Angel. His identity was established by another museum, a *black* museum, where pathologists compared his remains with the ankles of a woman who had been killed by an acid-bath murderer (her trotters were all that was left of her). Many have speculated that he was the inspiration for *Beowulf*, the epic verse of the Dark Ages which ends with the committal of its dead hero to a 'broad high tumulus, plainly visible to distant seamen'.

The Sutton Hoo ship-burial was one of the most important finds in Europe, even the world. To inventory the contents of the entire Sutton Hoo site was to count the ways in which it fulfilled the requirements of a locus of intrigue and drama, as well as providing a rare ornament of English subterranea. There were no fewer than seventeen burial mounds, of various sizes: they looked as though they'd been turned out of fish moulds. And to delve into them, with trowel and bodkin rather than fish slice, was to expose a matchless hoard. A limestone plaque from Alexandria; the bronze lid of a Nubian ewer; silver spoons and bowls from Byzantium; a French sword with a gold and garnet pommel; Syrian cloaks and other sumptuous textiles; an iron standard and a sceptre set off by a bronze stag; thirty-seven gold tremisses from the mints of Gaul; spears and clasps; a lamp containing 1500-year-old beeswax; a six-stringed harp and a cap of otter fur. The trove wasn't all so alluring, though. Digs also uncovered ritually sacrificed horses and the victims of bloody execution.

The kingly figure at the centre of Sutton Hoo had been dead for roughly as long as we've had Christianity in these islands. His background had been the cause of speculation since his grave was first properly excavated some seventy years ago. What was there to say of him today? What was the angle on the Anglo-Saxon?

As recently as 1983, his last resting-place was a ruin – 'catastrophic', according to a report compiled for the British Museum. 'Part of it had been scheduled [as a historic monument], and the notice announcing that it was "an offence to damage it" had fallen over and was half-buried in the bracken which was growing six feet high.' Now the undergrowth had been cut back and the National Trust had made the Sutton Hoo site interpretative, as is the modern way. In my own explorations, I had the invaluable aid of a local guide, Michael Argent, a big bloke with white hair and a check shirt. We were also joined by Paul, a historical re-enacter, whom I inadvertently offended by calling a Viking, whereas it was as plain as the iron visor on his face that he was in fact an Anglo-Saxon.

The Sutton Hoo visitor experience operated out of two purpose-built sheds. Beneath their vertiginously sloping roofs, rustic parliaments could almost be imagined holding their sessions before roaring faggots, accompanied by lashings of mead. For today's tripper, the cafeteria offered piping hot soup 'served with Anglo-Saxon style trencher bread'. Among the displays in the museum were graphics representing the elder in his eternal repose: a homunculus lying on what appeared to be a surfboard (presumably a shield). This recalled the unintelligible graphics that NASA used to bolt on to their galaxy-going probes, to bring other life forms up to date with what was happening here on earth. What was there to say about the Anglo-Saxon today? He had been made to look like the mascot, the poster boy, of the Voyager spacecraft. But then what were the mounds if not modules that had completed many orbits of the sun – time capsules – and what was their most illustrious occupant if not a time-traveller?

Sutton Hoo was interpretative, all right. Show up, and we'll do the rest, it seemed to say. Give us an hour or two and we'll give you the (ancient) world. The attraction had 'the character, quality or function of interpreting; serving to set forth the meaning (of something)', as the *OED* has it. But the dictionary offers a second definition of 'interpretative', and rather excitingly (I'm easily pleased) it's the exact opposite of the first. The term can also mean 'deduced or deducible by interpretation or inference; inferential, constructive, implicit'. In other words, you have to do the work yourself.

The joy of Sutton Hoo was that it was also interpretative in this sense, too. It wasn't only about the saga of an Anglo-Saxon warlord, so to speak, it was about your own personal journey as well. Sutton Hoo had a great story to tell, but it was one that had to be teased from its much-turned earth like a charmed worm. As the site's own director of research, Martin Carver, conceded, 'The trip to the burial ground is a pleasant one by any standards, but it is less clear why anyone should make it. There is no stone circle, no Roman walls, no crumbling castle; indeed a cemetery can rarely offer the grandeur of ruins.' On the contrary, one was confronted by 'the humps and bumps that cover so much English history'. Well, I for one was happy to try my hand at a little amateur phrenology, to feel my way. And the longer I addressed myself to the furrowed brows of Sutton Hoo, the more I realised that so much depended on how you chose to construe things – so much was open to interpretation.

To begin with the most obvious and fundamental poser of all: was there a positive ID on the incumbent of Mound 1? We might think we know him, from his helmet in the British Museum. But characterful as this bespoke millinery undoubtedly is – with its stuck-on tache, its noseplate cleverly worked to suggest the body of a bird of prey – it's only the representation of a man's features. Who was he? In my frustration, I swear, there were times when the very phrase 'Sutton Hoo' rang in my head like a mocking question.

In common with most of the literature, Michael, my guardian, was happy to pronounce the late longboatman Raedwald, King of the Angles. 'His palace was at Rendlesham, very near here, though nothing has ever been found. The idea that it was a palace was established by field-walking.'

'Field-walking?' It sounded a bit like psychogeography, the study of place with reference to the lingering resonance of the history that once happened there. But it was a lot harder than that, according to Michael: you actually had to try to get things right. 'It's about walking around the location with your eyes open,' he said. There was a reference in Bede's *Ecclesiastical History* to a court of the Angles at Rendlesham, and field-walking archaeologists proved its existence to their own satisfaction in the 1980s. Their interpretative work told them that it was the site of a Saxon cemetery as well as of the palace and an early church, though the latter constructions were still waiting to be unearthed. Researchers have also paced out the nearby spot of Snape, where a ship-burial on a smaller scale was found in the nineteenth century. They concluded that the Snape site was complementary to Sutton Hoo.

From his power-base in the Debden valley, Racdwald ruled over 'all the provinces south of the river Humber', Bede writes. 'This King Redwald [*sic*] was a man of noble descent but ignoble in his actions: he was the son of Tytila, and grandson of Wuffa, after whom all kings of the East Angles are called Wuffings.' You wouldn't want to get on the wrong side of him, nor of his three-foot-long sword. As King, he once sheltered the future Northumbrian monarch, Edwin, against his enemies, but at the same time listened to entreaties from the same people about turning poor Edwin over to them, or doing him in himself, for cash. Edwin was only spared after a spirit appeared to him in Raedwald's camp, warning him what was up and offering him safe passage if he would convert to Christianity on the spot. Edwin agreed and Raedwald suddenly came over all hospitable. The reason for his change of heart was the intercession of his queen, who persuaded him that 'it was unworthy in a great king to sell his best friend in the hour of need for gold, and worse still to sacrifice his royal honour, the most valuable of all possessions, for love of money'.

Michael led the way to Raedwald's old haunt over a crunchy carpet of pine cones. It was Heritage Open Day at Sutton Hoo. That meant free entry courtesy of the National Trust, and attractions including men like Paul kitted out in worsted thornproofs and a knee-length tunic, like a jujitsu outfit, the whole ensemble set off by a sheathed sword and a leather purse. 'He made that at his own expense,' said Michael. From beneath his visor, Paul exhaled fiercely.

It's been said of Sutton Hoo that 'the vista is rich with that rarest of modern pleasures – silence'. The Debden moved noiselessly below us and all was tranquil, save for the depredations of Suffolk's insect life and the bells of a September wedding. Oh yes, and the report of a gunshot from the direction of Woodbridge.

Michael looked pained. 'Everyone's unhappy that Heritage Open Day is clashing with Woodbridge Maritime Day,' he said. The rival diversions included races on the river and a display by 'professional knot-tier and rope-maker Des Pawson, who was recently awarded the MBE for services to the knot and rope-making industry'. (What was a professional knot-tier? How did you get an MBE for services to the knot industry? Did you have to lace the Prince of Wales's brogues on a minimum number of state occasions? When FA Cup finalists tested the sponginess of the Wembley sward in their Armani and their Prada, were you responsible for the traditional finishing touch, the Windsor knots as big as soup plates?) Michael swept his arm towards the river. 'Raedwald's boat was seaworthy. He'd taken it down the river and on to Canterbury when he went to meet St Augustine and be christened.' My guide was carrying on regardless, like the trouper he was. He said, 'The King came back here to his church and installed a Christian altar alongside the existing pagan one.'

Bede takes up the story. 'His last state was worse than the first: for, like the ancient Samaritans, he tried to serve both Christ and the ancient gods, and he had in the same shrine an altar for the holy Sacrifice of Christ side by side with a small altar on which victims were offered to devils.' A Wuffing called Aldwulf, a king of the East Angles after Raedwald, 'lived into our own times', said Bede, and reported that he had seen the shrine as a boy. Indeed, there's an argument that Raedwald not only went to his grave resisting the new religion, but that the tomb itself was a symbolic bulwark of idolatry, a bastion against the imperialism of the Merovingian kings of France, who were Christian converts. The earthworks were thus the landscape-gardening equivalent of a V-sign; a last hurrah, or perhaps ha-ha.

But was it really Raedwald who was buried on the banks of the Debden? The argument went that since he was the ruler in these parts in the early seventh century, which was the scientifically established provenance of the earthy sepulchre, and since only a man of high birth, or rather death, would qualify for a send-off like the one the Anglo-Saxons prepared at Sutton Hoo, it followed that Raedwald must be the dear departed. As indicated above, the occupant of Mound 1 was in no shape to help the historians with their inquiries. Indeed, it was an act of antiquarian bravado to persuade an inquest that there had been a body at all. Stuart Piggott, who worked on the initial dig in 1939, told the coroner's court that 'owing to the acid nature of the sand [in the barrow] no visible trace of the skeleton remained – a condition which is however familiar to excavators in such soils'. This argument carried the day, and it was reinforced in the 1980s when a man called Rupert Bruce-Mitford visited the Pathology Museum at Guy's Hospital, London, to study the heels of Mrs Durand-Deacon. These were the only bits of that unhappy lady to be pulled intact from the bath of acid which her murderer, John George Haigh, had prepared for her. Martin Carver writes:

> Bruce-Mitford went on to infer a similar process, if much more protracted, in the acid bath provided by the hull of the Sutton Hoo ship, and showed that in a central area, where the great old buckle and the baldric lay, the finds carried corrosion products that were slightly phosphate-enriched. The most likely explanation of this was that there had been a body, which had lain in rainwater collected in the hull and burial chamber, acidified by its passage through the acid sand of the mound; so over the years the body had been rendered invisible by decay. It could now be strongly argued, with scientific corroboration, that a body had lain or sat in the west half of the chamber.

But not even this stopped academicians from quibbling that the exclusive berm might just as easily have been occupied by a wealthy nobleman as by an out-and-out king.

The mounds of Sutton Hoo stood in a clearing behind a border of rope. Beyond this rose ears of maize. Ducking under the cord, Michael, Paul the Anglo-Saxon and I might have been in the makeshift baseball oche carved out of the corn in *Field of Dreams*, the feature film starring Kevin Costner.

Many of the mounds had suffered the effects of settlement and erosion, said Michael. They had experienced the often clumsy attentions of beast and man, centuries of nibbling and tilth. The first hillock that we came to had been 'almost ploughed away to nothing'. This was Mound 5. 'We know that a man in his twenties was buried here, and there's evidence of a bladed implement having been in contact with his skull.' By 'bladed implement', Michael meant 'axe'. The young man had sustained at least nine savage blows. Raedwald might have been the most notable tenant of Sutton Hoo, its 'excellent cadaver', but the field was rich in stiffs. This was more than a nice day out at a National Trust property, this was CSI: Suffolk.

There were the unsettling 'Sand People', Dark-Agers who'd dissolved as surely as the King himself, but who had left behind gritty silhouettes of themselves, macabre human sandcastles. According to a British Museum account, 'It became increasingly clear that most of these bodies were buried in positions that were odd: one was kneeling, head to the floor of the grave; one stretched out, hand above the head; another folded forward, another folded back, another sideways; and strangest of all, one splayed out in a hurdling position, accompanied by a wooden object that seemed to belong to . . . a primitive plough.' The Sand People were the victims of ritual killings. They were interred near gallows which operated from Raedwald's time until the eleventh century. In 'Burial 42', two women were buried face down on a decapitated middle-aged man, 'for reasons beyond the reach of current science', as Carver puts it.

I followed Michael up a gentle rise, the loamy flank of a cottage loaf: we were on Mound 1. I was doing my own field-walking on the resting-place of the mighty Raedwald, and pulling it off with an impudence I would never have dreamed possible only a few centuries earlier: trampling over Raedwald, trifler with princely life, the pagan who made a fool out of St Augustine, the outrager of enlightened Gallic monarchy right up to the end. The top of the loaf hadn't risen; there was a longboat-shaped dip in the mound. A rectangle plumb amidships was cordoned off. In the case of a lesser visitor attraction, a lesser vessel, this might have been a larky way of denoting the ultimate maritime VIP area, the Captain's Table. Here it wasn't Raedwald's groaning board that was being marked out but his slab, his burial chamber below decks. I was intent upon my field walk – the ground was surprisingly tussocky, taut, under foot – and also thinking about another archaeological technique that had been used at this location. It entailed cutting sections through the site, making transects, as they were known, but the best thing about this method was its name: it was called ground-truthing. What was the ground truth of Sutton Hoo?

The often gore-steeped history of what went into the earth here was only half the story; there was also the narrative of how it all came out again. Sutton Hoo: it's all very well as a name, sure, as a brand, but it doesn't begin to do justice to the full interpretative experience. Phone the sign-writers, get the T-shirt embossers out of bed: is it too late for *Sutton Hoo, What, When, Where and Why?*

A lot of credit for uncovering its secrets belongs to Basil Brown, a horny-handed countryman and my forerunner as conqueror of Mound 1. In 1939 Brown was retained by Mrs Edith Pretty, the owner of Sutton Hoo House, whose estate included the hillocks. It's been averred that shadowy figures frequent them at dusk, even an apparition of a horseman upon a white steed, but it was a more welcome visitation, a friendly ghost, that reputedly encouraged the excavations. Mrs Pretty had lost her husband Frank, and had taken to consulting a spiritualist in London. 'She's supposed to have had a visit from Frank in a dream, and he told her where to find the King,' said Michael.

Brown finds himself speculating along these lines when Mrs Pretty gives him his orders in a scene from *The Dig*, John Preston's 2007 novel based on events at Sutton Hoo:

'Well, I'm wondering to myself why you want the mounds excavating now. After all, it's not as if you've just arrived here, or anything like that.'

As soon as he had finished speaking he glanced away. I suspected he thought he might have overstepped the mark.

'You are quite right, of course,' I said. 'I often discussed it with my late husband. It was a subject that greatly interested us both. But unfortunately he died before we were able to make a start. Then, after he died, I found that it did not seem appropriate somehow. As for what changed my mind, I can only say that I felt that if I did not do it now, then it might be too late.'

It might have been too late because war was on the horizon. Michael said, 'The excavation had to be rushed because of fears of a Nazi invasion. They did it all in three months. It would have taken three years today.' Ironically, one lot of Germanic conquerors was threatening the repose of another. That was an Englishman's job!

Brown was a familiar if already threatened figure in the landscape, the self-taught all-rounder in hairy tweeds; 'Astronomer, Archaeologist, Enigma' in the somewhat over-yolked title of a hagiographic monograph about him. He believed that the essence of archaeology was 'a good spade and patience', and this philosophy was spectacularly vindicated in the excavation of the leavened loaf beneath my feet. Brown came upon rusting rivets: ship's nails. The longboat they'd once held together had long since rotted away, like her owner, but Brown's great insight was to trace her outline in the stains that her timbers had left behind in the sandy soil. In effect, he was uncovering an imprint of the boat, her photographic negative; the mound was a dark-room of the Dark Ages. Brown was part of a team that went on to uncover the King of the East Angles and his extraordinary grave gifts. Brown's cardinal virtue, according to his biographer Chris Durrant, was that he 'possessed very little, if any, sense of self-importance and was entirely at home with his helpers . . . on whom he relied to shift the countless tons of earth. Against this good-natured backdrop of steady spadework he was able to tease out the shadow of the great boat when others of a different style might have failed to capture the prize or, worse, trampled on the delicate image in the sand.'

When the unprecedented scale of Brown's find became clear, however, he was relieved of his leading role by the men in suits, or rather the men in *better* suits. The coroner who sat in judgement on the treasure trove found that it rightfully belonged to Mrs Pretty, Michael told me. 'She stashed a lot of it in her bedroom – under her bed. She eventually gave it to the nation, to the British Museum. They stored it in the London Underground until the war was over.'

It wasn't until years later that Brown achieved something like his due. In 1966 he was awarded a Civil List pension of £250 in recognition of the debt he was owed by the nation. The grant was made on the recommendation of Bruce-Mitford, who'd field-walked in Brown's pioneering footsteps. 'I'm so glad that we have been able to get this small token of appreciation of your work fixed up for you,' the younger man wrote. Until his death in the 1970s, Brown would travel up to London to see his 'treasure'. Durrant says, 'He would arrive in the forecourt of the museum neatly turned out, stiff white collar and shiny black boots, hearing aid whistling audibly from a distance.'

I heard the ticking of an agricultural sprinkler from somewhere in the maize fields and I considered an oak standing beside a barrow. Such a tree grows to a great age, of course, but in the context of Sutton Hoo, it might as well have been the greenest sapling. One by one, the mounds had been opened and examined by means of the best available archaeological techniques. Now that they were closed up again, the ground truth of them was that they had reclaimed what was mysterious about them. They had been restored to their archaic otherness.

Back at the visitor centre, I took afternoon tea on the sun-deck with Paul the Anglo-Saxon. As he slaked his awful thirst, the sinking Suffolk orb was at his back. Its strong, flat light made the delicate bone of Paul's drinking vessel all but transparent, I noticed, as he raised the horn to his lips.

7

CHUFFED NUNS

In English folklore, tunnels often connect buildings that have associations with power, religious or secular, such as churches, monasteries and abbeys as well as castles and great houses. Or a passage might go down to the sea or to a river, or disappear into the depths of a hillside, a hidden thoroughfare. On the other hand, its purpose might be bruited abroad – for example, for the movement of black-market goods, as in the case of the caves under New Brighton, or the warren said to connect old houses beneath the streets of Rottingdean in Sussex. Then again, Beeston Castle in Cheshire is one of a number of historic fortresses where besieged incumbents are believed to have dug defiles as a means of escape. The monks of Whitby Abbey are reputed to have quarried out a corridor to Robin Hood's Bay more than a mile away, as a getaway route in times of war.

Other legends hold out the delicious possibility that stumbling down a buried way will turn into tripping the light fantastic, culminating in the revelation of buried treasure, though a deadly threat often clouds this promise. In the nineteenth century, the Sussex anthropologist Charlotte Latham was told that a two-mile tunnel from Offington to the old hill fort of Cissbury Ring held a pot of gold which was guarded by a brace of monstrous serpents. It's claimed that the monks of Birkenhead Priory, the founders of the famous Mersey ferry, abandoned their living at the time of the Reformation and fled down a tunnel with the prior's gold, only for the roof to collapse, irrevocably entombing both novices and pelf.

Some legendary tunnels seem impervious to the earthbound considerations that would constrain the average twenty-first-century contractor. It's said that they pass under riverbeds or through marshy ground, the kind of terrain in which any venture would soon become flooded or choked. The supposed extent of such a burrow may also stretch credibility. In *The Subterranean Kingdom* Nigel Pennick writes, 'The average length of a legendary tunnel is about two miles, and to build one of that length would be a major engineering operation, the like of which was not seen in Britain before the eighteenth century.' The longest tunnel described to the antiquarian Granville Squiers in the 1930s was no less than twenty-five miles from one end to the other, further than the longest rail tunnel in service today apart from the Channel Tunnel.

The distorting influences of darkness and confinement may colour judgements of the extent of subterranean passages. F. C. J. Spurrell, a nineteenth-century authority on dene-holes (chalk caves entered by vertical shafts), recalled: 'I once came across a man who told me that he had fallen down a pit, in which he passed two days. On recovering from the fall he wandered down deep passages for immense distances, until, regaining the entrance, he sat under it and howled until someone heard him (for a path led near the hole) and he was extricated.' Spurrell asked the man to guide him to the spot where he had fallen, and he explored the hole for himself. But when he scrambled in, 'no passages presented themselves; but the size of the cavern, its great circuit, its buttresses and pillars, and high irregular mounds of earth fallen from the vault, fully explained the account of the poor fellow, who, bruised, starved and in darkness, had crawled round and round the cave "in wandering mazes lost".'

In *The Old Straight Track*, published in the 1920s, Alfred Watkins contended that supposed underground passages between ancient sites such as churches, abbeys, castles and camps often followed the paths of ley lines. He came up with the theory that these 'tunnels' were actually folk memories of old tracks linking these local features. The tunnel myth was really another way of saying that a straight track traversed a ridge to an invisible point on the far side of it.

One such case was a mysterious tunnel said to run along the Coldrum Ley in Kent. The tunnel, like the ley line, travels from a church in the village of Trottiscliffe to Blue Bell Hill, by way of the Coldrum stones, Snodland Church, an ancient ford on the River Medway and Burnham Court Church. At one time, all the locations along this route could be seen from any of the others, apart from Trottiscliffe Church and the Coldrum Stones. On Watkins's argument, talk of such a tunnel might have begun with well-meant neighbourly directions about how to reach the out-of-sight stones from the church. The existence of the Coldrum tunnel has never been confirmed, though one aspect of its mythology is that two brothers discovered it, one choosing to explore it while the other followed his progress on the surface. The first brother was playing a flute, and the music could clearly be heard by his sibling – until it suddenly stopped. The second boy was too scared to go into the tunnel himself, and his brother was never seen again.

This is a recurring fable, turning up for instance in the legend of the Blind Fiddler of Anstey. In a pit west of the village of Anstey in Hertfordshire is a dark recess known as Cave Gate, which was said to be the entrance to a tunnel. This was claimed to extend for the best part of a mile, all the way to Anstey Castle, a medieval keep which once stood on a promontory close to the parish church. No one dared explore this covered causeway but it was the talk of the tavern, the Chequers. One day, the pub's old fiddler Blind George agreed to venture into it for a bet. Taking his dog with him, he entered Cave Gate, fiddling as he went, so that the rest of his drinking companions and the other villagers could keep track of them. The Chequers regulars were walking on top of the tunnel, following the music. They were about halfway to Anstey Castle when the fiddling abruptly ceased. A horrific shriek cleft the air, followed by utter silence. The villagers rushed back to Cave Gate and were in time to see George's dog running out of the tunnel again. The hapless cur was howling, tailless, with all his hair singed off. The Blind Fiddler was never seen again, and the villagers decided to block up the passage. According to some, its course is still plain when snow settles, because it melts first along its route.

When a folklore collector called W. B. Gerish documented the tale in 1903, the suggestion was that it had originated before the turn of the nineteenth century, as 'elderly men remember their grandfathers telling them this story as if it had taken place considerably before their time'. Like the accounts of the Coldrum passage, the saga of Blind George was fixed in the topography and history of its setting. Church records show that Anstey did indeed have a fiddler whose surname was George, but he was buried in the churchyard, not lost in the murk beyond Cave Gate. It's also true that snow melts first in a straight line at Anstey; however, this signifies not the course of a tunnel but the route of a road. (This dates the present version of the legend to as late as 1830, when the road was moved by about a hundred yards from its former alignment.) As for the tunnel itself, it's thought to have been a prehistoric flintmine, and penetrates no further than thirty feet from Cave Gate. The far end of the tunnel is in fact quite a different thing: it's the old route for the water supply to Anstey Castle.

The misadventures of Blind George recall a similar yarn told at

Grantchester, Cambridgeshire, and other well-known versions are set at Binham Priory, Norfolk, and Richmond Castle, Yorkshire. The widely travelled legend of a forbidding tunnel and a vanishing violinist also clung to a medieval abbey in Kent, the home of an enclosed order of nuns. I came across the following tantalising reference to the Benedictine sisters of West Malling in the indispensable reference work, *The Lore of the Land: A Guide to England's Legends* by Jennifer Westwood and Jacqueline Simpson:

A rather sinister tale was noted by several writers in the 1970s and 80s; though only recorded relatively late, it has parallels in other parts of England which show that it follows an authentically traditional pattern. It concerns a long tunnel, the entrance to which, it was said, could be seen in the ruins of Malling Abbey. Some men once wanted to test the theory that it ran all the way to a cave on the downs near Ryarsh, so they got a fiddler to walk along the tunnel, playing his instrument as he went, while they themselves followed above ground, tracking him by the sound. Suddenly the music stopped, beneath a small wood called Fiddler's Copse, about midway between West Malling and Ryarsh. Nothing more was heard; the fiddler was never seen again; and the course of the tunnel remains uncertain, since nobody else was willing to explore it.

Well, I was willing to explore it, I thought. Especially as there was an added wrinkle in this particular tunnel myth. You see, the strolling player of West Malling, the musician who accompanied himself to his ruin through the abbey's underground passage, wasn't the only one to tread that clandestine corridor. Other pairs of feet, more shapely than his own, also skipped the same way, or so ungallant tongues had it. The tunnel was a gangway for errant nuns, escaping their bonds and seeking fleshly distraction in the world beyond. These mischievous sisters were taking advantage of their subterranean crawlway and driving a coach and horses through it. Talk about the dissolution of the monasteries. It's no aspersion on the blameless sorority of Malling Abbey today to say that generations of women who took their vows before them behaved as though life was for the living, and indeed vice versa.

In the Middle Ages, the King had the power to order something called a 'visitation', a kind of otherworldly OFSTED inquiry into a monastery or convent. In 1299 Archbishop Robert Winchelsey was sent to West Malling and was sorely troubled by what he uncovered. Too few of the women who took the veil felt a genuine calling; for many, it was the only way out of a life otherwise spent in spinster- or widowhood. This upset the rightful order of things in the community, where a nun's time was properly divided between worship, study and manual work. 'When this ideal broke down and work came to be regarded as undignified, large numbers of servants had to be employed,' according to the abbey's own history. 'This led the nuns to indolence, gossip, vanity, worldly behaviour and on occasion, sexual immorality.'

Hardly had Winchelsey brought the bad news back from the Kent countryside than there was further tumult at the abbey. In 1321 a cleric by the square-jawed title of Bishop Hamo de Hethe was ordered by Edward II to carry out another visitation. This was after the nuns had complained to the King that 'their house was being ruined' by the abbess, Elizabeth de Baddlesmere. Elizabeth tried to put Hamo off with a story about being too ill to get the old place looking nice, but he was not to be gainsaid.

In those days, a prelate carrying out a visitation – an OFNUN report, you might say – had all the 'teeth' that a *Daily Mail* leader writer could have wished for. With the full force of the royal seal behind him, the diocesan or the Archbishop, entering a dubious establishment, would insist that it be observant and wisely run or there would be hell (on earth) to pay. So instead of being taken in by the abbess's blandishments, Hamo paid a visit, and pronounced her guilty of maladministration. Elizabeth de Baddlesmere found herself leaving holy orders and collecting her marching orders instead, though some said the bishop was currying favour with the King and that Elizabeth was being punished as a blow by proxy against her brother, Baron Bartholomew de Baddlesmere, an enemy of the Crown. The new abbess, appointed by the Bishop, was Agnes de Leybourne, a member of a local family. 'Her behaviour appears to have been even worse than her predecessor's,' the abbey records reveal. 'She frequently left the Abbey in secret to visit her friends in Leybourne Castle and appointed them to offices in the Abbey.'

Was this where the stories of nuns flitting along the abbey tunnel had originated? It would appear so. I wrote to the nuns about coming to see them and received a reply from Sister Mary David. 'Yes, we have a tunnel (often called the "Secret Passage") which oral tradition says connected the abbey and Leybourne Castle – the Abbess Agnes de Leybourne was supposed to have used it to visit her brother, who owned the castle in the 1320s. This castle is about a mile from the Abbey.' The sister said that 'all modern archaeologists' who had braved the tunnel – the haunt of fruity nuns, it seemed, as well as blighted fiddlers – had doubted its usefulness in any getaway plan. 'This inconvenient fact has not, however, stopped any tales about naughty nuns creeping out of the enclosure.'

Certainly, there had been a lot of it about. There was a time when the mendicant minxes of Malling were hardly ever in their cells, and when they were, they weren't alone. On 2 October 1340, the Bishop was writing about the nuns' failure to 'keep enclosure'. The abbey's annals record that 'secular women and sometimes men who were not servants were allowed into the cloister, even overnight, and the nuns were using the pretexts of pilgrimages, visits to their families and godchildren and attendance at funerals to leave the enclosure'.

Putting yourself in a nun's habit for a moment, and

contemplating the contemplative life from the hurly-burly of your own scapegrace existence, you might suppose that an anchoress had all the time in the world. But on the contrary, her days are spoken for. If she's not practising her rituals of worship, she's tending to the needs of the abbey's guests. Her diary is entirely blocked out with prior prayer commitments and Bible study: it's chocka with PowerPoint presentations. This was the case with the time-poor but spirit-rich Sister Mary David. But from within her mullioned sanctuary, she somehow found me a window . . .

I duly knocked at the sixteenth-century gatehouse to Malling Abbey. One of the nuns appeared at a little side-door giving on to the gardens. 'You're here to see Sister Mary David?' she said in a gentle Scots burr. She was framed by the doorway, a vision on the cusp of the abbey proper, or so it seemed to me. Its hallowed halls and God-favoured greensward were a beatific backdrop to my interlocutor in her holy hoodie. I was shown all at once into the presence of the senior nun.

'I'll show you our secret passage!' said Sister Mary David, taking my hand in a cold, bony grip. It was difficult, not to say unchivalrous, to speculate as to her age, but she was one of the abbey's longest-serving incumbents. The white collar of her nun's raiment was coming away a little at the seam. She was carrying a large torch. 'Are you an archaeologist?'

'A journalist. Much worse.'

'Yes, it is,' she said. She was flinty, but she didn't appear to mind personal questions – or she answered them, at any rate. There was a suggestion of the mid-Atlantic in her voice. Sister Mary told me that she came from Niagara. 'I'm American, not Canadian, though back in those days, people moved across the border.'

Our talk of hackery led me to ask the sister how her community stayed in touch with the outside world.

'We take the *Telegraph*, *The Economist*,' she said, 'the *Tablet*. We have a sister who types up the BBC News.'

This struck me as an extraordinary symbol of the sequestered experience, the novice as a member of the religious partisans, a spy for God, decrypting the terrible chatter of the world beyond the cloister and passing the vocation-confirming carbons on to her sorrowing sisters. During its history, the community has found itself on the run from the rest of us, not just in retreat in the strictly spiritual sense of that term. As one account of Malling has it, 'the Benedictine tradition was driven underground for four centuries'. The abbey wasn't spared when Henry VIII issued his fatwa against the monasteries. It was seized on 29 October 1538. At the time, its annual income was a healthy £245 10s 2d, according to its own accounts. 'After the sisters had been turned out, the lead roof and bells of the church were stripped, while the stones were pillaged for local buildings.' As late as 1553, five of the nuns were still drawing their pensions. Some had presumably returned to their families, or gone into domestic service. They weren't allowed to marry until 1547, when the repeal of the Act of Six Articles released the 'ex-religious' from their oath of celibacy. The story of the abbey goes on, 'The nuns of Malling thus became just a tiny handful amidst the many thousands of dispossessed, uprooted religious. Their fate is known only to God.' It would be more than three hundred years before a Benedictine community was restored to Malling.

In 1540, in an exchange of property with the King, Thomas Cranmer, Archbishop of Canterbury, became the owner of the abbey, its manor and its rights in West Malling. The old place returned to the Crown at the beginning of Queen Elizabeth's reign. She gave it to one of her favourites, Sir Henry Brooke, who in turn bequeathed it to his nephew, Henry, Baron Cobham. But he forfeited his prestigious address when he was accused of being party to a treason stirred up by Sir Walter Raleigh and was sent to the Tower for his pains.

Sister Mary led me past the brooding stack of St Leonard's Tower, built by Gundulf, Bishop of Rochester, who founded the abbey about 1090. The Prior House at Malling had once been a leper colony. My own personal visitation also included the splendid Georgian mansion which was put up at Malling in 1746. The house was built in the then fashionable Gothic style, with windows and doorways purloined from the Abbey church.

'Are you the boss around here?' I asked.

'I'm happy to say I'm not. I wouldn't wish that for myself for anything.' Anyone who wanted the job would not be suitable for it, the sister said. It was the sort of thing that is said of popes. We discussed the Archbishop of Canterbury and his travails over such matters as gay priests. Sister Mary commiserated with him: 'Poor man.' She told me about an event at the abbey where someone had asked, 'Hands up if you've never met a gay vicar?' No hands. 'Hands up if you've never met a gay *bishop*?'

Sister Mary confirmed the pressures on her time – her span was indeed tightly allotted. 'It's a very structured life,' she said. 'The main work is looking after our visitors. We have about two thousand a year. One of our guests was a gentleman of the road. We took him in and his life is now in turnaround.'

'What time do you get up?'

'At four.'

'Don't you ever have a holiday?'

'Sure. I get up at five.'

'Have you ever had doubts about all this?'

'Once, for a period in my thirties,' conceded Sister Mary. It happened at the time she was 'professed', that is to say, took the vows of full nunhood. But that was a long time ago, she said.

You could see how it would be possible to become attached to this tranquil spot, but what were the rules about venturing over the wall? Well, things had clearly tightened up since the hairshirt-burning days of Abbess Agnes de Leybourne. 'The nuns are allowed to go home on urgent family matters, for legal reasons, and to vote,' the sister explained. She told me the staggering fact that, apart from such dispensations, she had been confined behind the walls of West Malling for thirty-eight years.

I was so shocked by this revelation, that the next thing I did was to ask Sister Mary if she could tell me the name of the Prime Minister.

She rolled her eyes, 'Of course!' There followed a vigorous, heavily footnoted critique of the cover of that week's *Economist*, which showed Gordon Brown as Michelangelo's David, naked save for a fig leaf. This foliage jockstrap was the PM's modesty-preserving policy on the EU, the sister clarified. For good measure, she shared her thoughts on the Bush administration. 'A bunch of numbskulls!'

The last time that she had made the short journey through the door at the side of the gatehouse and into the outside world, it was to vote in local elections, eighteen months earlier.

'Did you look forward to it?'

'I couldn't wait to get back. The litter! The traffic!' This didn't seem a particularly charitable, a particularly *Christian*, view of the outside world. You might expect a nun, a member of any self-denying order, to be more tolerant and slower to irritation than the folk outside the abbey walls. But on the contrary, perhaps you should anticipate that a lifetime of living removed from other people would make you set in your ways.

Another nun, Sister Anna, once made an appointment to see her GP. The local vicar was also in the surgery, with his little daughter, and he was struggling to make the child behave. As their names were called to go in and see the doctor, the priest looked across the waiting-room at Sister Anna and said in his carrying pulpit voice, 'Sister, whatever you do, don't *ever* have children!' As the author of the abbey's history, *Living Stones*, remarked, 'Small wonder the villagers have stories about the nuns!'

The travel privileges that the novices enjoy – or not, as the case may be – were introduced in the 1970s and 80s. Before then, the tone was set by the ascetic Frederick Vasey, the Anglo-Catholic chaplain of the community when it was restored in its present guise in 1929. He felt that in order for the abbey to be 'authentic' there needed to be all the trappings of high-churchery, including grilles in the nuns' parlour, solemn vows and strict enclosure. As the biography of the abbey observed, 'The quality of hiddenness, which Fr. Vasey considered an essential of the contemplative life, has remained as part of his spiritual legacy.'

The sister and I were now bearing down on one of the abbey's overlooked reservoirs of hiddenness, its subterranean passage. Slipping through another gate, we found ourselves in the garden of a chalet-bungalow, set aside for the visiting friends or relatives of the sisters. 'Here we are,' said Sister Mary.

But were we? There was no sign of an escape hatch, no candle-winking grot nor any arched entrance to a nun-favoured tunnel of love. However, as we drew closer to the abbey wall, a flight of mulchy steps sunk into the Kentish crust very satisfyingly revealed themselves.

'Off you go,' said Sister Mary, and handed me her flashlight.

Hang about! What was this? Did I understand the sister correctly, was I to carry on alone into the *souterrain* which had been the undoing of West Malling's lost minstrel and unknown numbers of nuns, albeit for somewhat different reasons? It seemed that I had her line and length absolutely plumb. I thought about the reference to the tunnel in *The Lore of the Land* and its gooseflesh-making payoff, 'Nobody . . . was willing to explore it.'

Perhaps Sister Mary read the look in my eye as my boot havered over the first slippery step. Was she seized by the same spirit of adventure that had led her as a young woman all the way from Niagara Falls to the Garden of England? Or maybe her solemn oath of charity simply got the better of her – at all events, she exhaled in mock exasperation and jinked past me into the tunnel. Lifting the hem of her habit a fraction, she disclosed a pale hairless calf, like one of my dad's.

I hunched forward and followed her in. As my eyes accustomed to the gloom, my impression was that we were entering a hut or bothy. The beam of our torch picked out great curved, broadly similar blocks of stone which had been used in the making of the walls and the canopy above our heads. The floor was earthen, or to put it another way, muddy.

The Benedictines might have been embarrassed by the dubious reputation that the tunnel had contributed to, but that didn't stop them from building a men's community almost on top of it. A brotherhood was founded in this corner in the 1960s, on the spot where a farmer had once kept apples in a barn, though this sodality had not proved as long-lived as its distaff version.

Sister Mary and I edged our way forward in the dank and dark. According to the devout or otherwise susceptible, powerful subliminal forces were at work close at hand. One writer has said, 'Malling Abbey is best described as a "haunt of ancient peace" . . . One recalls of Malling that "the silence was deep" and that "the currents of need and grace went to and fro".'

Robert Hugh Benson (1871–1914), a curate who visited the abbey, described a profound supernatural experience. He recounted praying before 'a high iron-barred screen in which there was no door'. After a time, he became 'aware of a motionless figure, a nun, kneeling in prayer'. He couldn't see her face and had no idea of her age – 'She might have been twenty-five or seventy.' As he meditated on this figure and on the enclosed life and its seeming 'uselessness', Benson became conscious of

> a vital connection from the Tabernacle to the woman . . . Now in the Tabernacle I became aware that there was a mighty stirring and movement. Something within it beat like a vast Heart, and the vibrations of each pulse seemed to quiver through all the ground . . . A moment ago, I had fancied myself apart from movement in this quiet convent; but I seemed somehow to have stepped into a centre of busy, rushing life . . .

I was aware that the atmosphere was charged with energy; great powers seemed to be astir, and I to be close to the whirling centre of it all . . . I perceived that this black figure knelt at the centre of reality . . . there ran out from this peaceful chapel lines of spiritual power that lost themselves in the distance, bewildering in their profusion and terrible in the intensity of their hidden fire.

That word 'hidden' again. Sister Mary and I were in one of the most hidden, most surreptitious nooks of the abbey, and the truth of it was that the full story of the tunnel was itself hidden to us; 'uncertain', as the authors of *The Lore of the Land* had noted. I don't know what I expected to find, exactly: a knob of rosin, abandoned when the lost violinist of West Malling was surprised in his sawing, perhaps, or even a compromisingly foxed wimple misplaced by a chuffed nun. Maybe 'all modern archaeologists' were right when they nixed the tunnel legend, preferring to see it, in their cold-water-pouring way, as a drain: a culvert that had served the abbey in the Middle Ages, allowing waste to run away into the local limestone, then as an ice-house in the eighteenth century.

What I did in fact find, blocking up the passageway some yards into it, was what looked like a landslip of brick and stone. I tested its strength – it didn't take long to establish that this barrier had the beating of me. There was a little aperture near the top of it through which you might peer dimly into the recesses of the route. But I knew that I would not now be able to confirm whether it ran all the way to a cave on the downs near Ryarsh, or linked the abbey to Leybourne Castle.

I wouldn't want you to think that I was disappointed – on the contrary. The chase was the thing, as the abbey's more wayward sisters might have said. On a more spiritual plane, I see with hindsight that by entering the tunnel I had unwittingly acted out a lesson that is urged on his followers by the abbey's ineffable patron. For do we not find this among the abbey's texts and teachings? 'St Benedict's answer is simple but paradoxical. The monastics, he says, are to seek God, but in so doing the workers are sought by the Lord: they are to do the work of God, yet it is God who works in them and they are to find their way to heaven through obedience and humility *whose symbol is the ladder they ascend by climbing down* [my italics].'

The ladder is long and rickety, and only the bravest and the best of us will pass its test, and I could not forbear, in my vanity, from asking Sister Mary as we climbed out of the secret passage again: 'I don't suppose you ever watch *Newsnight*, do you, sister?' Half-turning round on the leaf-slicked steps and looking down at me with the strong autumn sun at her back, this silhouette of a nun spoke to me, saying, 'I haven't watched television in almost forty years.'

Sister Mary invited me to stay for tea at the big house. I joined a group of guests a little older than myself, men as well as women, enjoying homemade scones and jam behind leaded windows. A woman in sensible coordinates was happily reading a primer on how to become a nun. Bent over a tea-caddy, the Scottish nun who had first shown me into the abbey was playing mother; or do I mean mother superior? She complained that she was losing her voice.

Sister Mary was halfway out of the lounge. She backed into the room, twisting herself around the door, playing with the handle. She was almost coquettish. 'That's not a problem I suffer from,' she said.

8

GLORY-HOLES

As well as being accused of going to ground in order to get up to no good, the religious have from time to time had recourse to the subterranean as a way of escape. This was never more true than in Tudor England, when Catholic priests faced arrest, trial and death for their Roman inclinations. The dramatic times of these desperate clergy and the faithful families who protected them have given rise to accounts of burrows and botholes. 'More than a hundred ancient Catholic houses in this country have crannies that are claimed as priest "holes" or hiding-places and scores of them are genuine,' as Jeremy Errand drily notes in *Secret Passages and Hiding-Places*. 'A large proportion of the houses are also endowed with legends of secret passages.'

The Elizabethan religious settlement was intended to usher in a kind of benign Protestantism, an early version of today's milquetoast Anglicanism, a spell of fair weather after the nation's religious barometer had plunged first one way, then the other, during the tempestuous dispensations of earlier Tudor monarchs. Henry VIII's seismic breach with the papacy was the point of reference for the regencies of Edward VI's reign, but Mary Tudor took the throne determined to rehabilitate the country in the eyes of Rome. When she was in turn succeeded by Elizabeth and the needle twitched again, Marian priests were not required to hide themselves, though many of them took the precaution of stowing their furnishings and vestments, the frills of their now frowned-on faith.

The state's real targets were the so-called seminary priests from the continent, Catholic missionaries who had graduated from English colleges in Flanders, Rome and Spain. They were landed in England from 1574 with a brief to nurture the seed in the hospitable environment of country estates belonging to sympathetic families, making the hearing of mass available to all interested members of the landed class and generally nudging the Counter-Reformation along. In 1580 they were joined by cadres of an elite new Catholic swat squad, the Jesuits, who had been founded with the express purpose of restoring the true Church in lapsed outposts of her empire.

The bent of the missionaries was scriptural rather than seditious, but the Queen's advisers were afraid of an alliance of Catholic powers against England. The priests were seen as early 'insurgents'. The discovery of plots against Elizabeth confirmed these fears. Priests began to be tortured and executed, and by 1585 a foreigner in a dog collar could be accused of high treason simply for setting foot in England. As for the Roman-leaning laity, a fine for missing (Protestant) church on Sundays was put up from twelvepence a week to a swingeing £20 a month, a conscience tax that was clearly targeted at well-to-do recusant households. Harbouring a priest became a crime punishable by massive fines, forfeiture of assets and even death.

It became extremely uncomfortable to be a practising Catholic. Leaders of the embattled faith met at Harleyford near Marlow in 1586 and made plans to disappear priests into the woodwork of the gentry houses where they were welcome. The scheme was masterminded by Henry Garnett, who was made

Jesuit superior that same year. Catholic clergy were moved around the country clandestinely, like the slaves smuggled out of cotton fields in America two hundred or more years later. This underground priest railroad picked up new arrivals when they were dropped on English beaches and supplied them with money, horses and disguises. They were guided away from the stony plantations of non-believers to the rolling green pastures of recusant estates. 'Here young priests could wait while postings were found for them, and older ones could meet for conferences and retreats and rest between fatiguing and nerve-racking journeys, often on foot, to remote villages and farmhouses,' writes the Catholic scholar Michael Hodgetts.

Priest handed priest on to priest in Garnett's human chain. For all that, he never did a better day's work in his life than when, in 1588, he performed the comparatively mundane chore of hiring a certain servant. He chose as his factotum Nicholas Owen, an unschooled carpenter from Oxford, who would go on to carve out a brilliant career in the priest-hole industry. In time, he had this admittedly niche market all to himself, demonstrating the kind of fiendish imagination that you might expect of a Jesuitical Jeeves. Of all the priest-holes in the country, more were built by Owen than by any other individual. 'A man of extraordinary wit and discretion, he was also deeply religious and never began his day of hide-making without first taking Communion,' says Errand. Owen is credited with saving hundreds of lives, among the laity as well as the clergy, and with keeping many recusant estates out of the hands of Elizabeth's bailiffs. Priests escaped more than once from houses where Owen had been active. Sometimes five or six of them at once weathered the storm of a search party in one of his specially adapted houses, one of his Catholic conversions. Owen's expertise extended to tunnels, or so some authorities have claimed. 'With incomparable skill [Owen] knew how to conduct priests to a place of safety along subterranean passages, to hide them in walls and bury them in impenetrable recesses, and entangle them in labyrinths and a thousand windings,' a historian called Fea wrote in 1908. The life expectancy of a runaway reverend increased significantly if he could only gain the safety of an alcove – a God-slot, if you will – attributed to Owen's matchless toolbag.

There are priest-holes at Chingle Hall, in the Lancashire village of Goosnargh. It was the family home of the Catholic martyr John Wall, one of the last two clergymen to be put to death in England. When the Walls acquired the property in the late sixteenth century, they set about redesigning it, laying out the new place in the shape of a cross, and they took the opportunity of installing holy hidey-holes. Others have come to light at Speke Hall, outside Liverpool, and across the Mersey in the Catholic halls of Poole and Hooton. Towneley Hall near Burnley was another safe-house. John Towneley was imprisoned nine times and fined a total of £5000 for his career recusancy. Priest-friendly hideaways have also been identified at Lawkland Hall near Settle, Ufton Court in Berkshire, Scotney Old Castle near Lamberhurst in Kent and at Braddocks, a Tudor house in north Essex.

Owen's masterpiece is Harvington Hall in the Worcestershire parish of Chaddesley Corbett. Very few places could seriously challenge its claim to have been the most priest-infested house in all England. If not that, it is almost certainly the most priest-hole-riddled property still standing, with half a dozen hides, including one which was said to lead to a haunted underground passage. There were trapdoors and false ceilings, sham panels and phoney floorboards: an entire repertory of *trompe l'oeil* devices and bits of business. The whole house was one great big game of Find the Lady (or Padre). Its gimmicks and gadgets were kept a deadly secret, of course, but had they been vouchsafed to the leading alchemists and necromancers of the day those distinguished men in all conscience would have had to admit that Garnett's servant had the beating of them. No blasé man of magik or jaundiced jester could fail to doff his jingling cap to Owen's handiwork.

Harvington Hall surveys you coolly from the middle of a moat as your minicab comes to rest on its gravelly strand. The sedge shifts in the water, a muscovy duck achieves lift-off, and a good likeness of a redbrick Tudor pile turns into the pieces of a kaleidoscope as you gaze into it. The defensive gulch was sunk in the thirteenth century to protect livestock from the wolves which roamed the Forest of Feckenham. You crunch towards the ancestral stronghold of the Pakington family mindful that it has successfully repelled invaders for centuries, that worthier adversaries than you have come to the West Midlands to pit their wits against this box of tricks, only to go away humbled. This is the seat of a battle-hardened family: Robert Pakington was shot dead in Cheapside one morning in November 1536, becoming one of London's earliest firearms statistics. The Hall sheltered Father Wall, though he was later hanged, drawn and quartered not far away at Worcester in 1679 after the Titus Oates 'Popish Plot' affair. He was canonised in 1929.

'In its day, Harvington could doubtless hold its own with the finest mansions in the country,' according to an account of 1901, 'but now it is forgotten, deserted and crumbling to pieces. Its very history appears to be lost to the world.' It was all but derelict and overrun with ivy. When Jeremy Errand visited for his 1974 book, restoration of the house had not yet begun. 'It smells strongly of old wood . . . faded photographs of the house at the end of the last century have an unearthly look about them. They seem to picture something between a house and a forest.'

I found that this Arcadian abandon still reigned at Harvington, albeit now for cosmetic effect. It was a few days before Christmas and the house was dressed for wassailing. There were pleasing links of borage, holly and mistletoe. On the groaning board were candles the size of a choirboy's thigh. Alan the accountant showed me over the place in his red – in his

Christmas – sweater. He squired me to a priest-hole in the restaurant. These days, school parties can be found here lunching on tubes of cheesy string, throwing their heads back like Greek herdsmen with skins of rough wine. The secret chamber was located in the breast of the fireplace. It was so good, there was absolutely no sign of it. 'I brought you in here to get your bearings,' said Alan.

The real priest-hole action was to be found outside. This part of Harvington was the solar, the original medieval hall, and the exterior wall of the solar faced on to a courtyard. Under a layer of brickwork, the panels of the wall had been filled with wattle and daub, but in the courtyard Alan indicated a fissure in this medieval aggregate. It had been crudely and – by the deceptive looks of it – freshly introduced. 'Slip your hand in there and you can touch the priest-hole,' was Alan's irresistible invitation. I lost no time in matching the action to the words, and was soon groping in the glory-hole, if you'll overlook the expression. To empathise with the furtive cleric in his predicament was to know that this was no time for smutty schoolboy jokes, I reflected, as I found that I could just reach the priest-hole by thrusting an outstretched arm towards it and not unbunching my fist until it was all the way inside.

This was an inspired marriage of function and design: to call it a hole-in-the-wall operation doesn't begin to do it justice. Through this chink in hearth and home, the fugitive could be passed food and drink to keep body and unlawful soul together. He could also keep watch for unwelcome visitors to Harvington.

The task of winkling out papists from the wormy wainscoting of old England fell to the secret service; in fact, it was set up for this very purpose. The agency was established by Walsingham, one of Elizabeth's ministers, and developed by another, Robert Cecil. Its cloak-and-dagger types included men in clerical garb, double-crossing Catholics. Narks were also retained in the homes where priests found succour. When the service believed it had run one of them to ground, a gang of pursuivants would descend on the manor house without warning and hammer on the door. 'Inside there would be a frenzy of activity,' according to one description of a typical bust. 'Opening the door was always delayed as long as possible. Meanwhile the chapel or Mass-room, probably in the attic, would have to be hurriedly cleared of its furnishings, which were hidden in recesses in the walls or beneath floorboards. The priest would then slip into his hidden compartment.'

Alan and I went back into the house and up a flight of wooden stairs. We were now on the upper floor of the old solar. About 1500, it had been turned into a two-storey building by the introduction of a floor which rested on massive moulded beams and stopped-chamfer rafters. Alan and I were now in the aptly named Withdrawing Room. He lifted up a hatch and we were gazing down upon a dark pit some ten feet deep. 'Do you want to go in?' he asked. I shinned down a wooden ladder.

'It's pretty cosy in there, isn't it?' Alan called down. 'But you wouldn't worry about things like that if you were in fear of your life.' My new surroundings were the same dimensions as a sentry box, which I suppose is what the priest-hole was. Here the churchman's vocation of bearing witness assumed a terrible literalness, and was in danger of being tested to destruction. The nuns of Malling Abbey might have called to mind a sort of Benedictine Free French, monitoring the bulletins of the BBC as if for news of their ongoing resistance, but at Harvington a real religious underground had kept faith in the most arduous of circumstances.

When a household that was shielding a priest at last drew the bolt on the door to let the monarch's men in, the family and servants were interrogated without benefit of the Queensberry Rules. Like a bunch of paramilitary estate agents, the priest-hunters set to work noting any interesting features or conversation pieces – this commodious inglenook, that loft extension perfect for a family

home, particularly if the family was hiding contraband
confessors – any detail which might betray a secret recess. Panelling
was torn down and inquisitive hands were thrust into suggestive
crannies, just as mine had been. And if none of that came up
trumps, the nostril-twitching bounty hunters were content to sit
and wait it out, to track pantry traffic for any sign of a covert
priestly snack, to starve the poor man out of hiding, if needs be.

I was musing on this in my popish snug when Alan hollered
down to say that he had to get away in order to appear in a
photo shoot. The *Kidderminster Shuttle* was looking for a
Christmassy spread from the great hall. (Alan offered the
photographer a fancy-dress look but she didn't want to go there –
they did that last year – so in the end he struck a relaxed and
informal pose with a gilded pear.) It was left to a series of Alan's
colleagues, a relay of nice ladies from the shop and office, to keep
me company around the parts of the Hall that I hadn't seen;
though by the end of my stay, I was allowed to come and go as
I pleased, like an old retainer or indeed a cherished chaplain. I
was entrusted with the key to the attic, a suitably cruciform piece
of ironmongery rather like an Elizabethan Allen key, and I stole
alone among the moaning rafters. To say that wanted priests
spent time under Harvington's roof is no more than the literal
truth, because rudimentary accommodation was found for them
beneath the eaves, where they took cover after scrambling up
from a pair of false chimneys in rooms directly below.

The house was flagrantly churchy. The spies who demanded
entry at Harvington would have known that they had come to
the right place. The walls were painted with motifs of
pomegranate and lily, familiar religious iconography, and with
extraordinary sanguinary teardrops, representing the blood of
the Passion. On a landing were indistinct daubs which appeared
to show Christ before Pilate, and the Resurrection. These days
the Hall is in the hands not of the National Trust or English
Heritage but of the Catholic Church itself. A former archbishop

was the patron of the Hall's restoration and a portrait of his successor looks down from a wall of the Great Chamber. A hide devised for the emergency concealment of Roman accessories can be found under some false floorboards in the Pakington family chapel. If time and the Queen's men were pressing intolerably and there was no hope of stashing robes and books and order frontals in the attic, then all this Catholic swag would have to go into the hide. The ruse evidently paid off, and Harvington's surviving tokens of recusancy include a 1631 missal and a pamphlet entitled *Testaments for the Real Presence* from 1566. A rosary was found beneath one of the floorboards. Like an article of sailor's scrimshaw, this comforter had been worked by hand out of holly berries, perhaps by St John Wall himself. It is dated to the early seventeenth century.

Nicholas Owen is thought to have been busy at the Hall while Humphrey Pakington, the owner, was having it extensively rebuilt in the 1580s. By 1588, the master of Harvington was considered to be one of the half-dozen leading left-footers in the county, and his name had been entered on Cecil's infamous *Note of the Papists and Recusantes in the severall shires of England.* Michael Hodgetts writes, 'It is noticeable that the more ingenious hides at Harvington, those which show the trademarks of Nicholas Owen, are all sited round the Great Staircase, which is an obvious insertion and datable from its style to about 1600.' On this wooden switchback of a stairway, a false tread shields not one but two Owen priest-holes. The stair lifts up and you are startled to see a crouching priest looking back at you in distress. He has a week's growth of beard.

'Hmm, he needs a dust,' said Sherida from the Hall office.

'Do you think so? I think it adds to his look.'

The stair-hide is a tribute to the sheer Catholic-camouflaging panache of Owen's work, because it extends beyond the pinched cubicle where the chasubled mannequin kneels. Indeed, this was really the ecclesiastical equivalent of the crumple-zone on a family car, because its real purpose was to protect a much more important space beyond, not less than six feet high and some six feet square – practically a studio apartment or a granny flat – which Owen created by lowering the ceiling of a butler's pantry adjoining the staircase. It seems unlikely that the wily Pakingtons would have warehoused a real live priest in the pit beneath the stair. Instead, they would have planted some expendable liturgical gubbins, confident that the pursuivants would carry off this prize and not think to probe further into Owen's magnificently devious lair. To look upon this priest-hole was like peeking into the mansions of the hide-master's very mind, the unassuming countenance concealing the frontal lobe, itself only a portal to what was truly precious within.

Owen acquired the nickname Little John, 'by which name he was so famous and much esteemed by all Catholics', according to a contemporary Jesuit telling of his legend. 'In making of secret places to hide Priests and Church-stuff from the fury of searches, he was skilful both to devise and frame the places in the best manner, and his help therein desired in so many places, that I verily think no man can be said to have done more good of all those that laboured in the English vineyard.'

This joiner for Jesus reinvented the priest-hole as he went along, knowing that Elizabeth's agents grew increasingly wise to his legerdemain with every hide they rumbled. He also excelled himself in Harvington's library, where he devised a hidden compartment to tingle the spine, the very stuff of the best yarns about secret panels in creaking manor houses, and yet carried off without compromising his solemn brief – to make a life-preserver. The book-lined room in question was known as Dr Dodd's library, though it also found fame as the study where a man named Henry Tootal wrote a religious history book. Here Owen set a veritable brain-teaser for Cecil's merry men. Inside the door of the library was a raised platform on which a five-foot-high oak cupboard had rested in Tudor times.

You could call it occasional furniture: the occasion would be a raid by the priest-hunters. When the alarm was sounded, one of Harvington's cassocked houseguests could cram himself inside the dresser and move a panel aside to expose the library wall. Then, if he pushed a particular beam in the wall, it would swing out towards him on an iron pivot, revealing a hole just big enough for a father of average build to squirm through. While Harvington rang to the shouts of England's finest, the object of their search would keep himself to himself in a cell eight feet long by five feet high and barely three feet across. Cramped it may have been, but it defied easy discovery. Following the Elizabethan pogrom, this particular priest-hole remained undisturbed for almost three hundred years, until it was found by accident in 1897. When an unsuspecting Victorian leant against the library wall and felt it tapping him back, the company was agog to make out an oak stool in the cobwebby defile.

I shoved the pivoted plank and squeezed into the lonely cell. Was this really the best, the most intelligent, solution that the adherents of the old-time religion could come up with? It had the excitement and unreality of a child's game, the reimagining of a house as a series of hiding-places, and all carried off with such thrilling verve and attention to detail. But it had the naivety, the literal-mindedness of childhood, too: let's *hide* Father Wall and never tell. Cross my heart and hope to die.

One last hideout was fitted with an escape route under Harvington. This was the one that was said to connect with a cursed tunnel. The cubbyhole itself had been slotted between a bread oven and a garderobe, a medieval privy, on the ground floor. A hunted priest could wriggle into a shaft that was as tall as the house, reaching from ground level all the way up to the roof. He could hunker down here, or he could make his escape. There was an old system of pulleys in the shaft, installed to turn the spit in the kitchen fireplace, and this could be pressed into service for a makeshift abseiling descent. The wanted man could then struggle through a hole at the base of the shaft and light out for the moat – and freedom.

With his pursuers at his heels, he would probably be willing to overlook the grisly history of this emergency exit, where the lover of a young woman was reputedly torn to pieces by dogs to satisfy her father's rage. Sir Peter Corbett, squire of Harvington at the turn of the fourteenth century, had been granted the privilege of hunting in the royal forests near the Hall. The place where he is said to have quartered his hounds, a stone-lined pit called the Kennels, can still be seen. The Kennels were supposedly linked to the Hall by a tunnel which passed under the moat. Sir Peter's daughter fell in love with a young man from the troglodyte town of Wolverley, where people live in caves to this day. The lovers used to meet in the tunnel because they were afraid that their relationship would incur her father's wrath if he found out about it. They weren't wrong. One night, alerted by the barking of the dogs, Sir Peter and his kennelman discovered the young lovers and overheard them planning to meet on the following evening. When darkness fell again, Sir Peter locked his daughter in her room and let the dogs loose in the tunnel. There followed the terrible snap of canine jaw on still-green bone, and in the morning nothing was left of the beau from Wolverley but his hands and a pair of stout boots (occupied). Sir Peter's daughter, inconsolable, tossed herself into the moat. The master of the house was himself stricken with remorse and hanged his dogs.

No sixteenth-century Sir Peter Corbett emerges from the annals of Harvington, and there is no tunnel under the moat: it was presumably a whimsical extension of Owen's priest-hole, not to mention a particularly ghoulish variant on the incorrigibly promiscuous tunnel myth. For all that, though, it's said that the wraith of a huntsman still stalks the grounds of Harvington, trailing a pack of fiendish hounds.

*

There was surer tunnel sport to be had not far away at Hindlip
Hall, or so I hoped. Hindlip had been the centre for priest-
smuggling for Worcestershire and the Welsh Marches. It was the
home of Humphrey Pakington's friend, Thomas Abington, and
a tunnel was installed there in 1572. Hindlip is near Worcester,
and just ten miles from Harvington as the crow flies – or the
priest flees. But I made the journey by train and taxi – actually,
by *two* taxis – a trek to throw even the most dogged pursuivant
off the scent. Some might think that this argued a lack of
planning and local knowledge on my part. But a
psychogeographer would be slower to blame. He would intuit
that this corner of Worcestershire was still distractingly a-quiver
from the trauma of Elizabeth's doctrinal witch-hunts. Moreover,
he would divine that the spell cast over its great estates by
Nicholas Owen had turned it into England's answer to the
Bermuda Triangle: I was lucky to reach Hindlip at all.

If tall tales of incense-soused crevices in old houses exceed
verifiable examples, the same is true when it comes to tunnels
frequented by men of the cloth in order to stay one step ahead of
their enemies. Kingsley Palmer, a folklore fancier who tramped
Wessex gathering this kind of wool, said that an area of Somerset
of about a hundred square miles yielded no fewer than sixty-
three such yarns. 'In Dorset there are nearly as many stories
about tunnels as about ghosts.' But it's one thing to say that a
venerable mansion could boast a stretch of tunnel, quite another
to prove a priestly link. Many of the tales can be explained by
our old friend domestic drainage, the sanitary breakthrough that
arrived at country residences at roughly the same time as
seminarians on the run from early James Bonds.

If you're looking for a God-fearing estate in possession of a
subterranean priest-passage, Little Moreton Hall in Cheshire is
among the more plausible candidates. In the nineteenth century,
the owners hired a chimney sweep to investigate stories of a
tunnel connected to a pair of secret rooms situated over the

kitchens. The sweep found that these former bachelor pads' mod cons included a shaft which dropped underneath the house, where it did indeed connect with a tunnel leading to the moat, in the style of the accursed hide at Harvington. Granville Squiers, visiting Little Moreton Hall in the 1920s, authenticated the shaft, but it's no longer visible, and the entrance to the tunnel has been filled in with stones.

There is an underground passage running for fifty yards beneath the yard of Irnham Hall in Lincolnshire. Irnham was a well-known nest of Roman Catholic sympathisers. A priest-hole was found there in 1884 containing a table, a crucifix, a prayer-book and the moth-eaten remnants of a soutane. The tunnel could be entered under a flagstone in the hearth of the main hall. The other entrance – or exit – lay under a stone slab beside a beech tree. Both ends of the tunnel were later sealed off.

At Harborough Hall in Warwickshire, there are records of a shaft plunging from the attic to the ground, perhaps a converted garderobe chute. If this recalls Owen's hide-making antics, it's little wonder, because Harborough is on Owen's old patch. From the base of the shaft, a brick-lined drain led towards a lake a short distance from the Hall. The shaft and the tunnel were lost after the house was rebuilt in the last century. Owen is also thought to have been responsible for a similar getaway route at the ancestral home of the Throckmortons, Coughton Court near Alcester in Warwickshire. A priest-hole containing an antique ladder, bedding and a folding altar was exposed in an ornamental corner tower. It's believed that the hole is the surviving section of an adit which went below ground level, to connect with a tunnel or drain.

On the subject of priests copying the moles that they somewhat resemble and travelling through the Tudor subsoil, students of the period have teased a nuance out of the term 'conveyance', which comes to light in correspondence between Cecil and his spies. Sometimes the word meant nothing more than a place of concealment, a static hide. But at other times it strongly implies a tunnel, as in the case of a secret dispatch from an agent called John Ferne, who was following the comings and goings at Grosmont Abbey in north-east Yorkshire as he made plans for a raid. 'The house being strong,' he wrote in 1599, 'large, and many secret conveyances underground to a brook running nearby, I may employ as great strength of people as I can from York, for I do not know of any faithful assistance in the country, for that the people are wholly defected from religion, twenty miles along the coast, and do resist all warrants and officers that come along with them.'

Sure enough, hardly had Ferne's invisible ink materialised before his paymaster's eyes than a raiding party of fully two hundred men was turned back by the abbey's supporters. But the point is that when they eventually forced their way over the threshold, there appeared to be corroborating evidence of tunnelling:

> There was found in the search all things for the furnishing of mass and divers popish books, but nothing else could be found, although all floors, ceilings, pavements, double walls were broken up and divers vaults of strange conveyance were found out. Among which . . . [a] stairhead, within a thick stone wall, was covered with a great post of the bigness of a man's body, which seemed to bear the house, but indeed did hinge only, and was removable to and fro, being locked with iron work, did stand fast, but being unlocked, would remove from the hole which it covered at the nether end, at which hole a man might easily descend.

Although Grosmont endured the clumsy attentions of the Queen's priest-catchers, nothing remains of the abbey today.

All in all, my greatest chance of finding what I was after appeared to lie in Worcestershire. 'It is at Hindlip that we find the best contender for the title of priests' passage,' wrote Errand. 'The tunnel is still in existence and is quite negotiable. Its Tudor brickwork is in a remarkable state of preservation.'

Father Garnett and his trusty manservant Nicholas Owen had both known Hindlip. Indeed, it was the backdrop to a gripping turn of events in their story. But this one-time rookery of Jesuits was now the roost of law-enforcers of a different feather: it was the HQ of West Mercia Police. I'd dropped a line about my interest in the tunnel to the Chief Constable, and his office got back to me by return with the dismaying news that Hindlip Hall had been flattened in the nineteenth century. But the word was not all bad: 'There are still the remains of a tunnel within the grounds at Hindlip that purportedly was used as an escape route. The condition of the tunnel is such that you would not be able to access its full length; however, if this were of interest to you, I would be very happy to arrange for you to view this structure.'

Were it of interest to me? *I'll* say it were. The house, the *new* house, is the square-shouldered creation of Lord Southwell, who came into Hindlip by marriage in 1797. The old Hall, with its once splendid turrets and wings and fluting chimney-pieces, was not much to look at by then. Like its neighbour, Harvington, it was badly neglected. 'The whole building had deteriorated. The house is at present in a ruinous state; many of the windows blocked up; the gardens all in disorder,' wrote J. A. Laird in 1812 in his *Topographical & Historical Description of the County of Worcester*. So Milord Southwell tore it down and replaced Abington's old safe-house with a spanking-new country residence complete with a full retinue of servants, parkland tended by three gardeners, and a private chapel (like earlier masters of the great house, Southwell was a devout Catholic). The Hall went on to see action in the Second World War when it was commandeered by the Ministry of Works as a back-up for the Air Defence Committee, and the police moved in during the late 1960s.

I reported to reception, where Southwell's guests, richly

caparisoned and dazzlingly bejewelled, had once disported themselves. In no time at all, I was making quite a show of myself, too, with my particulars brazenly displayed in a cellophane locket. I was met by Paul Wiseman and the intriguingly handled Simon Coldbreath. The pair of them were named like characters from Shakespeare: he, the Bard, had lived not far from this old spot when Hindlip was in its priest-secreting pomp. Paul and Simon were wearing suits teamed with windcheaters. Simon was a surveyor acting for the force; Paul handled finance and admin for the buildings department. We went out through the magnolia-coloured colonnades of the madeover Hindlip – 'They're iron,' said Simon, 'they'll clang if you tap them' – and were soon on the springy turf of the rear lawn. The fields of Worcestershire, her agrarian story, unscrolled ahead of us as far as the Malvern Hills.

Thirty yards or so from the house, I found what I'd come for. In a dip on the boundary of the property was the wound-like opening of a tunnel, said to have been reserved for Elizabeth's Most Wanted. Here our motley crew was augmented by rude mechanicals in the shape of Stuart, an affable groundsman/ janitor in his blue overalls, and the silent Chris ('He hasn't got much speech,' said Stuart kindly). Truly, we might have sprung from one of the Swan's forgotten folios. What a sight we were, as we dithered and dickered at the mouth of the tunnel, checking and rechecking our torches, consulting the works of reference on recusancy in my haversack ('the tunnel . . . winds away from the house down the hill in the direction of an old farm . . .'). Anything to delay the evil moment of entry, of confinement. In every man's heart there is a fear of overextending himself, of encountering a challenge that is beyond him, and losing face in front of his peers. My own unspoken dread at this time was to become pinioned in the tunnel and to require evacuation by the very emergency service that was hosting me that afternoon. In the privacy of my imagination, I rehearsed the drear sequence: the exploratory rasp of the Alsatian's tongue on my already salty cheek; the hot, sweet tea with the Family Support Officer; the disobliging picture caption in the *Kidderminster Shuttle*. But such morbid fancies seemed to evaporate in the unseasonal sunshine as we stood about jawing. What a hoot it was, in the end, for five grown men to spend a Friday afternoon in exploration of a secret passage.

Stuart and Chris had removed a length of corrugated iron and some screening foliage that deterred uninvited ingress to the tunnel. As a further safeguard, it was sealed by a gunmetal wicket. This was the stretch heading back towards the house. In the other direction, towards the fields, the tunnel became a much narrower channel. There was a grille over the mouth of it. 'I had it sealed up,' Simon told me. 'I mean, can you imagine? A kid gets in there, a drain, and dies under police headquarters? I can't think of anything more appalling.'

When the tunnel really couldn't be put off any longer, Chris unlocked the wicket. Simon zipped up his windcheater – to protect his suit – and led the way. I followed in single file. The wicket was ajar now, but there was still its frame to negotiate. You had to dip under a steel bar, to limbo beneath it . . .

On Robert Cecil's orders, the original totterdown Hindlip Hall was raided when his quarry, in the shape of Garnett and Owen, was within its walls, and the spy chief urged a thorough sub-terranean search when he gave his instructions to the sheriff of the county. The Gunpowder Plot against the King and Parliament had just been foiled and the idea of the Jesuits legging it to liberty across the plains of Worcestershire could not be entertained:

> First observe the parlour where they dine and sup; in the east part of that parlour it is conceived there is some vault, which to discover you must take care to draw down the wainscot, whereby the entry to the vault may be discovered. And the lower parts of the house must be tried with a broach, by

putting same into the ground a foot or two to try whether
there be some timber, which if there be, there must be some
vault underneath it.

Cecil's snitches may very well have warned him about the tunnel.
It was sunk fifteen feet below the floorboards of the house. It was
between three and four feet high, big enough for a man to
scramble through. At every twenty yards, vertical shafts led up to
ground level, perhaps connecting to garderobes. This at least is
what I'd read. But were Simon and I really going to venture into
a corridor quarried out for the priesthood more than four
hundred years ago? That word 'garderobe' troubled me. It was
hazardous to my prospects, almost as threatening as it had been
for the unfortunate Tudors who had to frequent the primitive
sanitaryware itself. Was the tunnel no more than a drain, like so
many of the other so-called priest-passages? Would my quest end
in the bathos of the bog?

I was wondering whether I'd need to crawl, but in the event
the olde worlde spec was bang on: the clearance was as much as
four feet, plenty of room for us to get about on our haunches.
Simon and I remarked upon the dry, well-finished, regular
brickwork surrounding us, and under foot too. Surely it couldn't
be sixteenth-century? But so what if it had been repointed? It was
going to take more than that to spoil the story. I was pleased to
see that there was no sign of a shaft descending to join the tunnel,
as though from an outhouse of old.

The passage became a little wider and there was a noticeable
incline. 'It's quite steep,' said Simon.

'What is it, do you think,' I asked him, 'sixty?' (Sixty *what*,
Stephen? I think I meant an angle of sixty degrees to the
horizontal but I wasn't confident enough to spell this out.)

'Oh, I dunno,' muttered Simon, perhaps not entirely sure what
I was going on about.

On reflection, the gradient was much gentler than I was

suggesting. This was another example of the confusing effect of darkness and enclosed space. In time, our Bardic band would dispute the length of the tunnel we had traversed. We had a tape measure with us and we should probably have run it up the hole, but in the event we didn't.

There was no faffing about when the sheriff's goons shouldered their way into Hindlip on the trail of Garnett and Owen. Sheriff Sir Henry Bromley arrived at the Hall with about a hundred armed men on 20 January 1606. The gates were barred, of course, and the ladies of the house were sent out to try their pretty hand at persiflage and obfuscation. But Bromley was having none of it. 'Sir Henry, impatient of this delay, caused the gates, with great violence and force of men, to be broken down', as a priest called Father Gerrard wrote in his *Narrative of the Gunpowder Plot*. The fugitives had taken advantage of the ruckus to secrete themselves, but the hunt for them went on.

The red mist lifted from Bromley's gaze long enough for him to appreciate Owen's craftsmanship. His official report of the incident records 'cunning and very artificial conveyances in the main brick wall, so ingeniously framed and with such art as it cost much labour ere they could be found ... eleven secret corners and conveyances were found, all of them having books, massing stuff and popish trumpery in them, only two excepted which appeared to have been found on former searches and now therefore had less credit given to them'.

It was now four days since the raiders had descended on Hindlip. They hadn't found the priests and they hadn't found the tunnel. Owen and another servant, a man called Ashley, broke cover, perhaps to make a run for it down the secret passage, or else to turn themselves in and so sacrifice themselves for their masters. They had been hiding in a long gallery where they had been able to observe the movements of the pursuivants, watching them take turns about this chamber. When they thought that their scourges were at the far end of the gallery, Owen and Ashley tiptoed from their hide 'and came out so secretly and stilly and shut the place again so finely that they were not one whit heard or perceived', according to Gerrard. Unfortunately, the King's men chose that moment to turn round, and so came face to face with Owen, cabinet-maker for Christ and public enemy number one. The game was up.

Down in the tunnel, the game was also up for Simon and myself. After no more than about forty yards, and perhaps as few as twenty-five – distances seemed greater when you were taking pigeon-steps rather than manly strides – we were brought up short by a barrier of breezeblocks that had been oozingly cemented in our path. It was hard to say when these might have been assembled. Close to this obstruction, the roof of the tunnel was distinctly higher than before: perhaps it met a perpendicular shaft at this point. But it too was closed up.

Now in the gardens, Simon walked on top of the tunnel, pacing out its length across the lawn. From his manmade knoll, he speculated that the police had had the tunnel sealed so that cables from an electricity substation could be laid through it, or over it, and into an office block.

It's not meant as any slight on my new-found friends on the force to say that they treated me as though I wasn't there. I don't think it was rudeness. It was the natural preference of people (of men especially) for talking to people that they already know. Including the outsider is hard work. But I like to think that our little Friday afternoon odyssey had the others at HQ genuinely interested, or at least genuinely distracted.

It was Simon's idea to go down into the basement of the Hall. He wanted to see if we could find the mouth of the tunnel. Descending the flags to the undercroft of West Mercia Police HQ, I was surprised to smell the cellar of the house I grew up in, my parents' house. What *was* that odour? It wasn't unpleasant, though you wouldn't bottle it and sell it. It was trapped air, I suppose, the whiff of things that had got cold and damp and never quite dried out.

In a corner, old files were stacked pell-mell in boxes. Sprays of stationery grew wildly from them. 'Are these the closed cases, then?' I asked. Nobody laughed. In the years to come, I may kick myself for not following up this tantalising signal of trouble brewing over West Mercia's clear-up rates.

Having brought his suit through the chalk and dust of the tunnel without incident, Simon was understandably disappointed to snag his elbow on a nail standing proud from one of the boxes. It was a little way beyond this that lay the object of his interest – a ladder that climbed the wall until it disappeared into darkness. Simon thought that the rungs might lead to the tunnel. Taking my cue from him, I fought my way to the far side of the smothering paperwork. At the top of the ladder, I could see utility cables winding their way out of the basement through a tiny aperture where a cornice might have been.

Did the priestly passage lie beyond? Stuart, for one, was sceptical. 'I bet when they built the new house, the workmen just filled in the tunnel, or smashed it. They wouldn't have been bothered with it.' I could only concur. Our interest in conservation, in exposing and curating the past, is a recent enthusiasm. In fact, the entrance to the tunnel must have been some distance from where we were standing, on the site of the original Hindlip Hall, which made the hidden pathway an even more substantial feat of Tudor engineering. But perhaps we were looking at the point where the old tunnel passed by this basement.

Simon led us back up the stairs to the ground floor of the police nerve centre, with its universal atmosphere of phone chatter and coffee waft. The five of us now stood in front of the architect's plans. This was how the Hall had looked before the police moved in. One of the chambers was listed as 'Lord Hindlip's Room'. There was excited, or at least focused, talk about who or what occupied the various rooms today. 'The girls are in there,' said Paul, tracing a finger over the blueprint. 'Then Jim's there . . . then Andy.'

From the charts, we made an important discovery: the tunnel was marked. It was listed as a 'conduit'. Its measurements were given as four feet by two. It ran away from the house towards four or five o'clock. This all chimed with our experience: it looked like the Tudor dugout we'd been in, all right. The plan didn't appear to show the tunnel going under the house: this too was consistent with Stuart's idea of it having been summarily filled in.

But hang on a minute, what was this? A second listed and illustrated conduit, apparently touching or intercepting the first. Was this the point below ground where Simon and I had literally come up against a brick wall? Don't tell me we were actually in *this* tunnel, not the first one at all? It appeared to end up in the corner of the grounds where we had been exploring. But on the other hand its measurements were surely too dainty (three feet by two)? Another incongruous aspect was that it was moving away from the big house towards six o'clock – that is, due south.

Simon decided that he wasn't happy about the scale of the chart. He took a step or two back on the constabulary shagpile. 'We were here,' he said emphatically, holding his hand out. Where we had entered the passage was off the graph, or rather the plan. So the point on the diagram showing the two tunnels meeting was some distance from where we had been burrowing. As I might have anticipated, a secret subterranean thoroughfare which had confounded the Cecil's secret service, as well as everyone else who came after them, was never going to be a cakewalk.

Simon wondered aloud about surveying the site, seeing how the soil had been disturbed. There might have been a chance of a further probe if the old Chief Constable had still been in post, I gathered. 'He would have been down there with us in his wellies like a shot,' said Paul. But unless West Mercia Police unexpectedly targets archaeology, unless the current Chief gets up at a press conference one day to say that his vision of community policing starts in his own backyard, the last secrets of Thomas Abington, Father Garnett and Nicholas Owen will surely remain interred beneath the Worcestershire sod.

Three days after Owen was captured at Hindlip – and a full week after Sheriff Bromley had kicked the door in – Henry Garnett finally emerged from hiding with his co-religionist Father Oldcorne. Mrs Abington had kept them supplied with soup and hot drinks through a quill from her bedchamber, but the priests were cramped and in great pain. As Garnett wrote later from the Tower of London, 'If we had but one half-day's liberty to come forth we should have so eased the place from books and furniture, that having with us a close stool [chamber-pot] we could have hidden a quarter of a year. For all that my friends will wonder at, especially in me, that neither of us went to the stoole all the while, though we had means to do *servitii piccoli*.'

The priests were executed. Owen was imprisoned. Cecil's men hoped to make him talk, to give up the almost-Swiss mechanisms of his stealthy tradecraft. Cecil was counting on a 'great booty of priests' and ordered that 'Little John' (Owen) should 'be coaxed if he be willing to contract for his life' but that in any event 'the secret is to be wrung from him'. The circumstances of his death remain opaque. The official version is that he committed suicide with a knife but there are suspicions that he died under torture. 'No secrets were wrung from him,' says Errand, 'and he took with him the knowledge of scores of shadowy hides – and perhaps a few underground ways as well.'

9

THERE GOES THE NEIGHBOURHOOD

It was getting on for one o'clock in the morning and I was lying in bed when it started bucking like a bronco. And not just bucking; it was practically snorting and pawing the bedroom carpet. In the kitchen, cutlery chattered: it sounded like a dispute about billing in a knife-thrower's dressing-room. I reacted as anyone would have done in my place – which they were more than welcome to at that moment. I rued the last drink I'd had before retiring, and then wondered if I was having some kind of seizure. But fear was followed by a different emotion, one that would have gripped few others that night, I hope. It was disgrace, and what's more, it was accompanied by the disturbing presentiment of a posthumous payback. It was all coming back to me: the chortling conversation that I'd had with my sister earlier in the day; the pair of us tittering with laughter about a family member and her visit to a clairvoyant who had told her that she was in contact with a 'Rosie', which just happened to be our late mother's nickname. 'Apparently, Rosie's very worried about her house,' my sister managed to say, despite the knuckle that was crammed into her mouth.

Oh my God, it all made sense, I realised, gingerly planting a foot on the rippling floorboards. It was almost a year since Mum had died, and we still hadn't sold her house. It remained full of her stuff. That was it! She was giving me a boot up the backside from beyond the proverbial coil. My dear old mum had come to me ectoplasmically in the night and was chucking my bits and pieces around in an attempt to make me do something about hers. This didn't strike me as the sort of thing she would do, admittedly, unless she thought it might amuse me. But there was still a part of me that continued to wonder if I had been visited by my mother's house-clearing spectre, even after all the shaking stopped and the radio was reporting an earthquake that had been felt through swathes of eastern England. I hadn't entirely discounted this possibility myself, back when I was still clinging to my neighing headboard. After all, a tremor had tossed me out of bed once before, but that was in New Zealand, and even those of us who were fully on side with the climate change message had never bargained on quakes in dear old Blighty.

In fact, the country's susceptibility to tectonic shifts is documented in its folklore, as surely as in the skittish zigzags of the seismograph. Indeed, great upheavals of the earth are offered in explanation of one of the most peculiar and yet thrilling aspects of our subterranean scene. I speak of the lost cities of England. Cosmopolitan entrepôts, storied metropolises, thriving towns, homely hamlets: familiar settlements all, in their day, they have faded from view or slipped out of sight completely, with little to show for their long tenancy of terra firma. They are a shadow of their former selves or else they are utterly emptied, extinguished, as good as forgotten. Places where people once raised families and earned their livelihood – places of getting and begetting – persist in the landscape only as symbols on a map, names on weathered wayposts.

But where some of those lost cities are concerned, there is more to be discovered, or rediscovered. There is the nub of an old church, the last surviving cornerstone of a lost community; perhaps a ragged stretch of graveyard. Sometimes houses are spared, whole streets, almost an entire 'burb. The rest of the neighbourhood has been carried off by a trauma in the earth's crust, so the story goes, or else by sandstorm or flood. Very often, these freakish conditions are believed to be supernatural in origin, a bit like my own hairy experience on the fault-line of filial duty. In the case of lost cities, the otherworldly scenery-shifters include the Devil and his busy sprites, mischievously moving complete conurbations in the night without so much as a word to anyone. Conversely, it may be the work of the Deity Himself. If a particular populace has incurred His displeasure, He will command that the wretched hometown in question be consumed by water: it will be damned, and at the same time undammed.

Lost cities exert a strange pull. Men with metal-detectors consider their outdoor Hoovering very heaven if it snaffles them a ducat or a doubloon, and sod-botherers like Basil Brown back at Sutton Hoo wait a lifetime to disinter one Anglo-Saxon king who has seen better days: how much more exciting, then, to happen upon a whole city. And they really do exist, right here in England. They lie somewhere beyond the tangible if somewhat limited evidence of a post-hole, and not quite so far as the realm of faeries switching postcodes on you while you sleep. One of the highlights of my underground odyssey was to go in search of the lost cities of England . . .

In Nottinghamshire, a farm on the road between Oxton and Southwell is all that's left of the village of Raleigh, long ago gobbled up by a quake. In 1827 a man called 'C. T.' contributed an item to the *Every-Day Book* – a kind of almanac – that contained the following:

> Near Raleigh . . . there is a valley, said to have been caused by
> an earthquake several hundred years ago, which swallowed up

a whole village, together with the church. Formerly, it was a custom for people to assemble in this valley, on Christmas morning, to listen to the ringing of the bells of the church beneath them! This, it was positively asserted, might be heard by putting the ear to the ground, and harkening attentively. Even now, it is usual on Christmas morning for old men and women to tell their children and young friends to go to the valley, stoop down, and hear the bells ringing merrily.

A sudden gap in the earth's floor was also blamed for the loss of the nearby community of Grimstone, between Newark and Ollerton. There are records of Grimstone up until 1434, but none since.

Vicars and their flocks are particularly susceptible to quakes. In the 1850s the Reverend W. Thomber, whose living was in Blackpool, described the disappearance of neighbouring Kilgrimol, two miles along the south shore from the resort. Of the incumbent and his parishioners there was nary a sign, wrote the clergyman with a fine fellow-feeling. But just as in the case of Raleigh, its location was recalled in local tradition. 'On Christmas Eve every one . . . on bending his ear to the ground, may distinguish clearly its bells pealing most merrily,' wrote the Revd Thomber.

England positively clangs with the tolling of her subterranean spires. In *The Lore of the Land*, Jennifer Westwood and Jacqueline Simpson state that 'most sunken church legends belong to earthquake lore'. Generally speaking, the effacing of places of worship is told in 'exaggerated tales . . . of down-dropped trenches or "grabens", these last being great chunks of the earth's crust which lie between faults and, at times of great vibration, may be shoved downward into the earth', along with everything that happens to be standing on top of them, such as churches.

A lost house of God is a recurring feature of the nation's

gazetteer. On Swinside Fell near Black Combe in Cumbria is the prehistoric monument of Sunkenkirk Circle, made up of fifty-two stones set close together. In 1794, a local historian called William Hutchinson said of this and other stone features at Swinside that 'the neighbouring people call those places by the emphatical names of Sunken Kirks'. Sunkenkirk Circle itself was supposed to be the building materials of a church that Old Nick had helpfully driven into the ground at night. The more prosaic explanation is subsidence. The Swinside circle was 'pretty entire', according to Richard Gough, a contributor to William Camden's *Britannia* (1610), but he noted that a few stones had fallen 'upon sloping ground in a swampy meadow'. Over the centuries, others may have followed them into the bog.

It's a similar story at Sancliff in Lincolnshire. In July 1696, a man called Abraham de la Pryme wrote in his diary, 'The 18th instant, being Sunday, I went to see a place, between Sanclif [*sic*] and Conisby, called the Sunken Church, the tradition concerning which says that there was a church there formerly, but that it sunk in the ground with all the people in it, in the times of popery. But I found it to be only a fable, for what they shew to be the walls thereof, yet standing, is most manifestly nothing but a natural rock.' Despite de la Pryme's scepticism, Sunken Church continued to be known by that name centuries later, and the story went that on the anniversary of the day the church was lost, its bell music could be heard early in the morning, calling the faithful to mass. At Fisherty Brow in Westmorland, a natural hollow marks the spot where 'a church, parson and all the people' fell into a fissure long, long ago. 'And anyone who doubts it,' according to one vernacular telling, 'may put his ear to the ground on a Sunday morning and hear the bells ring!' In the eighteenth century, a story was told of a deep hole, perhaps elf-dwelt, at Dilham in Norfolk. A church which was built over this fault apparently slid into it without trace, and after rushes grew up in its place, unwary oxen who trod there went the same way. A similar tale did the rounds at Oby, also in Norfolk, perhaps because there was a churchyard in the village but no sign of a church.

The most important lost city in the country, a place with as many absent yet still audible bell-towers as all the parishes above put together, is Dunwich on the Suffolk seaboard. And just off it, too, come to that. Dunwich is England's answer to Atlantis. In its pomp, before it was all but gathered to the icy bosom of the North Sea, only five other cities were more prosperous – London, York, Norwich, Lincoln and Northampton. Dunwich stood on eight hills – England's non-eternal city went one better than Rome. It was limned by Turner. It excited the imagination of writers from Daniel Defoe to Samuel Pepys; from the Romantic poets to the Jameses, both Henry and M. R. An early chronicler, John Stowe, wrote in 1573, 'The common fame and report of a great number of credable persons is, and hath been for a long time paste; that there hath been in the town of Dunwiche, before any decay came to it, 70 pryshe churches, howses of religion, hospitalls, and chapelles and other such lyke, and as many wynde milles, and as many toppe scheppes, etc, etc.'

Medieval Dunwich, with its own mint, was a bauble to which any self-respecting robber-baron aspired. In return for his protection, the townspeople offered up a dowry of cash and fish: traditional tribute. Robert Malet, the man installed at Dunwich by William the Conqueror, received each year rents totalling £50 – this was when £50 *meant* something – and 66,000 herring. So glutted was the city on its fishy harvest that there was more than enough to stink out the royal smokery with the King's share. As Daniel Defoe observed, 'Hereabouts they begin to talk of herrings . . . and we find in the ancient records, that this town, which was then equal to a large city, paid, among other tribute to the Government, 50,000 of herrings.' And fish were by no means the only raw material to circulate through Dunwich. The city enjoyed the fruits of trade with the other great ports of northern Europe, for which it was so advantageously situated. As one account has it, 'Every day, in those times, the ships came and went, to London, Stavoren, Stralsund, Danzig, Bruges, Bayonne and Bordeaux.'

This lively scene was captured by local historian Nicholas Comfort. 'Ships threaded their way to the Daine [harbour] through a throng of fishing smacks, Iceland barks, merchant ships and naval galleys. Having got ashore past piles of merchandise and huddles of men seeking work or arguing over the price of fish, travellers could look up the narrow, twisting streets towards the market-place. The lower town was looked down on in more ways than one by better-off folk at the top.' As Comfort suggests, Dunwich's population of some five thousand souls didn't always rub along harmoniously, and so a hierarchy of legal institutions was established, from a magistrates' court to a court of admiralty and a coroner's court. Even a man of the cloth could find himself up before the beak. Walter, Rector of St John's, Dunwich, stood trial for rape in 1407 and got away with a fine. The town gaol has been compared to the sheriff's office in a Western, and petty crimes were punished with a spell in the stocks. They were still standing in the late eighteenth century and bore the following minatory engraving:

> Fear God and honour the King,
> Or else to these stocks I will you bring.

Nor were disturbances confined to the odd unruly denizen. Malet, and others who got their feet under the table at Dunwich in their day, had to be vigilant in defence of their prize. The city had to repel assailants on more than one occasion. It sheltered behind its eleventh-century earthworks, the Palesdyke, and a bristling stockade of pikestaffs, though even these fortifications were scant sanctuary when the storms blew in and the onrushing waves seemed to stack and teeter overhead.

I can't remember when I first heard of Dunwich, the city beneath the sea; when I conceived the quixotic notion to go to a place that wasn't there (or was only barely there). It was a real-life version of the lost land of Lyonesse, the mythical home of King Arthur's Guinevere. In *Brideshead Revisited*, Charles Ryder looks back on his days at university, 'submerged now and obliterated, irrecoverable as Lyonesse'. But outside the pages of Waugh's novel, Oxford has not been suggested as the true location of the absent Arthurian haunt. Some scholars have linked Lyonesse to legends told about the Breton coast in the fifth and sixth centuries, while others suggest that it's off Land's End. The Scilly Isles are the mountaintops of Lyonesse in yet a third version of the tale.

Dunwich was the next best thing. There's documentary evidence of the lost Suffolk citadel in the shape of black and white photographs of its receding landmarks: the old church on the shrinking headland; the belfry that once rose from the beach like the conning tower of a scuttled sub. But something about these pictures recalled the famous, or infamous, snaps of the Loch Ness Monster. And they seemed to invite similar questions. Did Dunwich exist? Had wily locals staged the sightings, mocking up naves and chancels with oil drums and planks, in order to attract credulous trippers? As in the case of Nessie, the monochrome images of Dunwich reinforced a suspicion that the lost city had little substance outside tall tales and overheated imaginings. There was a sense that if you made the journey to Dunwich, you might just get lucky and see it; but there again, the chances were that you probably wouldn't. It was the Brigadoon of East Anglia.

It was imperative to go and look for it now, though, to go while you still could. As mythic and romantic as it was, Dunwich was also a memento mori, a reminder of a real and recurring threat to the land of which it was once such an ornament. In 2007–8 English Heritage was mapping and cataloguing thousands of coastal structures that were endangered by climate change, rising sea levels and the attendant depredations of erosion. Some at-risk spots would have the benefit of established sea defences, a spokesman said, 'but in areas of rural coastline the policy is more likely to be to allow the sea to reach its natural level. There will come a point at which we will have to decide which sites to defend and which we will simply lose.' A Roman cemetery found in the sand at Beckfoot in Cumbria would soon be washed away, and Blakeney Chapel, a medieval church on the Norfolk coast, was facing 'inevitable destruction'.

The National Trust estimated that 60 per cent of its stretches of coastline would be affected by erosion by 2010. In March 2008, it emerged that there were plans to surrender a great swathe of the Norfolk Broads to the sea. The waves would be allowed to breach fifteen miles of coast, between Horsey and Winterton, and flood inland for five miles, as far as the villages of Potter Heigham and Stalham. Hundreds of homes, 2500 acres of National Trust land and Hickling Broad would disappear under sea water before the turn of the century. The MP for Norfolk North discovered that a substantial part of his constituency might be submerged. 'The implications are pretty horrifying,' said the reeling representative. Even on millionaire's row, Sandbanks in Dorset, there was a distinct chance of inundation. On their exclusive but low-lying sand spit of a home, the risk of flooding rose from 1 in 200 in 2007, on the calculations of the Environment Agency, to 1 in 87 by 2027, and 1 in 10 by 2050.

The coast is often the first part of a landmass to be settled, not least on an island like our own. It's rich in evidence of human activity over thousands of years, much of which still waits to be discovered and examined – and now never will be, as like as not. Tantalisingly, the sea offers glimpses of this fugitive trove only to snatch it away again, as in the case of the Lincolnshire seaboard, where submerged forests and medieval saltworkings have been temporarily exposed, as well as the wreck of an ice ship that plied between Grimsby and Norway but sank in 1901.

I stayed in Aldeburgh the night before I went to Dunwich. It was a strikingly clear night in September, with a cool breeze off the North Sea. I couldn't decide whether the spangled Suffolk canopy was crushing, rendering all who looked upon it antlike; or conversely, that it was all-enfolding, a big tent. Wasn't it, in fact, exhilarating to gaze at this sight and begin to apprehend what it all might mean, as an ant, presumably, could not? At all events, it was a timely reminder that Fenland is big country, and it didn't seem at all unlikely that a city the size of Dunwich could be lost in it. The legend of its lost bells seemed to chime, if you'll overlook the expression, with the seashell sculpture on the foreshore of Aldeburgh, a memorial to Benjamin Britten. It's engraved with a line from his *Peter Grimes*: 'I hear those voices that will not be drowned.'

This was part of the old kingdom of Raedwald, monarch of Sutton Hoo. He was connected to Dunwich by a legend concerning three holy crowns, hallowed headgear which had been buried in the land of the Angles and were said to preserve England against invasion so long as they never left these shores. The yarn was disinterred by M. R. James in the bone-chilling *Ghost Stories of an Antiquary* (though some scholars believe that he made it up himself). A sixty-ounce silver coronet found in 1687 at Rendlesham, Raedwald's seat, was said to be one of the sacred crowns, and a second was long ago washed away at Dunwich, or so the legend has it. The third, secreted at a spot still unknown but perhaps Aldeburgh itself, was credited with having kept the Kaiser at a safe distance during the Great War.

I went to my hotel room and took up W. G. Sebald's *The Rings of Saturn*. Didn't he write about Dunwich? Had I in fact read what he says about Dunwich, but forgotten it? I flipped back through the pages that I'd already dog-eared but failed to find a reference to the forgotten city. With a sigh, I resumed reading from where I'd got to: at once, Sebald was on to Dunwich, setting the scene perfectly for my trip: 'The region is so empty and deserted that, if one were abandoned there, one could scarcely say whether one was on the North Sea coast or perhaps by the Caspian Sea or the Gulf of Lian-tung. With the rippling reeds to my right and the grey beach to my left, I pressed on toward Dunwich, which seemed so far in the distance as to be quite beyond my reach.'

Sebald approached from the north, along a disused railway line and through a marsh. Though Dunwich 'now consists of a few houses only', a traveller arriving from the same direction a thousand years earlier would have been impressed by the spectacle of a great city, the capital of East Anglia, and by a coastline which was fully a mile further out to sea from today's cliff edge. It was claimed that a Dunwich tailor, running up a jerkin in his quayside fitting-room, could look out upon the rigging of merchant ships plying the Yarmouth Roads, as the straits of that stretch of the North Sea are known. In fact, this honest tradesman would have had to be several miles out to sea to accomplish that feat, but the story spoke to the reputation of Dunwich as a great floating bazaar, moored somewhere between England and the rest of Europe. In reality, the matelot-loud medieval port was within a sheltering bay, the 'Haven', which was created by a long spit of land, the Kingsholme. Dunwich proper was separated from the sea by no less than twelve square miles of oak forest. This was Eastwood, where the gentry hawked and hunted by kind permission of His Majesty. The story of Eastwood, of which only a small copse survives today, recalls the thickly forested past of another coastal outpost, St Michael's Mount, which is known in the Cornish tongue as 'Cara Clowse in Cowse', 'the old rock in the woods'. Wistful archaeologists believe that submerged forests often contain many unrecorded structures, such as causeways, fish weirs, burial chambers, clay huts used in the refining of salt, oyster pits and shipwrecks.

For my part, I reached the lost city by road, through Dunwich

Heath. Here Sebald became confused on his trek, unable to follow a straight line because of the heather, 'woody and knee-deep'. He wrote, 'In the end I was overcome by a feeling of panic. The low, leaden sky; the sickly violet hue of the heath clouding the eye; the silence, which rushed in the ears like the sound of the sea in a shell; the flies buzzing around me – all this became oppressive and unnerving. I cannot say how long I walked about in that state of mind, or how I found a way out.'

Even by road, Dunwich wasn't easy to find. Some byways off the Ipswich road, the A12, turned out to be blinds, false leads. When I finally arrived, on the main drag of St James's Street, there was no one about, but then the electoral roll for Dunwich is a headcount of just eighty-eight. There were the half-dozen houses that Sebald had mentioned, and the town museum and the pub. The road was named after the last surviving church. St James's was built in 1832, by which time the few hardy Christian souls had been without a parish church for sixty years. Dunwich St James's looked hale enough – flint-clad and with arched windows – though poignant wreckage of the old city stood alongside it in the churchyard.

No theatrics were needed to draw the eye to these – the ruins of a leper hospital – but as chance would have it, what survived of it was a proscenium of three walls *sans* roof. The stone hospital, which incorporated a chapel, was some twenty yards long and eight wide. On either of the longer walls there had once been rough cubicles, each containing its own bed 'on which a sufferer lay'. The hospital went up at the end of the twelfth century but the chapel was older, a Norman place of worship which was itself built over the site of a Saxon church. It may have been one of the Dunwich churches inventoried in the Domesday Book, only to be cut off from the rest of the community when the Palesdyke was thrown up around the city limits in the late eleventh century. St James's demonstrated the shrinkage of the once proud seaport: at one time, the leper hospital and its chapel had literally been beyond the pale, to protect citizens from infection. But thanks to the incursion of the sea over the years, it was now at the heart of modern Dunwich: a short walk from the beach.

Elsewhere in the churchyard, a stony column stood apart. This outstretched finger of masonry was the last handhold that another church, All Saints', had maintained on the Suffolk coastline before the elements had prised the building off. A weathered plaque fitted to this forlorn digit revealed it as 'The North West buttress of All Saints Church . . .' – and then the message began to fade, like a distress call Morsed from a wallowing ship. 'The last trace of the churches of the first East Anglian capital and see . . .' I made out, as well as 'Removed' and 'cliff' – and then the SOS cut out altogether. Four tombstones were clustered around the base of the buttress, including one engraved 'In Memory of Robert Easey who departed this life May 7 1793 aged 45 years'. The buttress and the headstones had been salvaged from cliffs less than half a mile away and placed in the grounds of St James's in 1923. The lost church had its origins in the fourteenth century but it was closed in 1778 amid fears that it was about to fall victim to erosion and subsidence. As a notice-board put it with brutal brevity, 'The church fell over the cliff between 1904–1919.'

Here we approached the source of Dunwich's fascination, I felt, the idea that its churches could just drop off the edge of the land and into the sea. I'd found the same proposition stated just as baldly in a reference book: 'The last medieval church . . . started to fall off the cliff in 1904.' It was all the more heady for being so plain-spoken, somehow. The loss of any building in this way had to be spectacular and unsettling, didn't it? But all the more so when it happened to a church, with its implicit promise of divine protection, its warranty against acts of God.

It was a brilliant morning, and a few dog-walkers were abroad on the beach. The café was opening. Once known as

Flora's Tea-Room, it was originally built from the timbers of a barge (*The Flora*) which sank just off Dunwich. The café had gone up near the site of the long-forgotten almshouse of the Maison Dieu, the home of the poor, the infirm, the disturbed. The Maison Dieu had the ring of the Deep South about it, and that wasn't entirely out of place, you felt. You were gazing out at the breakers of the North Sea but you might have been looking at the over-topping levees of New Orleans.

Or indeed the Gulf of Lian-tung in China. Unless you count the environs of the Sizewell nuclear plant, Dunwich boasts the longest stretch of unspoilt coastline within hailing distance of London, which is estate-agent-speak for saying that no one in their right mind would dream of building anywhere near it. The belfry-strewn beach was the right place to contemplate the fall of Dunwich; the fall was inherent in the rise. The very topographical quirks that had made the city such a success as a seaport had also settled its fate. The North Sea washed away the coastline surrounding the Kingsholme, the isthmus which sheltered the harbour, until it became a wall, all but sealing Dunwich off.

That was the beginning of the end for this great trading post, the place where a man like Robert Malet could once enrich himself hand over fish. Two tremendous storms set the decline in stone, literally. The first dumped thousands of tons of shingle into the harbour on New Year's Day, 1287. It carried off houses, businesses, livestock, people – as well as laying waste to Dunwich's ecclesiastical real estate. A similar effect followed a hurricane-force north-easterly which blew in on 14 January 1328, on the night of the highest tide of the month. People fled with whatever they could carry. Before the gale struck, there were two hundred houses in the well-to-do parish of St Nicholas. But it blew them into the sea or smashed them into kindling where they stood. By morning, only thirty houses remained. Much of St Leonard's parish simply sank. Sebald writes:

All night the waves clawed away one row of houses after another. Like mighty battering rams the roofing and supporting beams adrift in the water smashed against the walls that had not yet been levelled. When dawn came, the throng of survivors . . . stood on the edge of the abyss, leaning into the wind, gazing in horror through the clouds of salt spray into depths where bales and barrels, shattered cranes, torn sails of windmills, chests and tables, crates, feather beds, firewood, straw and drowned livestock were revolving in a whirlpool of whitish-brown waters.

As if whipped on by Satan himself, in some diabolical Derby, the steeplechasing churches of Dunwich pursued each other across the final dwindling furlong of clifftop before setting themselves for the last: clearing the edge and plunging down the far side into the water. One by one they went: St Bartholomew's, St Felix's, St John the Baptist, St Leonard's, St Martin's, St Michael's, St Nicholas's, St Patrick's, St Peter's and All Saints'.

In his *Tour Through the Whole Island of Great Britain*, published in 1724–6, Defoe wrote of Dunwich:

This town seems to be in danger of being swallowed up; for fame reports, that once they had fifty churches in the town; I saw but one left, and that not half full of people. This town is a testimony of the decay of public things, things of the most durable nature; and as the old poet expresses it,

By numerous examples we may see,
That towns and cities die, as well as we.

The ruins of Carthage, or the great city of Jerusalem, or of ancient Rome, are not at all wonderful to me; the ruins of Nineveh, which are so entirely sunk, as that 'tis doubtful where the city stood; the ruins of Babylon, or the great Persepolis, and many capital cities, which time and the change of monarchies

have overthrown; these, I say, are not at all wonderful, because
being the capitals of great and flourishing kingdoms, where
those kingdoms were overthrown, the capital cities necessarily
fell with them. But for a private town, a sea-port, and a town
of commerce, to decay, as it were of itself (for we never read of
Dunwich being plundered, or ruined by any disaster, at least not
of late years); this I must confess, seems owing to nothing but
the fate of things, by which we see that towns, kings, countries,
families, and persons, have all their elevation, their medium,
their declination, and even their destruction in the womb of
time, and the course of nature. It is true, this town is manifestly
decayed by the invasion of the waters, and as other towns seem
sufferers by the sea, or the tide withdrawing from their ports,
such as Orford ... Winchelsea in Kent, and the like: so this
town is, as it were, eaten up by the sea, as above; and the still
encroaching ocean seems to threaten it with a fatal immersion
in a few years more.

As Dunwich slipped from sight, it re-emerged as myth, a city
beneath the surf, its location given away by the reverberation of
sunken church bells. 'Quite a common belief amongst laymen
regarding the condition of submerged Dunwich, is that the streets
and market places with their houses and shops remain intact, and
the numerous churches stand complete with their bells still
hanging in the belfries,' Jean and Stuart Bacon note in *The Search
for Dunwich*.

This undersea knelling was celebrated in verse:

> Oft 'tis said
> The affrighted fisherman a steeple spies
> Below the waves; and oft the mariner,
> Driven by the whirlwind, feels his vessel strike
> Upon the mingled mass.

A Victorian skipper, John Day, claimed that he knew when he was off Dunwich because of the eerie tintinnabulation of a bell several fathoms down. Some versions of the myth have it that the watery changes were rung to warn against the kind of weather that had felled the bell-towers in the first place.

Dunwich is not alone in being covered by the North Sea. It's one of many lost towns, real places drowned within recorded history. Because these losses are comparatively recent, legends of divine punishments are rare: more characteristic is the by now familiar folklore accenting the world of underwater camp-anology. A nineteenth-century archivist, Lady Camilla Gurdon, found evidence of this tradition at Aldeburgh and Felixstowe. It also attends a lost fishing port, Shipden, near Cromer on the Norfolk coast. Shipden, also known as 'Shippedenmere' or 'Chippendenmere', dipped beneath the rollers in the early fifteenth century. It was said that the debris of the old church, St Peter's, was sometimes visible when the tide was unusually low, lying about four hundred yards offshore. This outcrop was referred to locally as the 'Church Rock' or 'Shipden Steeple', and in the nineteenth century the idea got about that the bells of St Peter's could still be heard when bad weather was about to sweep in.

In the North East, more than thirty places mentioned in the Domesday Book have disappeared. Near the mouth of the Humber, beyond the Sunk Island Sands, lies Ravenser, which was also referenced in old Icelandic literature. It was a prosperous port until the fourteenth century, but was flooded in 1361, and all its merchants decanted for Hull and Grimsby. By 1390, not quite thirty years later, most traces of the port were gone. An old stone cross at Hedon, East Yorkshire, is supposedly from Ravenser, as are church bells at Easington and Aldborough, south of Hornsea. Off the Kent coast, the Goodwin Sands are said to be the last remnant of the lost island of Lomea. Once a great estate belonging to Earl Godwin, father of King Harold, it succumbed to a flood in 1099 because Godwin had failed to maintain the sea defences.

At Dunwich, I wandered the breakwater, straining to make out the muffled boom of an engulfed clapper. I eyed the dunes for a splinter of rood-screen, a glimpse of apse. This wasn't as fanciful as it might seem. Although fashionable upper Dunwich has been entirely lost, its des reses having cascaded to the beach and dashed themselves into a million pieces, the hugger-mugger quarters of the old town – the fish markets, the rude tailors' cutting-rooms – had less far to fall, and there was cause to hope that their hard-scrabble foundations endured. Three hundred years ago the salt-tongued sea, in its licking and snuffling at the Suffolk coast, duly turned up the buried remains of houses and chapels, the pattern of watercourses and a stretch of quayside that had been overwhelmed by the disastrous storm of the fourteenth century. When the cliffs abruptly shed more of themselves, in 1739 and again in 1904, they exposed the extraordinary sight of what looked like rows of factory chimneys on the beach – these standing stones were actually the deep draughts of old wells.

Fishermen hauling in their nets have brought up lumps of masonry from the ruined choirs of Dunwich. Frogmen have recovered parts of a church window and a fragment of a tomb honouring a fourteenth-century knight. Stuart Bacon, who claims to have dived the waters off Dunwich a thousand times, said in 2008 that he and his team had located the resting-places of three churches and a chapel down there in the wringing murk. The remains lie between ten and fifty feet beneath the breakers. Bacon announced a project to take the latest underwater cameras down to the sunken spires.

But the Dunwich churches haven't taken all their relics with them to the bottom of the sea, I discovered. All Saints' was the last of the places of worship to go, a little over a century ago, but not all of its late parishioners made the journey; or they haven't

yet, at any rate. I went to see where the church once stood. I
walked over the clifftops, through the grounds of a thirteenth-
century Franciscan friary, marked out by a flint wall. Beyond the
wall was the graveyard of All Saints'; all but fallen away now, but
lingering on in the shape of a few square feet of powdery coast
which somehow sustained trees and bushes. Though the church
had been declared unsafe before the end of the eighteenth
century, it was such a landmark to shipping that the lighthouse
people at Trinity House saved it from collapse for a further
century. Its lonely melancholy was catnip to Victorian aesthetes.
When Turner painted it, he shifted the tower to seaward to suit
his composition of men putting to sea in a rough swell.
Swinburne wrote of the church:

> Here is the end of all his glory –
> Dust, and barren silent stones,
> Dead like him, one hollow tower and hoary
> Naked in the sea wind stands and moans.

Henry James defied anyone 'at desolate, exquisite Dunwich' to
be disappointed in anything. 'There is a presence in what is
missing,' opined the master, not for the first time putting his
perfectly manicured pinkie on it.

Across the stony wall of the friary grounds, what remained of
All Saints' ossuary was roped off. Signs warned of 'dangerous
cliffs'. Among the scrubby undergrowth, within a yard or so of
the tottering cliff face itself, rose a headstone. It was squared off
and strangely anthropomorphic, suggesting or representing a
man's head and shoulders, like the packaging you find in a shirt
box. I ducked under the rope and tested the dry earth for
traction. I read the inscription on the greening gravestone: 'In
Memoriam . . . Jacob Forster who departed this life March 12
1796 aged 38 . . .' The word 'Years' followed, on a line all to
itself. A short distance away, I found another memorial lozenge,

ripely verdant and sunk so deep in the soil that its inscription was buried too. It looked as if it had already been relocated to Davy Jones's Locker. Here was a sighting of England's Thebes, I felt, an encounter with littoral Dunwich – 'There is a presence in what is missing' – suspended between Suffolk and the North Sea, transmogrifying from the old capital of East Anglia into the seabed's lumpy mattress.

The cliff fall of 1904, which began All Saints' slide into the briny, also calved human remains from its consecrated precincts. 'From the black earth and yellow sand gaunt bones protruded – not one but dozens,' the man from the *Daily Chronicle* filed from the scene. 'I counted a score of fragments of human limbs, there a thigh bone, there a part of a pelvis, and there, perched on a mound of earth and masonry, a broken, toothless skull, the sockets where the eyes had been staring out at the restless waters.' Nicholas Comfort writes, 'Erosion . . . tore bones from All Saints' graveyard, some seemingly from communal graves, dug hastily during the Black Death or when other churchyards were endangered.' Alfred Scott Thompson, the long-serving vicar of Dunwich (1903–33), would tour the foreshore with his verger after every landslip and load the skulls and bones they found into a coffin, for reburial at St James's.

All Saints' itself succumbed to gravity arch by shattering arch. The Easter Island obelisk of its tower crashed to the beach in November 1919, though it wasn't until January 1922 that the last of it was lost (all except the buttress that was providently removed to St James's churchyard). 'Now the ruins are in a gully . . . not far from the shore in a silent, mainly dark world with a large congregation of crabs, eels, small fish and a few lobsters,' according to *The Search for Dunwich*.

The passing of Dunwich from the land to the sea was a relentless flux. During the twentieth century, the water was still encroaching at the staggering rate of a yard a year, though one tide in 1976 snatched five feet of cliff away; one day in February

1989, it was six feet. Now, in 2007, I contemplated the tombstones: bad teeth in the crumbling jaw of the coast. I gave it a couple of years at most before the vicar of Dunwich, the verger and their bone-gurney, must go down to the sea again.

10

DROWNED TOWNS AND CORPSE ROADS

It wasn't only ports like Dunwich that were overcome by flood. Underwater cities have been a feature of dry land, too. Most of these deluges took place many years ago. As a result, they were often associated with biblical wrath. Semer Water in Rydale, Yorkshire, is said to cover a city which was drowned for its sins. A traveller variously identified as St Paul, Joseph of Arimathea, or Christ himself, arrived at this black spot seeking alms. His entreaties were spurned until he reached the cottage of some kindly if impoverished OAPs, who gave the stranger their own frugal repast of milk, cheese and oaten cake. Blessings duly attended the honest couple, but the man of the road bid the waters cover the Sodom of the Dales, crying:

> Simmer-water rise, Simmer-water sink,
> And swallow up all but this lisle house,
> Where they gave me bread and cheese, and
>   summat to drink.

Sure enough, the earth began to hiss, a deluge engulfed the city, and it remains waterlogged to this day.

Another Yorkshire village sent to a watery grave because of its depravity now lies under Gormire in the Hambleton Hills. In the Lake District, a similar reputation clouds a place called Talkin. Many years ago it was a large and prosperous town, notorious for the greed and cruelty of its inhabitants. Yes, the word of mouth on Talkin was terrible. This Cumbrian Gomorrah stood on the site of the present Talkin Tarn. In an effort to persuade the townsfolk to mend their wicked ways, an angel descended to Talkin in the guise of an old beggar. But not only was this ineffable gentleman of the road reviled and refused food and drink at every turn, he was pelted with stones in the market place and forced to flee. As he was making his exit, a poor widow took him in and gave him water and what little food she had. Her houseguest prayed that God would punish the village but pass over the widow and her home. 'Presently the sky darkened and a tempest began to rage,' writes A. Hall in *Lakeland Legends and Folklore*. 'At the height of the storm, an earthquake shook the town and it sank into the ground. When the sun rose next morning, the entire town had vanished and in its place was a deep, still lake. The only place that had been spared was the house of the widow. It is said that if you row into the middle of the tarn when the weather is calm and the water unruffled, you can see the drowned buildings.'

I had a fancy to see some drowned buildings. Dunwich and its see-sawing clifftop graveyard, its dear departed who had very nearly gone altogether, had whetted my appetite for the vestiges of England's lost communities. I would go looking for them in Lakeland. I'd been reading about a lost village called Mardale, a real sunken town. In the 1930s Haweswater valley was flooded to create a reservoir supplying the North West, and the hapless Mardale had been in the way. It was the village that died for

Manchester. It might not have been on the end of a biblical bolt but it had taken some punishment all the same, in the shape of a comprehensive levelling by the military. First it was evacuated; then it was flattened by the sappers. Finally, the dam was closed and what was left of Mardale gurgled out of sight. Although thoroughly inundated now, it only became one of the region's signature water features within living memory. Mardale had been a hardy Lakeland community, as recreated by Sarah Hall in her novel *Haweswater*:

> The buildings . . . were squat, stout and tucked into woody enclaves, designed to withstand the ravages of the seasons, the rough, unpredictable weather common to this part of the country. There was an inn at the south end of the village called the Dun Bull which advertised in the Midland papers for boarders and occasionally received them. At the Dun Bull Inn gatherings took place, the shepherds' meet, the Mardale Hunt, evening assemblies where old men sang ballads with their rough, low voices softening like the air in spring. The inn was as much a centre for congregating as the church. And it stood almost opposite St Patrick's church on the other side of the main, mucky, wheel-rutted road.

Now it had all gone. But during hot spells, when the water level dropped, the village eerily reappeared, or so I'd read. In photographs taken during bone-dry summers, trippers were seen promenading its avenues and enjoying the view from a hump-backed bridge. The stony streets were miraculously resurrected from the bottom of the lake. The Mardale area was also celebrated by fans of the film *Withnail and I* as the location where the eponymous principals holidayed at Uncle Monty's cottage. And there was a further attraction in going to look for Mardale's resurfacing remains, in that I could combine the trip with walking the Corpse Road. This was a route which had been scored into the hills by the regular transit of men and beasts bearing a heavy burden: the dead. A corpse road was a well-established feature of remote parts in the days before cars. It might alternatively go by the names of bier road, burial road, church way, coffin road, coffin line, lyke or lych way, funeral road or procession way. Some settlements could only be reached on foot or by horseback. The deceased might have been a hill farmer on a wild and woolly spread, or the matriarch of an isolated hovel, but a burial in consecrated ground was required, all the same. The nearest church might be miles away. So the late local would be strapped to a horse or placed in a sling and borne haltingly off to an appointment with the parson and a reckoning with the Almighty, windswept mourners following the jolting bier up the fellside.

Ramblers who tackle the popular coast-to-coast walk from the Lakes over the Pennines to the North Yorkshire Moors and on at last to the ravening North Sea, stomp past Haweswater, and may catch a glimpse of a hairpin track snaking up the hill on the far side of the lagoon. This was the Corpse Road. In an earlier phase of Mardale's history, a distinctly drier epoch, the route embarked from the village church, St Patrick's, across Selside Pike to the graveyard at Shap. St Patrick's, also known for some of its history as Holy Trinity, stood on a promontory, Chapel Hill. Sarah Hall's *Haweswater* describes St Patrick's as

> a beautiful, ancient church, built at the end of the fifteenth century on sacred ground, where a tall, mossy Celtic cross had already stood for centuries. Upon the building of the church in 1499, the cross was incorporated into the graveyard and there it remained, older than even the two yew trees which backed up against the dry-stone wall circling the headstones within the graveyard. The building was tiny and dense, with enough room for only a handful of worshippers.

The land that St Patrick's stood on might have been sacred, but unfortunately it wasn't consecrated, and for more than two hundred years it was bordered not by a graveyard but a simple churchyard. Though no doubt admirably godly, Mardale didn't have a dispensation from the church elders to inter their dead where they had lived, hence the recourse to a corpse road across the fellside to the parochial boneyard.

A corpse road was a 'holloway', a harrowed path or a sunken road, from the Anglo-Saxon *hola weg*. It was one of the antique thoroughfares scored into England through repeated usage. Robert Macfarlane writes in *The Wild Places*: 'Few holloways are in use now: they are too narrow and too slow to suit modern travel. But they are also too deep to be filled in and farmed over. So it is that, set about by some of the most intensively farmed countryside in the world, the holloways have come to constitute a sunken labyrinth of wildness in the heart of . . . England.' In terms of the English underground, my excursion on the holloway to Mardale had everything going for it: it was a perfect storm of subterranean conditions. I would be travelling on a road taken by the dead, by the buried; I would be on a *buried* road taken by the buried, in fact; and it would take me all the way to a buried village.

For, you see, I had decided to make the journey in reverse, beginning at Shap and finishing at Mardale. The submerged settlement was the true prize, the due destination. It seemed right to end my walk there. I was also excited by the troubling idea that if you go the wrong way down a corpse road, you're liable to meet the dead coming towards you; an idea that was marginally qualified, you may think, by the fact that I'd thought it up myself (or I *thought* I had – what I didn't know then is that it's considered bad luck to take a corpse over a bridge twice, which presumably means going in the opposite direction to the one it has already taken). You could be forgiven for suspecting that this is a tall tale introduced to disguise a last-minute detour

down the Corpse Road on my part, an itinerary planned without
due cognisance of historical convention. And you'd be right. I
was on a day off, a licensed leave of absence, but all the same, a
midweek hike in late-summer Lakeland felt like a sublime sickie.
Mindful of the unpunched space in my clocking-in card, I
congratulated myself on lead-swinging of majorette virtuosity.

The reason I was in the Lakes in the first place was to cover a
news story that couldn't have been further removed, at first sight,
from funereal holloways. BBC2's analogue signal had been
turned off to the inhabitants of Whitehaven, as part of a rolling
changeover to digital television. Not only had I reported this
watershed for *Newsnight*, I'd also accompanied the official
responsible to the sheep-girt relay station where he practised
throwing the switch for the final fade-out: Richard Percival
would go back on his own in the small hours to do the job for
real.

Mr Percival larked it up a little at the behest of the
photographers who'd made the long journey from Fleet Street; he
went along with the ribbons that someone had laced into the
transponders. But he impressed me as a rather correct figure:
ramrod carriage, moustache, narrow tie, possibly ex-military.
The modern world has no truck with ceremony, with the
vestments and baubles of office. But I presumed to intuit that the
proper Mr Percival shared my instinct that he should by rights
have had some sort of title: Keeper of the Queen's Signals,
perhaps; that after a simple, abstinent dinner at his hotel he
should have been piped to the broadcasting bothy by a lone
clansman; and that there was time for a reflective moment, as his
hand trembled over the plunger, for a few well-chosen words,
possibly school of Neil Armstrong. Like any right-minded
Englishman, I would have been reassured by these little touches,
and then it would probably never have occurred to me to ask Mr
Percival if he could be trusted not to run amok, alone at the
controls, and jam transmissions to Whitehaven, pumping BBC2

signals past their sell-by date into its all-unknowing homes. 'If I did that, it would mean summary dismissal and a big inquiry,' he laughed nervously.

Mr Percival was scorch-makingly close to the white heat of technological revolution, and yet he had a lot in common with the pall-bearers of the Corpse Road, it seemed to me. Like the stricken of Mardale, he found himself beating a lonely path up the fells to carry out his solemn and onerous responsibilities, to bear witness to a light snuffed out, to be in at the death. Of course, his pristine information highway will still be giving reliable service long after the Corpse Road has finally returned to the mire, or so we are led to believe. But they said the same thing about the old telly signals, and they were being turned off for good. The shades that they conjured from Whitehaven's cashiered cathodes are condemned to wander the ether for eternity, not unlike wraiths forever revisiting a roadway of lost souls, you might think. I wouldn't be writing off the Corpse Road quite so quickly, myself: what was it, after all, but a means of communication, not so unlike digital TV? One was all about a pure stream of binary code; the other, good old-fashioned two-footed slogging. For all its morbid associations, the Corpse Road would survive for as long as people were inclined to pace out the Via Dolorosa from Mardale to Shap. Or indeed vice versa.

We've joked, you and I, about the spiritual dimensions of vanished villages and lost cities: the phantoms ill-met on a far-flung track; the uncanny bonging of waterlogged church bells; even the vapourisings of my dear late mum over her abandoned homestead. As I was going to Shap, I reflected on the first of these phenomena – which, as I say, I had lately called into being by dreaming it up. There could only be one thing as boggling as encountering the dead coming towards you on a corpse road, I thought, and that would be to meet oneself in the same circumstances. Oddly enough, that's what happened to me. I ran into my past.

On the way to Shap, I was stuck behind a tractor as we dawdled into a village – and was happy to recognise it as a place where I'd stayed five years earlier. I hadn't known about Mardale then, nor the *Withnail and I* connection – otherwise I would have been pleased to know that the lonely callbox I had patronised, with no mobile phone signal available to me, was the one from which Withnail places his antic call to his agent. This brush with the bygone wasn't the last that awaited me in the fells.

Leaving the car on the Shap side of Haweswater, I made my way up to a farm, scattering plump, tawny hens as I went. The farmer was emerging from his house. He'd lived at the farm for thirty years, he told me. He was pulling on wader-style green galoshes. He looked as though he'd shaved in the dark: over his strong cheekbones were crop-circles of beard that the ploughshare of his razor had missed.

'I'm looking for the Corpse Road,' I told him.

'You're standing on it,' he said. 'You just keep going up this road, you'll come to an old farm building and a signpost saying "Corpse Road" and then you turn right and head up the fellside there.' I followed his gesturing finger beyond the metalled road, to a steep incline of scree. There was a pungent, an earthy – a farmy – smell about him. I dilated on my conceit that if you crossed the road from the wrong side, you might run into people who had gone over to the *other* side.

The farmer said, 'Oh, there are many ghost stories about the road.' He had a warty chin, I noticed. 'Oh yes, there's one packhorse still up there, with a coffin on its back.' Once more, we looked along the road to Mardale, but only one of us swallowed involuntarily. The winding and gladed route was dappled with October sunshine. What could be more inviting? What could be more restorative than a walk across the hills on a day of Indian summer? And yet wasn't it all a little *too* enchanting? It was a rare hour of brilliant light, but weren't the colours a little too rich, too saturated? The path that lay ahead

of me looked like the Yellow Brick Road; yes, I was a doubtful
Dorothy as I set out on that witchy way.

There are indeed many ghost stories about corpse roads. They
echo pagan notions of spirit paths and shamanic 'soul flight'.
Neolithic man built cursuses, like the one at Stonehenge, to
connect burial mounds. It was considered bad luck for a funeral
cortege to deviate from the established route of a corpse road,
because this meant that the deceased would never find rest, and
would return to haunt the living. In his *Glossary of the Cleveland
District* (1868), a historian called Atkinson describes a funeral
party struggling through great drifts of snow in order to cleave
to the traditional route over high moors. In Scatchard's *History
of Morley* (1874), the people of Walton, near Wakefield, refused
a convenient path to Sandal Church in favour of a route through
a field because that was the established 'Corpse Gate'. If a body
was carried over a cultivated meadow, the crops failed and the
land fell barren. Because a corpse road leads to a cemetery, the
route was thought to share the characteristics of the destination,
to be a place where the spirits of the dead thrive. A 'corpse
candle' was an omen of death, a sphere of light that was observed
to travel just above the ground from the cemetery to a dying
person's house and back again, in a fatalistic flarepath. One
makes an appearance in *Moonfleet*, though young John
Trenchard is sceptical: 'I considered that the tales of Blackbeard
walking or digging among the graves had been set afloat to keep
those that were not wanted from the place, and guessed now that
when I saw the light moving in the churchyard that night I went
to fetch Dr Hawkins, it was no corpse-candle, but a lantern of
smugglers running a cargo.'

'Corpse fires' broke out in graveyards. They were interpreted
as *son et lumière* curtain-raisers to impending committals; as
the playful phantasms of the dead; even as other occult forces
intent on leading travellers astray. These will-o'-the-wisps
attracted aliases such as Jack o' Lantern, Joan of the Wad,

Jenny Burn-tail and Spunkie. In *A Midsummer Night's Dream*,
Puck declaims:

> Now it is that time of night,
> That the graves all gaping wide,
> Every one lets forth his sprite,
> In the church-way paths to glide.

The likely explanations of these phantasms are scarcely more
plausible than the old wives' tales themselves. They were fireballs
of methane gas released by decomposing bodies, or barn owls
flitting across the darkling landscape bearing a fluorescent fungus
on the tips of their feathers.

As the Mardale Road wound its way into the hills, its
parameters were marked out by lichen-covered dry-stone walls
and lengths of fencing. In places, the spars of this railing had been
thriftily nailed or lashed to new uprights, perhaps by my friend
the farmer. To catch my breath for a moment I sat down on a
broad flat stone, the size of a pouf. Garishly mossed, it was the
sort of flag that a pixie or a leprechaun should by rights occupy,
perhaps with a hookah raised to his impish lips.

In the old days, shifting a stiff in the fresh air had been a push-
me, pull-you affair. On the one side were the bereaved, with their
cadaverous cargo; on the other were the clergy. Unlike the Saviour
Himself, the Church was not universally available to its flock, but
it nonetheless demanded burial fees for the right to repose in one of
its distant graveyards. In late medieval England, a growing population led to a boom in church-building, but established mother
churches and minsters viewed with alarm this encroachment on to
their well-remitted turf. Instead of allowing outlying congrega-
tions to bury their own where they dropped, the ecclesiastical
hierarchy instituted a churchy version of Park 'n' Ride, or perhaps
Ride 'n' Park. Families could lug their loved ones down corpse
roads all the way from satellite chapels to the parish church.

St Peter and Paul at Blockley, Gloucestershire, held the ancient burial rights to two outlying hamlets, neither of which had blessed allotments of their own. They were Stretton-on-Fosse, where there was a chapel which didn't become a rectory until the twelfth century, and Aston Magna, which had a chapel in the form of a modest chantry. All fees came to the parish church at Blockley, to which the people of Stretton and Aston were obliged to bring their dead. The corpse road from Stretton to Blockley was four miles long and crossed two streams. The route from Aston was half as long but led across three streams. (It was considered a good idea to take the dead across a bridge, because spirits couldn't cross running water. They also had difficulty with other liminal locations including crossroads and stiles.) In 1351 the Bishop of Worcester received a petition from the people of Stretton, asking for consent to bury their kith and kin in the village, to avoid paying 'dues and mortuaries' into parochial coffers. The bishop turned them down, and Stretton wasn't granted the burial right until the Reformation.

These villagers weren't the only ones to kick up a fuss. At Hinton in Wiltshire, the corpse road was boycotted because it passed through woods infested with robbers. By 1405, the locals had founded their own chapel, with land set aside for a cemetery. In 1427 the requiem mass was being said at Highweek in Devon, and worshippers couldn't see why they had to follow it with a long and dangerous journey to a distant boneyard. The fishermen of Revelstoke in Cornwall similarly declared that they were renouncing the corpse road because foot-slogging funerals cost them days at sea.

Such processions also had to contend with landowners. One reason why they seldom shied from the true path was because the squirearchy discouraged it. Like the priesthood, they had their own interests to consider. They were aware of a widely held belief that a corpse road, once trod, was inviolably established through any estate that it happened to cross. There are stories of gardeners at great houses grappling with the grieving as they tried to stretcher bodies across the greensward. For the landholding classes, this was a sensitive issue: obstructing or resisting the passage of a corpse was also sure to bring bad fortune.

On Mardale Road that day I could hear the gurgle of water running off the hills, and the soughing of the wind. Sunlight pierced the canopy of gnarled trees – and I was surprised by joy, as the poet has it, or perhaps I mean I was transported afresh by the bliss of escape. Escape from London, from the travails and contortions of sackings at the BBC, a story that I'd otherwise have been reporting. A hardy, doomed hornet alighted on the non-business end of my darting biro – the insect and pen mimicking each other.

I thought of how my mum would have enjoyed this outing; my dad, too. I used to go walking with him in the Lakes, and on a wild fellside always had a sense of communing with him. What do you do with a moment like this, I wondered, a moment you're in no hurry to see the back of – quite the reverse, in fact – but which is pregnant, so to speak, with the knowledge that it can't and won't last? It'll cloud over, it'll rain, night will fall and I'll be on the train back to the Smoke again. And yet, what the dead – corpses, indeed – would give to be in my place, on this stone on this marvellous reclaimed day, a day dragged somehow out of the cold and wet and dark to come, and gloriously present as one last day of summer.

It occurs to me now, as I'm writing this, that I was taking a breather not on some petrified toadstool, some dwarfish occasional furniture, but on a coffin stone. This was a slab on which a weary burial procession could set its burden down. Coffin stones or crosses were a feature of corpse roads, hallowed by long habituation or blessed by priests, so that bodies could safely be laid on them without fear of the spirits escaping and haunting their places of death. Also in Lakeland there was a well-known coffin stone on the corpse road from Rydal to Ambleside.

Once, a solemn column treading the Hambleton Hills in North Yorkshire deposited its mortal payload at the side of the road, during a comfort break. When the refreshed bearers returned to shoulder their charge once more, they found to their horror that it was gone. The site of this particular coffin stone was known ever after as Lost Corpse End. Another story has it that a much reviled old man died in Devon years ago and was carried across Dartmoor to Widecombe. He was placed on a coffin stone during the march. The company was aghast to see a ray of light zap the old boy's casket, reducing both it and its contents to ashes, and rending the stone in two. The devastating bolt from on high was taken to be a sign from God that there was no room in Widecombe cemetery for the old bastard.

It's rather thrilling to think that, all the while I was keeping company with my own revenants, I had been unwittingly polishing a coffin stone with my rear end; a clueless Aladdin brushing up against a magic lantern. Which is what the old rock was: a repository of hope, a point of light in the darkness. The sanctified stone warded off evil, radiated only good.

I found the ruined building the farmer had told me about, the signpost, the scramble of slate. It was marshy on the tops, and I made a soggy going of it through the mud, the kelp and the champ, the undersea algae. A peewit made a break for it from under the sole of my boot and three grouse (grice?) rose flapping from cover: I was a ghillie on a great estate, beating for the shots. A sheep's skull, picked clean and blanched, lay on the rutted way of the old Corpse Road – if that's where I was. It was hard to keep track of the route, in the unpeopled slough on the bare moorside. There were moments when I felt like crying, with the imperishable Withnail, 'I've come on holiday by mistake!' As entrenched as the holloway was in the valleys and even on the top of Selside Pike, the elements constantly threatened to efface it where it was most exposed. The rain scoured it and the wind scourged it. The souls of Mardale were doubly shriven.

I came across fencing that staked out a queer patch of ground. The enclosure was in the shape of a ship's hull, recalling Raedwald's tomb at Sutton Hoo. At first, I assumed that the barrier was protecting a nascent copse, some soused saplings, but when I got close I saw there was no sign of them. Perhaps it was a make-work project or an Outward Bound assignment. Or maybe it was a terrible sucking bog, a trap for the unwary on the old Corpse Road.

I wasn't expecting a lot from Mardale – I was hoping, but I wasn't expecting. The lost village lay in up to 18.6 billion gallons of water. It's been calculated that you could draw three baths for everyone on earth before you'd empty the lake. Mardale was 'only visible in long, dry summers', I'd read, and this was to all intents and purposes autumn; autumn in Cumbria, at that. So when I finally looked down on Haweswater, I was astonished to see fields, meadows, bounded by dry-stone walls. Admittedly, these structures were partially submerged – it would be as accurate to call them wet-stone walls – but the great thing about them was, they partially weren't. There was no mistaking them for anything else. They weren't glacial or other natural deposits of rock and stone. The points where one wall met another, their neat hospital corners, were patently crafted. There at the southern tip of Haweswater, the reservoir was by no means full, and in places it was clear. You could see through water the colour of weak tea to the atolls and reefs of long-lost Mardale.

Apart from the remains on the bed of the lake, all there was of the place, as far as I could make out, was a car park, where a notice of unknown date warned that no bus would be leaving Mardale all summer long. The point about Mardale – the paradoxical reason for coming to see it – was that it wasn't there any more. Though some came to walk dogs or scramble leanly up the scree, such as the man I saw, the white-haired and startlingly topless man, who was now changing into a shirt at the boot of his car. I was going to guy him about going in for a swim, but thought better of it or bottled it, and instead said 'Are you local?'

The topless man reacted with justifiable Lakeland pawkiness to this barely finessed version of 'Do you come here often?' He allowed that he knew 'a little about the place'. It was at his suggestion that I shinned up the opposite hillside 'for a clear view of the fields'. It proved to be a fine vantage point, and I doubt that I'd have thought of it myself. What I would have thought of was to access it by the most direct route possible – straight across the mudflats of Mardale. Except that my half-naked friend had rather forcefully (by force of character, I mean) directed me to the path which skirted the reservoir instead. This was more sanitary for Mancunian water-drinkers, but a longer way round for me.

I waited until the now fully clothed man had driven away before padding out on to the pulling mud. I walked down the choked lanes of Mardale. The village was half sticking out of a tundra of sludge. There was an old wooden table leg and the lure, the trap, of an abandoned pair of Wellington boots, barely protruding from the morass. They were drawing me to them like the fenced-off, dangerous ooze high on the hillside had drawn me. Straining to take a closer look at the wellies, I nearly lost a boot myself to the slurping goo. The Corpse Road ran from here to Shap until 1736, when villagers finally acquired the burial right. For two hundred years, they went to their reward where they had lived, here beneath this now-squelching sediment.

But in 1929, Parliament passed an Act allowing the Manchester corporation to build the Haweswater reservoir. The village was cleared, the people of Mardale were rehoused elsewhere in Lakeland, and the army went in. The church, St Patrick's, proved one of the most obdurate stumbling-blocks to their campaign of razing, at least in the pages of Sarah Hall's novel:

Dust began to settle over the wreckage of Mardale and it was only the battered tower of St Patrick's that remained at any substantial height. It shook and crumbled with each bomb detonation but withstood the shocks, and though by the end of the day it appeared that only one ounce of explosive would have brought it crashing down, there was no explosive left in the guarded tent to be used. So, finally, the Army let the church be. It was gradually knocked down with sledgehammers and pickaxes over the next few months . . . reduced to a pile of brick and stone and stained glass.

You could clearly see where St Patrick's had stood: the tree-covered mound of Chapel Hill rose higher out of the reservoir than the remainder of the village that the church had once served. This bluff was visible the year round, come rain or shine, or at least the trees growing on top of it were. But the rubble of the church itself went into the making of the dam. The latter was considered an engineering feat in its time, almost five hundred yards long and more than eighty feet high, and assembled out of more than forty separate buttressed sections, held together by flexible joints.

As for the long-awaited graveyard, it was itself rendered moribund by the advent of the reservoir. With the coming of that flood of biblical proportions, the dead rose up, leaving their coffins: they were exhumed and driven to Shap where they were reburied alongside their ancestors and kinsmen who had gone there the hard way. The village emptied; it was used for target practice by the RAF; it was sunk.

At the edge of the lake, above the high-water mark, I found a wooden cross: 'In Loving Memory of GREG MEWS 6-1-49–15-6-02 Aged 53', put up not far from where the Celtic cross was erected before the old church of St Patrick's was built.

I paced out the length of the old village walls. They were almost too good to be true. Could they really have withstood years, decades, of immersion in the cold, vast draughts of Haweswater? Where the water was too high, the tops of the walls became my stepping-stones.

On the banks of the lake was a lonely hotel. It was familiar; I'd been there once, before I'd ever heard of Mardale, the sunken village. The hotel was under new ownership. John, the owner, bent a rule and let me have a cup of tea – with 'chef's biscuits' – even though afternoon tea was finished. I drank it on the balcony, where I wouldn't be under foot and could look at the lake, the remnants of Mardale. John stomped over to me on his cane. 'I'm running in a new knee,' he said. He was wearing a white Fred Perry tennis shirt and a rakish neckerchief. John was prepared to overlook the house rules about high tea every once in a while. Under the previous management, he said, 'Jagger was here – with the daddy.' But mine host hadn't recognised the Rolling Stones' frontman, let alone his father, and the Jagger party were turned out into the raw Cumbrian evening without so much as a chef's biscuit. 'They'd stopped serving, you see.'

After I'd finished, I thought the least I could do was to take my tea things back to the lobby. On a table inside the front door was a scale model – complete with bell-tower and the finally consecrated graveyard – of St Patrick's, the lost church of Mardale.

11

HELL FIRE AND HAIRPIECES

In a perfect world, this chapter would be quilled by monks in the vigorous couplets of Chaucerian English, and available in limited-edition vellum. For what concerns us in the following pages – alas, of wood pulp! – is a gentil and courtly tale which might have been limned by the bard of the *Canterbury Tales* himself. It features a humble knight of the road, your present reporter; a lady in a great house; and a chivalric quest. It also involves that most romantic and noble feature of the English subterranean, the grotto.

Stancombe Park is metaphorically hidden away in the Cotswolds, but actually marooned in the sylvan Neverland of the English pastoral. A fine eighteenth-century house built of fudge-coloured Gloucestershire stone, it has been claimed as the model of Brideshead in the novel by Evelyn Waugh, who is said to have been a houseguest there in the mid-1940s when he was writing it. On the day of my visit, cattle are grouped under the spreading summer trees and the fields roll away almost to the banks of the Avon. I've been driving for ages, looking for the place: as I descend from the weary steed of a hire car, my lance of curiosity is deckled and unfit for purpose. And yet I must hoist my pike anew and raise my game, for I'm a man on a mission. It's said that a clergyman once lived here, that he created not one but two gardens with the generous dowry that he trousered on his wedding day. First, there was the elegant rose garden where he and his wealthy wife promenaded *en famille*. And there was a second, secret arbour, hidden in a distant fold of the undulating estate, where the cleric erected a grot with passages too tight for his portly spouse to negotiate. Small wonder – in this latter, water-splashing grove, the parson had installed a bewitching gypsy girl as his live-in naiad.

Here is Mrs Barlow to meet me: a slight but elegant woman with a corona of white hair, she is dressed for gardening in slacks and a puffy green gilet. But there is no mistaking the lady of the house. She is originally from Austria but has lived at Stancombe for forty-five years.

'For the grotto, go down there . . . by the deer fence,' she says. She declines to accompany me, blaming bad knees. A less discerning visitor might detect some impatience, even asperity, in Mrs Barlow. But I see a sadness nobly borne, a fair lady who can hardly bring herself to send another doomed paladin off bearing her favours. She knows that I am bound to go down to the grot, in search of the truth about the errant churchman and his bawdy maid, the first of the mysteries of the English subterranean that concern us here. Mrs Barlow tells me that we will take tea together when I return. This is in the nature of a promise – a keepsake or charm that might bring me luck or at least comfort on my lonely way. But if my lady has servants – and why should she not? – I imagine her counselling them, in a soft and sorrowing voice, not to bring out the best service just yet. One look at Mrs Barlow and I know that my gallant errand is in vain. What is a grotto, if not a folly? And how does the dictionary, that puncturer of dreams, define a folly? Why, as a thing of no practical benefit, as a waste of time. And yet I cannot resist. I cannot abandon my chivalrous undertaking. And I'm more than half under the spell of Stancombe already.

The formal gardens are a delight, with their avenues of pollarded trees, their putti disporting themselves around a love-seat. There is an intoxicating atmosphere of reverie, of unreality: it may owe something to ornamental shrubs in the shape of a gorilla and a squirrel, sculpted in Mrs Barlow's own very free hand, apparently out of Fuzzy Felt. Soon I'm following the deer fence as it describes a broad, descending arc of the hillside; it's a flimsy strap plunging the pillowing breast of the estate. There's the soughing of the wind, the tambourining of a bird, the odour of box and fox piss. After several minutes' walk, I reach a weedy pond, a brick arch and Doric columns over a gurgling waterfall. Then something like a pagoda, with a goat's skull – is it? – set in a brick arch. It is all very colourful, in a slightly unnerving way, but where is the underground chamber, where the narrow, wife-excluding tunnels?

In its heyday in the eighteenth century, the grotto was the last word in gracious living, the must-have conversation piece in the well-appointed garden. It was the decking, the water feature, the gas-fired barbie, of the age. It was an amusing variant on the gazebo or summerhouse as a refuge for one's guests on a hot summer's afternoon. They would be refreshed and restored in its cool confines – but also surprised, perhaps even shocked, by the curios on show within. Masons often laboured to achieve parodies of cave decoration. There was even a name for these sham features: pseudostalactites. Mine host might delight his friends with his collection of stones from around the world: in atavistic fashion, men tended to create grottoes underground, out of rock, while the fairer sex favoured sunlit cabins up above, festooned with shells. 'The "male" grottoes contained stark white statues of nymphs or lions, with poetic inscriptions appended, while "female" grottoes often boasted full tea- and coffee-making facilities,' claims the landscape historian Tim Richardson. Either way, the grotto was the plaything of the well-to-do, though there is evidence of a more vernacular origin in a now vanished summertime custom, observed on or about 25 July, when children would make small 'grottoes' out of mud, sticks or wood, and prettify them with oyster shells before begging coins off passers-by. A traditional verse of doubtful scansion, sung to accompany grotto day, was in honour of St James (Sant' Iago) of Compostela:

> Please remember the Grotto,
> It's only once a year,
> Father's gone to sea,
> And Mother's gone to fetch him back,
> So please remember me!
> A penny won't hurt you –
> Tuppence won't put you in the workhouse!

On fashionable estates, grottoes began to appear about the time of the Grand Tour's greatest popularity. For some, the grotto was a throwback; a retreat, in the sense of a conscious recreation of a lost Graeco-Roman idyll. Hence the statuary, and the plashing plumbing. For others, the grotto was a more forward-looking box of tricks. Alexander Pope, a great grottoist as well as an evergreen versifier, installed his under a busy street at Twickenham. It was a practical solution to the problem of accessing his riverside gardens without being flattened by a passing hansom; the poet even had to obtain planning permission. Pope's grotto was as functional, and yet as visionary, as an underpass, the grotto of our own car-centric society, where pearlescent lamps do duty for seashells. 'I have put the last Hand to my works of this kind, in happily finishing the subterraneous Way and Grotto; I there found a Spring of the clearest Water, which falls in a perpetual Rill, that echoes thro' the Cavern day and night.'

It was like something out of the teachings of Plato, the cave in which we dimly apprehend the world without, as Pope explained in a letter to Edward Blount:

When you shut the Doors of this Grotto, it becomes on an instant, from a luminous Room, a Camera obscura; on the Walls of which all the objects of the River, Hills, Woods and Boats, are forming a moving picture of their visible Radiations: And when you have a mind to light it up, it affords you a very different Scene: it is finished with Shells interspersed with Pieces of Looking-glass in angular forms; and in the Ceiling is a Star of the same Material, at which when a Lamp is hung in the Middle, a thousand pointed Rays glitter and are reflected over the Place.

Pope was not impervious to fashion, to the taste for dressing grottoes up as genuine caves. A shooting party was dispatched to Wookey Hole in Somerset, where the fine stalactites on view were culled in a cannonade of grapeshot and lugged back to Twickenham like tusks, to decorate the poet's retreat. Though in some ways his grotto was retro, with a taste for optical illusion which would have gratified the ancients, in other respects it was avant garde, established underground and boasting genuine if poached geological features.

In Mrs Barlow's cobwebby coppice I wander on in search of the grail of the grotto that the Revd David Purnell-Edwards built, indifferent to the hayfever ague that racks me. And then suddenly it's upon me – a bend in the path reveals a dark portal set in the undergrowth. Sure enough, it's none too wide, though on the other hand, you wouldn't have to be a slip of a gypsy girl to pass through. I enter a stooping brick tunnel and come face to face with a great hound, a stone dog couchant, in a rotunda at the centre of a manmade hill. This beast is uncurled at a crossroads, inviting me to select from tunnels at its left and right paws. I make my choice and head right, into another hall or portico with a mirror surrounded by shells.

Purnell-Edwards must have known the Goldney Grotto in Bristol, which is behind a wooden door on a hill above that city – surely all the best enchantments begin this way, with an unremarked wooden door set in a wall. That grotto was created by the Quaker Thomas Goldney III between 1737 and 1764. Young Goldney, scion of one of the merchant families that made Bristol – or the other way round, according to preference – pestered his father's widely travelled business associates for their beachcombings. These abalones and scallops, cowries and conches, duly found their way into Goldney's broad-brush facsimile of Aladdin's cave, where they were 'built out in high relief swags with a wonderfully rococo exuberance', in one justice-doing account. Goldney's phantasmagorical snatch of the Orient included splendid specimens of brain coral, also scrounged from mariners. (It was a ship trading under the Goldney ensign that in 1709 picked up Alexander Selkirk, the real-life Robinson Crusoe, from the uninhabited archipelago of Juan Fernández.)

Other notable English grottoes include the jewel and glory of Margate, which was discovered, or rediscovered, in 1835: 'while workmen were digging on the brow of Dane Hill, Margate, a spade fell from the hands of one of the workmen into what was regarded as a disused well. A boy being lowered into the well to recover the spade got the shock of his life when he found the shell-ornamented Grotto.' It has been claimed by some as the work of 'wanderers from Ancient Crete'. One account argues that 'few of the sight-seers realised that they are walking in the footsteps of travellers who left Mediterranean shores possibly 1,800 years or more before the birth of Christ', but most scholars contend that the grotto is not of genuine antiquity.

Back at Stancombe, the tunnel that I've selected now gives on to a slabbed path, which in turn delivers the visitor to another confluence of routes. It seems a temple has been sited here, marked by a stone ewer on a pedestal. Under a pitched roof, a pharaonic head glowers from its plinth. It wasn't enough for Purnell-Edwards to establish a secure trysting nook for himself and his sylph-like sweetheart – he evidently wanted to show her that their love was at the centre of the universe, by surrounding the pair of them with architectural influences from the great civilisations of Egypt, Greece and China.

There's a further stretch of brick tunnel, in which the priest installed the stirring if redundant feature of an archer's embrasure. I elect to retrace my steps, to stand once more before the marble watchdog. This time, I turn left – and break cover on the banks of a beautiful, dragonfly-skimmed lake. It reflects a perfect, pint-sized Doric temple. A wild boar, petrified in the moment of rearing up to attack or run away, is at the far end of this long water. The July sun is hot, and the humidity of evaporating groundwater makes it sticky in this damp parterre. A curving stone bench beneath the temple is big enough to seat ten – certainly, to accommodate Purnell-Edwards and the ladies in his life, even the stoutest of them – though today I share it with none but the dragonflies, who alight to sun themselves. The vicar had the grounds done to his erotic specifications in 1820, and the hot charge of lust that supposedly rearranged the features of this glen finds a throbbing reverberation in the temple, which has been kitted out as a honeymooners' hide, a place to play away. It was restored by English Heritage in 1996 and is available to rent. Is this where my virtuous trek must peter out in bathos, I wonder, with me peeping through the windows of this caravan of love at the admittedly well-proportioned nude on a wall, at the tray of drinks with a single red rose in what appears to be a shared toothmug?

I climb the three-quarters of a mile back to the house, transported by the faery dells of Stancombe, and yet overtaken by an obscure sense of despondency, of failure. As the honey-coloured colonnades come into view once more, there is no sign of Mrs Barlow. My eye is taken by another stone dog – a lapdog this time, in the shadow of a tree, marking the resting-place of a beloved pet – and when I look back again, Mrs Barlow is at the balustrade in dark glasses, filling a barrow with clippings.

She apologises for her gardens. 'They are not at their best. The staff are on holiday, you see.' She's pleased when I insist that on the contrary, all is splendid. She intends to honour her pledge of afternoon tea: 'Please wait in the garage.'

'Oh it was a love nest!' Mrs Barlow – 'Gerda' – is pouring from a large, slightly foxed, china teapot. The temple on the lake was a love shack, but not one patronised by the Revd Purnell-Edwards and his hot-eyed Romany, it seems. 'No. This man was too steady.'

I munch my Digestive in the garage. I imagine the late Mr B. stabling his motors in this whitewashed lean-to: a Rolls perhaps, maybe a shooting-brake. A racy little MG? My valiant cause has come to nothing; or rather it has missed its mark. The true love story was right in front of me, all along.

I ask Mrs Barlow if she could have imagined, as a girl growing up in Austria during the war, that she'd end up in a place like this. She makes a gesture of weighing up – literally, on the one hand, on the other – between her two beaux: the Englishman who won her and another, failed suitor, perhaps a hometown hopeful.

'Well, you made the right choice, then,' I say, or ask.

'I've been very happy here,' she replies, not quite looking at me. She had a happy marriage, she said, as much as to say, 'Well, *that* was lucky', which I suppose it was.

Her husband was a Lloyd's underwriter. In response to my musings about the saloons which had once occupied the garage, Mrs Barlow confirmed that he'd driven a Rolls. She herself had a convertible Bentley. 'But we gave them up. The roads around here are too narrow.' There was a sense of a thankful release, perhaps after her husband's death, from an attachment to appearances. 'In those days, driving a top car . . .' She doesn't quite finish.

'But it doesn't really matter,' I say, catching her mood, or hoping to.

'Of course not.' She now ran a thrifty Audi.

Evelyn Waugh used to write down at the love nest, says Mrs Barlow. He often stayed at the house, though this was before her time. He was a guest of the Creighton-Smiths, from whom Gerda and her husband bought Stancombe.

'He was a bit, you know—' Mrs Barlow sniffs the air.

'Snobby?'

'Snobby, yes. So he was happy to stay here.'

A belief held locally was that the memorable opening scene of *Brideshead Revisited* was based on the park. We agree what a great writer Waugh was. 'Oh that book! I love it,' says Mrs Barlow.

It's all a lovely dream, of course, no more substantial than Mrs Barlow's cloud-like topiary. Waugh lived nearby in Gloucestershire, it's true, but at Stinchcombe rather than Stancombe. And the real model of Brideshead has been claimed as Madresfield, a pile in Worcestershire.

Mrs Barlow offers a surprisingly firm, if bony, handshake. She won't have her picture taken ('I *do* mind'). She's anxious to let her dog out into the gardens – a large dog, I gather. 'A Rhodesian ridgeback,' I think she says. 'He can be rather overwhelming!' A knight-errant schooled enough in valour to know what the better part of it is, I bolt for the car.

For perhaps too long, I fear, I've stood aside and kept my counsel while historians have overlooked the connection between Sir Francis Dashwood (1708–81), the man responsible for the infamous Hell Fire Caves in Buckinghamshire, and the comedian Frankie Howerd. One was a camp joker, the other a master of ceremonies at dubious, historically themed revels. Ah yes; but which was which? There's the rub!

At one time, I must admit, I myself looked no further than the most glaring of parallels between the pair. That's right: Dashwood's anything-goes clubroom was concealed beneath the forgiving sod of his country estate, as was Howerd's wig, at his own. Oh yes, and the two men shared a Christian name. But dig a little deeper, as the self-respecting moler must, and you discover that the one whose life's work was nothing if not hair-raising, and the one whose legacy lay in quite the opposite direction, would have found each other simpatico in a thoroughly unexpected way. Not only that, but both are bound up in knotty puzzles to do with underground England.

Outside Howerd's bedroom window, hailstones the size of macaroons ricocheted off classical statuary. Beyond the hoary sward, beyond the fig tree which was reputedly reared from a sprig taken from Sir Winston Churchill's garden, loured the darkling Mendips. 'I can still see him out there, on one of his walks,' said Chris Byrne, fondly stroking the houndstooth topcoat which the late comedian had favoured on his constitutionals. 'People would see him marching up the lane with a sheaf of paper and a walking stick. He was learning his lines. What they didn't know was that the walking stick was hollow: he used to pop into the pub and get them to fill it with gin.'

Howerd died in 1992, but his shambolic presence still haunted his old country seat in Somerset in 2006, where Byrne was living as carer to the entertainer's elderly and reclusive former partner, Dennis Heymer. Wavering Down, the comic's very Franciscan-sounding pile, was preserved just as it was when he left it. It was utterly pickled, in fact, and I use the term advisedly. Byrne was candid enough to admit that the place was left untouched while he was battling alcoholism. But then he woke up one morning and realised that he and Dennis were sitting on a showbusiness treasure trove. They had the idea of opening the house and grounds to the public, with all proceeds going to charity. An entirely sober Byrne placed one of the more unlikely telephone calls to be taken that year in the offices of *Newsnight*: 'Would you like to be the first reporter to see inside Frankie Howerd's cottage?' he asked.

It was small wonder that he had struggled with drink. Life chez Howerd had been a bibulous one. As a titular signifier, Wavering Down was an address that gave Dunroamin and Ersanmine a run for their money. After a hard day's filming, it was Frankie's custom to lay his hand on the Bible in the hallway, mutter a word of thanks to the Almighty for sparing him from the Labour Exchange for another day, and help himself to a generous tot of Gordon's. Not for Frankie any old optic. His shot of mother's ruin ran from a mannequin of an old drunk naked but for the rain barrel he was hiding in: best not to ask where the spout was. The comedienne June Whitfield, once a regular houseguest, recounted that she would often see Frankie knocking back several doubles before an evening out, though it was his practice to abstain for the rest of the night.

The critic Kenneth Tynan, an admirer of Howerd, called him 'the subtlest clod', and a sense of teetering chaos was present in the fixtures and fittings of his home, which was put on the market in 2008. Publicity stills of the young Richard Burton, of Frankie kissing Liz and Frankie squeezing Elton, jostled for space on the unkept-up cottage walls with warm wishes from cardinals on Vatican notepaper and Ancient Egyptian arcana. The latter knick-knacks and gewgaws attested to Howerd's triumphs in classical roles – who can forget his Lurcio in *Up Pompeii*? – but they also reflected the belief shared by the comic and Heymer that they had trodden the sands of antiquity together in another life.

In the country, Howerd enjoyed rambunctious sets of tennis, a game at which he would have worsted John McEnroe himself for racket-battering peevishness. In a quieter frame of mind, he would steal alone into the parish church, a favourite, resonant spot for mastering those apparently ramshackle routines. He went to his reward beneath the churchyard at Weare. But he didn't make the final journey intact, it transpired. There was the ticklish question of Frankie's effects, specifically the most ticklish of all: the Howerd hairpiece. It was claimed that when he went to a better place, the rug went somewhere else again.

Howerd was never seen in public without his counterpane, though he inadvertently wore it at a jaunty angle from time to time. 'He used to scratch the back of his head when he was talking to you sometimes,' said the distinguished gagsmith Barry Cryer, 'and the hairpiece would go up and down like a pedal bin.' June Whitfield recalled working with the comedian on one of his earliest television shows. She was playing the part of his date, who became amorous and planted a kiss on her reluctant swain. As she took him in a passionate headlock during rehearsal, he cried, 'Would you mind putting your hands a little lower, please?' June said. 'He was obviously worried about his toupee coming off. I'm afraid it hadn't occurred to me.'

The posthumous fate of this confection of gum, matting and horsehair was shrouded in as much intrigue as if it were a hank off the top of a saint. One account, published in a national newspaper, discounted the legend of the stray syrup out of hand, and insisted on the contrary that the late funnyman was impeccably caparisoned when he met his Maker. The paper went on to make the outlandish claim that the 'wig has been exhumed', adding that this would furnish Frankie's old seat with a rare attraction for visitors. Another version, which bore the unarguable imprimatur of the Catholic Church, told of a clandestine coiffeurial burial in the grounds of Wavering Down: a corner of this field would indeed be forever Frankie. But Father Peter Slocombe, in his newsletter to the Clifton diocese, spoke not of one weave but rather of several. Chris Byrne, a Catholic who attended mass at nearby Cheddar, had been at the good father's right hand as he composed his lively write-up. And yet it had been Chris Byrne himself who was also the source of the article in the *Daily Bugle*. The tenant of Wavering Down certainly knew how to tell a good yarn. And I heard yet another rendering of it from his own lips: there was a plurality of pelts – a veritable dreamcoat of equine clippings – and some form of hirsute interment had occurred, he swore, somewhere within sight of the hail-darkened window before us. But it was later undone, he said, it was later reversed . . .

Byrne steered me towards a sideboard. The eye raked over more trinkets and keepsakes of the showbiz life, the *objets* and mementoes of an English bachelor of a certain era and disposition: a postcard of the pyramids, a teapot, a pair of— A *what*? A *teapot*? And what was on it? A strangely shaggy cosy. On second thoughts, you wouldn't want to say that it was *on* the teapot so much as clinging tenaciously to it. Byrne smiled reassuringly as he took my hand, guiding my now-unfeeling fingers. With a lurch – in equal parts, glee and horror – I realised what I was looking at, what I was limply stroking . . . 'It was Bette Davis's idea,' I heard Byrne's voice saying, as if from far away. 'It was her tip to Frankie. The steam kept it in shape, you see.'

Dissolve . . . to the sound of water dripping, I'm now probing something coarse, more granular. The chalk wall of the Hell Fire Caves is wet to the touch. There's a filigree of grey in it, but wherever I come across a seam and press an enquiring finger to it, it vanishes: the face is restored to pristine boniness. Howerd's faithful retinue apparently committed his hairpiece, or hairpieces, to the Somerset loam, then dug them up again and revived them with the softening caress of water vapour from a teapot. Here at West Wycombe, playground of the Hell Fire Club founded by Francis Dashwood in the late 1720s, they've known intrigues of their own involving body parts. Is that a skull I see before me, or merely a trick of the half-light as it strikes the calcium carbonate of the caves?

Suddenly, I'm buttonholed out of the gloom by Paul Whitehead, or at least by a marooned mannequin of the poor fellow. He was a minor poet who became steward of Dashwood's society, as his taped testimonial records. The club's cellar book survives, presumably written up in Whitehead's hand, though a graphologist who consulted this scored and spidery ledger could be forgiven for thinking that here was Jack the Ripper's (Bridget Jones's-style) diary of his tippling ('3 bottles claret; 1 murder . . . v. bad!'). Before Whitehead died in 1774, he cast about for a suitable farewell gift for his patron, 'a token of his warm attachment to the noble founder'. In the end, he left his heart to Sir Francis. This extraordinary deposition, eerily anticipating in several particulars the crooner Tony Bennett's signature hit some two centuries later, was complete when Whitehead endowed an urn in which his organ might reside. It was duly placed in this heart-shaped pot, which was itself installed in a mausoleum. But the cardiac crockery was disturbed, the heart went missing, and a shade of Whitehead even more insubstantial than his troglodyte likeness is said to traipse Wycombe to this day, looking for his lost lights.

Nor are corporeal tribulations confined to the afterlife in this part of the world. The parish priest of Dashwood's seat, a Father Allen, said of the caves, 'My tummy wobbles like a jelly every time I pass the entrance.' Perhaps it was the flint façade of the entry-way that gave him the collywobbles, with its incongruous suggestion of the Gothic arch of a church, though this is now largely hidden behind a café. The entrance is but a dim memory to me now; still, I know what the good parson meant. If I'm honest, I can never enter an earth in a hillside like this one without a catch in the throat. It's by no means an unpleasant sensation, though it would be nothing without a presentiment of danger. In the Hell Fire Caves, I put my finger on it at last: it's the fear of being buried alive.

And though it's surely all in the mind, I do sense an atmosphere, an oppressive aura, in these clammy tunnels. Television's *Most Haunted*, that unbending lightning-rod of supernatural activity, sensed it, detecting 'orbs of light' and an ethereal female in a dress, perhaps the wraith of a jilted bride who had been lured into the caves on a false promise of marriage. In the recent past, a handyman was spooked by a fall of chalk and gave notice.

Legend has it that when the caves were quarried out in the eighteenth century, it was in order to indulge the occult inclinations of Dashwood and his freemasonry of well-connected oddfellows. The Hell Fire Club, otherwise known as the Knights of St Francis of Wycombe, would proceed to chambers at the heart of the escarpment, in the very direction that I'm going, and there they would punish the grape as well as hand-picked doxies, rounding off the night with a little high-spirited blasphemy. Dashwood, later Lord le Despencer, was for a short time (1762–3) Chancellor of the Exchequer, and his fifty or so Club confrères included MPs, the Lord Mayor of London, military top brass and the son of the Archbishop of Canterbury. You'd be hard pressed to find movers and shakers who lived up to the name quite as energetically as did this crew. David Mellor, the one-time Tory Cabinet minister and sports columnist, is distantly linked by marriage to this set: his wife, Viscountess Cobham, was formerly spliced to a scion of Lord Lyttelton of the Hell Fire.

'The exploits of the Hell Fire Club are still notorious today,' writes Nigel Pennick in *Subterranean Kingdom*. 'The object of the society was to hold sensual orgies in the spirit of the Gothic delight in medievalism,' says Jeremy Errand in *Secret Passages and Hiding Places*. In *Subterranean Britain* Barbara Jones goes on, 'Many follies or groups of follies are famous . . . but the most famous of them all, at West Wycombe in Buckinghamshire, is a most entertaining group of assorted follies, with over everything the glamorous spell of the legends of the Hell Fire Club and its assorted sins.'

Perhaps it's the thought of Frankie Howerd's much travelled thatch, of Whitehead's missing ticker and the Revd Allen's quivering belly, perhaps even of the fleshly recreations which took place long ago in this hillside; but as I wind deeper into it, I find that the caves themselves take on the aspect of internal organs, of one great body, primed and prepped for gratification. The showpiece inner cave, Dashwood's cone-shaped 'Banqueting Hall', is itself an unconscious recreation of the human stomach. From its apex, the walls fall perhaps fifty feet to a rounded base, and they run with water like the inspissating secretions of a giant gut. What unconscionable appetites were sated here?

The house rules allowed every member to introduce 'a lady of cheerful lively disposition to improve the general hilarity'. Assuming the costume of a holy fraternity, the men were dressed all in white. Their companions were masked, to avoid any embarrassment in the event of spouses unexpectedly running into one another. Part of the frisson for Dashwood and his set was in concealment, in seeing without being seen: in a word, they liked to look. And the visitor is himself observed, viz. by the blank eyes of a furry-looking goddess, a statue that is peeping through the metal bars of a cell, a private room. However, the image that really caught the sensibility of the Hell Fire Club to a tee was a 'very grotesque figure', as described by John Wilkes, who was a noted social reformer by day and an improbable mainstay of the diabolical gang when night fell. Evidently, it wasn't the proportions of the effigy that had preoccupied the sculptor, so much as its portion. Over to Wilkes: 'In his hand a reed stood flaming, tip't with fire, to use Milton's words; and you might trace out *Peni Tento non Penitenti* . . .' The tag translates as 'a stiff penis, not contrition'.

Here, I think, we circle the nub of the question, if you'll allow me. Are we really dealing with horned satyrs, with dastardly devil-worshippers, or rather with a bunch of naughty schoolboys? Unquestionably, Dashwood was a man who enjoyed a full life. His family motto was *Pro Magna Carta* – the concept of liberty in all things – and this found expression even in the gardens he laid out at West Wycombe. Tim Richardson notes that his Temple of Venus, a rotunda on a knoll, only begins to make sense when you look at it from the viewpoint of a hardened roué, so to speak. 'It dawns on you that this is an evocation of female anatomy . . . the two "legs" that are the curved flanks of the entrance doorway . . . the mound (*mons veneris*), the oval-shaped entrance to Venus's parlour' – yes, well, we get the picture, I think. But for Richardson, Dashwood 'was not some Priapus of South Bucks, or the precursor of "black magician" Aleister Crowley, which some commentators have turned him into'.

On the contrary, Dashwood was more Bertie Wooster than Dennis Wheatley. You could call him clubbable, except that that wouldn't begin to do justice to his passion for get-togethers, his ardour for brotherhoods and lodges, his *rage* for fellowship. A keen traveller in his youth, he was the veteran of no fewer than six Grand Tours, and put his experience overseas to good effect – well, to effect, anyway – in the founding of associations devoted to ever more self-indulgent and skittish pursuits, of which the Hell Fire Club was merely the best known and most horse-frightening. The Dilettanti Society was a dining club dedicated to promoting the love of art. That at least was the official mission statement, though Horace Walpole said of the group that 'the nominal qualification is having been in Italy and the real one being drunk; the two chiefs are Lord Middlesex and Sir Francis Dashwood, who were seldom sober the whole time they were in Italy'. Members were required to have their portraits done, and Dashwood was seen as a monk, 'San Francisco di Wycombo', raising a foaming beaker to a naked Venus. The president of the

Dilettanti attended meetings in a Roman toga and matching crimson gown; by comparison, the secretary was a wallflower, obliged to turn up dressed as no one more eye-catching than Machiavelli. According to the splendidly bufferish memoirs of the 11th Baronet, a man who in the twentieth century did much to restore Sir Francis's seat, including the Hell Fire Caves themselves, the Dilettanti meet to this day, and the present Prince of Wales is an honorary member. 'The officers still wear their traditional elaborate dress, but only for the election of new members. On such occasions the original quixotic and amusing ritual – no doubt it was thought up by Sir Francis himself – is still observed and remains a secret.'

After Dashwood toured the Ottoman Empire by boat, he inaugurated the Divan Club, open to 'none but such as can prove that they have been in the Sultan's Dominions'. This time he appeared in oils as 'Il Faquir Dashwood Pasha' in a blouson of gold brocade, thickly medalled with gemstones, the ensemble set off by a cloak trimmed with ermine and a jewelled turban. Also committed to canvas was Fanny Murray, a noted strumpet. 'There is no record of what transpired at the meetings,' writes the 11th Baronet, 'but Fanny Murray is shown in the painting with one bare bosom and a nipple – surely a pun on the word "sultana" – and it is unlikely that the activities were wholly intellectual.'

The Lincoln Club grazed and swilled in that low-lying city, in clubrooms at the base of the Dunston Pillar, a 92-foot column, 'the only land lighthouse ever raised', which Dashwood erected to guide travellers across his trackless estates. Its great lantern remained lit until 1788; it fell to the ground in 1809 and was replaced by a marble statue of George III which was itself felled in 1939 as a service to low-flying aircraft. When he wasn't launching his own societies, Dashwood was at the Beefsteak or White's, where he recruited members of the Hell Fire Club from the ranks of the great and the good. They held early meetings in the discreet banquettes of the George and Vulture pub in the City. But it was at a ruined monastery on the banks of the Thames that this abbot-aping crew began to get well and truly Cistercianed. Indeed, many of the antics which supposedly took place in the caves actually occurred at Medmenham Abbey instead. A tag from Rabelais – 'Fay ce que voudras' (Do as you wish) – was chiselled into the lintel, and this served as the motto of the unfrocked order.

But deep in the Wycombe hillside, I still don't fully appreciate the club's creed until I cross a dry riverbed – 'the River Styx' – and penetrate to the furthest recess of the caves. I am three hundred feet underground, and half a mile from daylight. I'm touching bottom now, as Sir Francis might have it – Sir Francis Howerd, I mean. Here, in the Inner Temple, Dashwood and his cronies cavort in wax with a stuffed mandrill, forever regaling us, and themselves, with their most celebrated caper. On the eve of one meeting, Wilkes secreted this baboon on the premises, dressed it in 'phantastic garb, in which childish imagination cloths devils' and hid it in a chest. He attached a string to the chest's handle, and ran it under the carpet to his accustomed chair. At the height of the fun and games the next night, Wilkes tugged on the cord, the beast sprang from its box, and it piggy-backed on to an appalled Lord Sandwich, who thought that a sprite had come to claim him for that other Underworld. Sandwich shrieked and wriggled, but the greater the struggle put up by the inventor of the working lunch, the more determined the simian straddling. His lordship somehow found the breath to gasp, 'Spare me gracious Devil: spare a wretch who never was sincerely your servant. I sinned only from vanity of being in fashion; thou knowest I never have been half so wicked as I pretended: never have I been able to commit the thousandth part of the vices which I have boasted of!'

This, surely, was the *cri de coeur* of the whole sorry sodality. They weren't really wicked, they were just playing at it. It was merely the in-thing, like the caves themselves. As Barbara Jones says, 'In the eighteenth century, tunnelling became fashionable for those who not only desired but could afford it as a last sublime touch to the landscape park.' For sublime, read saturnalian. The Hell Fire Club liked to get together in the caves for a little roistering, and ginger it up with a demoniacal theme, as we have seen. But if push came to shove, they could get by with just the getting together and the roistering.

For Dashwood, the real sport lay in guying the religious establishment. The monkish habits affected by his society were in the nature of an advertisement rather than a disguise: anyone taking the road to Wycombe would have been able to see their chalky figures. The colour-coordinated caves to which they processed were in full view of the highway. (Without the caves, there would have been no road from which to look back at them, incidentally: they supplied the aggregate for the thoroughfare.) Furthermore, Dashwood had form as a scourge of Church authority. During a visit to the Sistine Chapel as a young man, he had been amused to see pilgrims belabouring themselves with whips. It was a ritualistic ceremony only; the whips were small and harmless – the adepts might as well have been flagellating themselves with fly-whisks. Showing a precocious taste for masquerade, among other things, Dashwood got himself gussied up as a Vatican guard, joined the congregation – then 'suddenly from under his cloak he drew out a stout horsewhip and cracked it up and down the aisle,' writes his scion. 'In the dim candlelight, the poor penitents thought the Devil himself had appeared', a prank which antedated the predicament of poor Sandwich, saddled with a monkey-jockey in its satanic silks.

The Hell Fire Club 'was more than anything else a satire on organised religion', according to Richardson. 'This faux brotherhood of monks living what was probably a "virtual" immoral life reflected Dashwood's own deep suspicion of the established Church and the hypocritical cant associated with it, not in a spirit of atheism but of deistic belief.' Somewhat surprisingly, his lordship had collaborated with his friend Benjamin Franklin on the publication of the latter's noted prayer book, and in the 1770s had also helped to build one of the first Unitarian chapels in London, 'so perhaps, paradoxically, there was a serious moral intent to the club'.

In truth, *épater les bourgeois* was Dashwood's thing, or it would have been if there had been many *bourgeois* around in his day. He enjoyed cocking a snook at society, though as we've seen, a snook was the least of it. In this, as in much else, Dashwood was the kinsman of the other, *soi-disant* Sir Francis, the squire of Wavering Down. After all, what were Howerd's gin-filled shooting-stick, his ribald read-throughs in the nave, the heathen interring of a toupee or two, if not his own little acts of devilment carried out under the noses of his conservative Somerset neighbours?

On the hill above the Hell Fire Caves is the mausoleum in which poor Paul Whitehead reposed his trust as well as his heart: both, alas, misplaced. The sepulchre is grand but also ugly: the National Trust's own guidebook to West Wycombe, pressing a lavender-soused handkerchief to its pulse points, calls it 'eccentric, somewhat nightmarish'. It was built hexagonal, *sans* roof, to no clear architectural template. Curling at the edges, in a drawer somewhere, is a receipt proving that the mausoleum was erected in 1764–5 by the reliable family firm of John Bastard the Younger (not thought to be the historical template of Bob the Builder). Dashwood's wife Sarah is buried there, and he himself is remembered by a plaque in the columbarium. Whitehead's much shrivelled bequest, said to be 'about the size of a walnut', was purloined by an Australian soldier in 1829.

Overlooking all things is a Norman church, surmounted by Sir Francis's Golden Ball, a phrase Howerd himself would have savoured. I clattered up the wormy steps to the church tower where Dashwood installed this gilded heliograph, eight feet in diameter, in order to signal to his friend John Norris. A fellow member of the Knights of St Francis, Norris lived thirty-four miles away, at Camberley in Surrey, where he had raised a matching orb of his own. When Dashwood was not in his underground nerve centre, he was patrolling the gargoyled steeple. Like a prototype James Bond villain, he struck fear and awe into the populace with his graven replica of the sun, harnessing the rays of the true star for his terrible purposes: to marshal his chums for sessions of the Hell Fire Club.

12

ROYAL SHAFTINGS

Dashwood's descendant, the 11th Baronet, came to the conclusion that his ancestor originally had the caves dug out as make-work projects, to relieve high levels of rural unemployment. The same has been said of some mysterious caverns in the North West of England. The Williamson Tunnels were excavated in Liverpool after Dashwood's were dug, and are their only serious rival for the title of the most unfathomable passages in all England. They have been called the largest underground folly in the country. Nobody knows for sure why Joseph Williamson created them. Reclusive to the point of agoraphobic – he was as insular as Dashwood was expansive – Williamson didn't care to ventilate his reasons and left no written explanation, not so much as a diary or a map. The idea of a Keynesian job creation scheme is based on one of his rare public utterances, but there has also been speculation that the tunnels were really tied up with the lucrative smuggling operation that was roaring away across the water in Wallasey at this time; even that Williamson was an end-of-the-worlder, digging out his last bolthole as another man might one day pound Oxford Street beneath the yoke of his eschatological sandwich-board. Nor can anyone claim to know for sure the true extent of the tunnels. Many of them have filled up with rubble, and not even the sophisticated soundings of a microgravity survey have resolved the matter.

The story of the tunnels is full of drama. Williamson's crew once pickaxed their way through rock and earth to come face to disbelieving face with navvies who were quarrying out a railway line for Robert Stephenson. Even today, more than 150 years after Williamson's death, his tunnels are still the scene of incident and controversy. According to my sources in the city, they're at the centre of a battle for precedence between rival groups of friends and supporters which could scarcely be less amicable if they were squaring up to one another in hobnails and shirtsleeves.

Williamson arrived on Merseyside in 1780 at the age of eleven, a year before Dashwood's death. Unlike the burrowing baronet, he had no inherited wealth to fritter: it's said that he had less than half a crown in his pocket. But he found work in the tobacco-importing business, later married the boss's daughter, and became one of the most prosperous men in town – though you might never have guessed it to look at him. He favoured corduroy breeches, a patched brown coat and a well-worn black beaver top-hat, 'a shocking bad one'. His shoes were 'black and slovenly'.

Williamson was comfortable enough to retire at fifty, and spent the next thirty-five years earning and then burnishing the nickname of 'the Mole of Edge Hill'. That quarter of Liverpool is just to the east of the centre, and only a few hundred yards from where the Roman Catholic Cathedral stands today, though in the early decades of the nineteenth century it was practically the countryside. Williamson began by extending his own cellar under Mason Street, before turning his attentions to the foundations of other properties in the environs. Liverpudlians who had fought in the Napoleonic Wars came home to unemployment, but Williamson intervened. He didn't so much rescue these men from the scrap heap, as set them to work on one of his own. The King of Edge Hill, as he was also known, is said to have paid men to dig holes and then fill them in again, to shift rocks from one place to another, and back to where they came from. At this time, he was still participating in public life, with a seat on the Poor Aid Committee. Perhaps mindful of his own humble beginnings, he was irritated by what he saw as the humbug of his colleagues on the subject of their charitable activities. On one occasion he leapt to his feet and demanded, 'How many of you employ labourers?' before taking the committee on a tour of his philanthropic, if otherwise pointless, works.

In time, Williamson bought out all his neighbours, making ad hoc alterations to their former homes or simply tearing them down. And if his ever-expanding bunker became more and more idiosyncratic in appearance from the outside, try to conceive of what was going on within. Perhaps because of a window tax which was then in force, by one account Williamson saw to it that several houses were left without a single pane – 'and therefore dark and uncanny'. Like the most reckless jerrybuilder working within the most benign and light-touch of regulatory environments – which, come to think of it, is exactly what he was – Williamson constructed interconnecting walkways between some of his houses, while haphazardly bypassing others. A long passage ran from one town house through others with which it did *not* communicate, to a sealed-off suite of rooms in another address entirely.

Williamson's original home was one of several with as many as half a dozen floors of cellars hollowed out of the sandstone beneath them. There were 'strange gulfs, arches over arches and passages innumerable', according to one contemporaneous source. If Dashwood's excavations evoke the organs of the body,

Williamson's suggest the pathways of the mind; a florid and untrammelled mind, at that. These tasks were undertaken entirely for the inscrutable ends of the man who was paying for them all; the edification was all Williamson's. Seldom was anyone else allowed to wander through the Edge Hill labyrinth.

But all these years after it was hollowed out, it was my plan to do exactly that, and coming along with me would be my old friend Gerry the Green Badge guide, my helpmeet and companion in New Brighton. The story of the Williamson Tunnels was bound up in the history of the railways in Liverpool – and the rest of the world, too, come to that – so it was no bad thing to have my favourite trainspotter at my right hand.

En route to the tunnels, Gerry proposed a congenial digression to the grave of the first man to be killed by a train. 'It happened right here in Liverpool,' he said. 'They can't take that away from us.'

In fact, the death occurred on the very line that Williamson and his crazy gang had stumbled upon. The unfortunate man was William Huskisson, MP for Liverpool, and he was buried in the shadow of the city's Anglican Cathedral. This hulking house of worship was designed by Giles Gilbert Scott, who also created the much loved, pee-scented red telephone box. Gerry said, 'Scott himself is buried right here, you know, in the driveway. He was a Catholic, you see, so he couldn't go inside.'

Treading softly on Giles Gilbert Scott, Gerry and I went to find Huskisson. He lies in a cemetery which pre-dates the cathedral, being attached to an old parish church, St James's. The graveyard was itself installed on the site of a former sandstone quarry, which provided the raw material for Liverpool Town Hall and a number of the city's churches. The Elysian Field is gained by means of a delicious short tunnel which runs down a steep slope at the foot of the cathedral. This feature is marked as a 'natural arch' on Ordnance Survey maps, but the nicks and grooves of quarrymen's utensils in the roof and the walls give the lie to this. The tunnel is twenty yards long, three or four yards high, and its sharp declension follows the bedding planes of the rock.

Huskisson died in 1830. He was struck by a train undergoing a trial run on Robert Stephenson's Liverpool and Manchester line. It was the first railway anywhere in the world – no thanks to Joseph Williamson, who had inadvertently done his best to hold the whole thing up. On the day of the fatal accident, there were two trains running parallel to each other, perhaps not at very great speed, when Huskisson hopped off one of them in order to ask Stephenson a question. The other train ran over his legs. They were amputated on the spot. An emergency run down the line to a hospital was improvised. 'They broke the land speed record that day,' said Gerry, 'I don't know what it was, but when you think about it, it must have been a new record.' Alas, the wretched Huskisson could not be saved.

The old mercantile citadels of the North of England all have their flamboyant tombs, and Liverpool is no exception. At St Andrew's Presbyterian Kirk in the city centre, for example, is the pleasing, sooty sight of a pyramid said to be the final resting-place of a gambler named Mackenzie. The story goes that this inveterate chancer made a pact with the Devil during a particularly high-stakes card game that was in danger of getting away from him: if Old Nick helped him to scoop the pool, then he could have his soul once he was in the ground. The gambler duly won the game, but when it came to keeping his side of the bargain, he had other ideas. He had the pyramid built for himself – and there he reposes upon a chair, having staked his very soul on one last bet, that the Devil cannot claim it so long as he remains *on* terra firma, as opposed to in it. This story has its echoes in other parts of the country, including Brightling in Sussex, where a wealthy landowner and MP, Gerry 'Mad Jack' Fuller, left orders that he was to be mummified and immured in a pyramidal tomb on his death, which took place in 1834.

Dressed in a top-hat and surrounded by bottles of claret, Mad Jack had the floor of his tomb sprinkled with shards of broken glass, to slice at the Devil's cloven hoofs if he should ever come to claim him.

As well as early railway casualties, St James's cemetery holds sea captains who perished on voyages and were buried in Liverpool after their vessels gained the port, and infants who succumbed in orphanages and workhouses. A stream that rises underground in the city emerges in the cemetery. It flows from a slot in the wall beneath a weathered inscription which once read:

> Christian reader view in me
> An emblem of true charity
> Who freely what I have bestow
> Though neither heard, nor seen to flow
> And I have full returns from heaven
> For every cup of water given.

There was a leaf tucked into this aperture; it was acting as a kind of spout. Gerry made the singular observation that he always found a leaf in the slot whenever he led a walk through the cemetery. 'Someone must put it there.' He bowed before the stream and drank. 'It's sweet,' he said. I followed him: the spring water was indeed light, tangy. I thought of the illustration on tins of Tate & Lyle Golden Syrup, the mangy old lion breathing its last, the circling bees and the slogan: 'Out of the strong came forth sweetness.'

From Lime Street Station, Gerry and I caught the train to Williamson's old manor of Edge Hill. 'Edge Hill is the oldest working railway station in the world,' said Gerry as we chugged through the chasm of the Lime Street tunnel. 'It opened in 1835. All the others have either been moved or renamed.' The way the railway worked in the early days was that trains from

Manchester to Liverpool had to stop and decouple from their locomotives at Edge Hill, before being lowered down a slope by cable to their final destination at Lime Street. They came back the same way, all by means of an 'endless rope' made of hemp. In the half-light, I could discern Gerry's familiar expression of beatified calm. '"Getting off at Edge Hill" used to be Liverpool slang for coitus interruptus, you know,' he said.

From a bridge on Gladstone Drive – 'It used to be Gladstone Road but now it's been gentrified' – Gerry and I were able to look out across some of Liverpool's pioneering railway works. But only after Gerry had been round knocking on a few doors for a set of steps. He had a regular contact, he explained, but there was no reply from this man's house. Hanging over the side of the old redbrick bridge, we could watch repairs taking place on an almost identical one a hundred yards or so down the line. A short time later, I brought up the matter of the steps with Gerry, saying 'We got the ladder—', only for him to finesse the point by saying, 'We *sourced* the ladder first', as though he was talking about a range of ostrich-burgers.

The Williamson Tunnels had been opened by the Friends of the Tunnels; or better to say, some of them had been opened, by some of the Friends. As I indicated above, all was less than cordial where the amigos were concerned. Independently of one another, two groups of people had pledged to do their best by the tunnels, but they didn't quite see eye to eye, for reasons almost as historically opaque as Williamson's cryptic motives themselves. Into this combustible mix I now unknowingly introduced the sceptical Gerry – it was his scepticism I didn't know about – who politely but unbudgeably declined to tour the tunnels and sat over a cup of tea in the café instead, though with no apparent loss of his almost transcendent equanimity.

Without Gerry at my side, I was thrown back on an admirable lady from the Friends; so far as anyone could, she led me in Williamson's unknowable if 'slovenly' footsteps. An early account of the tunnels, by a man called James Stonehouse, shed some light on the Mole Man's methods. Comparing what he saw with Edinburgh and even Petra, Stonehouse said that Williamson's war veterans and other labourers – their numbers ran into the hundreds if not thousands – had scooped out the sandstone on which Edge Hill stood and replaced it with piers of brick or stone, to support the roofs of their various digs. At one time, whole terraces of gardens rested on these plinths. There was a double tunnel, with one arch on top of another; even a triple-decker tunnel. Down in his labyrinth, Williamson was an unlikely Minotaur, capable of prodigious feats but entirely unguessable and unrestrained.

His upside-down estate penetrated so far into the Liverpool substrata that it was said that one four-bedroomed house stood on top of another. There was a large arched vault 'in which two carts could pass side by side' and a coal hole with a capacity of two hundred tons. At odd intervals, this sunken city was illuminated by pools of light from vertical shafts descending from the streets above. The southern perimeter of the complex, Smithdown Lane, was characterised by its ruined appearance and falls of rubble, a condition in which it has languished to this day. Stonehouse documented 'tunnels cut out of the living rock, pits deep . . . wherein the fetid stagnant water throws up miasmic odours, arches of weighty and solid structure, stable almost as the earth itself. Tiers of passages are met with, as dangerous to enter as they are strange to look upon.' Once, a woman drowned in a crater that had filled with water. Much later, a lorry reportedly disappeared into a hole in Smithdown Lane. It was never seen again.

My guide and I saw what Stonehouse had seen: the canyons and gulches of Williamson's world. We forded its ravines, negotiated the outlandish cacti of its sandstone excrescences – and all the while, we were walking through the termite-ravaged Sierra Madre of a man's mental landscape. Williamson's wife died in 1822, while his underground empire was still quite modest. 'I was sorry to part with the old girl when she did go,' he remarked. The couple had supposedly worshipped together at St Mary's, Edge Hill – naturally, they went to church through a tunnel from their back garden, or so it was said – though some have speculated that they belonged to a religious cult which anticipated the end of the world, and dug the tunnels as a place to shelter from the fire and brimstone until the moment of their salvation. At any rate, without his wife around, Williamson rather let the place go. It was said that his bedchamber was 'like a den for a wild beast'. Casks of port and sherry were stockpiled in a corner.

At the turn of the twentieth century, a Liverpool lad called Charles Hand scared himself rigid with candle-lit scrambles through the tunnels. Fascinated by the man who had created them, he did his best to pinpoint the whereabouts of the elusive Williamson during the excavations. From city directories, Hand found as follows:

1807, he [Williamson] lived in number 10 Mason Street
1813, he lived in number 13 Mason Street
1816, he lived in number 24 Mason Street
1821, he lived in number 18 Mason Street
1825 and 1827, he lived in Williamson's Buildings, Smithdown Lane
1829, he lived in number 18 Mason Street
1833, he lived in number 20 Mason Street
1839, he lived in number 20 Mason Street [final entry]

Though the King of Edge Hill moved his solitary court from house to house, he didn't live entirely in isolation. There were tenants. One complained of damp in her house. A few days later, as her maidservant was lighting the fire, a trapdoor flew up in the floorboards and Williamson's bald pate intruded itself upon the startled company, with a reassurance that he was digging a sewer to drain the water away. He took a shine to another female resident, a neighbour of his. He liked to call her 'the Queen of Edge Hill' and added an extension to her property – by carving her off a substantial slice of his own living-room. 'The same lady reported that she frequently heard strange noises from the vaults below,' notes Scouse historian Jim Moore.

'We call this the kebab,' said my guide. It wasn't hard to see why. It was an iron post, once swaddled in concrete; but the concrete had deteriorated and the metal had corroded, giving the whole the aspect of a skewer of meat, especially one bought after chucking-out time on a Friday night by a not entirely discerning punter. The kebab was actually a stanchion, part of an elephant trap of pilings which were sunk in the 1990s to support new houses overhead.

We now entered what the guide facetiously called the 'air-raid shelter'. You might think that the tunnels would have lent themselves ideally to civil defences in the days when the Luftwaffe was bombing the docks on the Mersey, but in fact they were considered too unstable. Much more recently, the section we were walking through was elaborately walled up to create a switchback, making the tour a circular one, in order for it to be health-and-safety compliant. Not only did my guide have to put up with me that morning, but she was also expecting health inspectors whose brief was to rule on whether the tunnels were sufficiently accessible to disabled visitors. My escort was hopeful. 'Let me put it this way. The best example we've had is a double amputee who got all the way round in one piece. We were made up.'

Through a beautiful arched chamber we went, a space suggesting a pharaonic tomb; and so to a repository of the shards of pottery and porcelain, jam jars and old horseshoes, recovered by the Friends. My Friend said, 'We've found lots of oyster shells. Maybe that's why they had so many children in Liverpool.'

I enjoyed the tunnels because they were so underdeveloped, so rudimentary, compared to many show caves, and also because of the remarkable contrast, or convergence, of different techniques and spaces: the hollowing-out of the easily yielding sandstone, done without machinery, so not smooth-edged but bearing a grainy, unfinished quality; the stone in turn abutting Victorian brickwork, much of it installed by Williamson's labourers but elsewhere part of the original cellars of old Edge Hill.

Over his third cup of tea, back in the café, Gerry told me the story of how his hometown had inspired the nonsense poems of Edward Lear. The humorist was a frequent houseguest of Lord Derby at Knowsley Hall, seven miles north-east of the city. The trip to and from this prestigious address would take Lear along the Prescott Road through Knotty Ash, which used to be known as Little Bongs, 'bongs' being an ancient word for rubbish or spoil. He would pass a gnarled ash tree, the Knotty Ash immortalised many years later by Ken Dodd, and this became the Bong Tree of Lear's verse.

I said, 'Why didn't you come into the tunnels with me, Gerry?'

'Because they're a folly,' he said. Gerry was a practical man, an engineer, a railway enthusiast. I tried to argue with him: the tunnels were interesting, I said, because they shed light on the extraordinary historical figure of Joseph Williamson, and more broadly, on fascinating subjects such as the human mind. 'Yeah,' said Gerry, distractedly. Gerry the Train Man, acknowledging what I was saying for form's sake, but secure in his preference for rail.

Before leaving the Mole Man behind for good, it's only fair to the old boy to report that he wasn't entirely lacking in the social graces. From time to time, he remembered himself sufficiently to dole out ale or porter to his workers, and glasses of wine to his visitors, infrequent as they were. Once he gave dinner to a group of people, who were served a frugal platter of beans 'in a none too sumptuous setting'. This was a beano, all right, but not as

Williamson's guests knew it. Several of them got up and left. 'Now that I know who my friends really are, pray follow me upstairs,' said their host to what was left of the party, before showing them to a banquet in his 'Goblin Hall', a vast refectory measuring 65 feet long, 14 feet wide and 27 feet tall.

No less a personage than the Prince Regent, who once met Williamson at a function on Merseyside, went so far as to call him the only gentleman in Liverpool. At this point, I humbly present yet another historical scoop. After the jaw-dropping similarities I teased out earlier between Frankie Howerd and the leader of the Hell Fire Club, let me say this of his Highness's generous appraisal of Williamson: it was a matter of one tunnel man recognising another. The King of Edge Hill and the blood prince both appreciated the form and function of the underground passage. George, Prince of Wales, had a corridor – perhaps more than one – dug out beneath his Royal Pavilion at Brighton. And just as in the case of the hidden Merseyside matrix, rumour and speculation rushed to fill the void; though if truth be told, this vacuum was in men's minds, all along.

Mindful of George's prodigious reputation as a sybarite and seducer, an account from 1862 suggested that the clandestine route was 'the medium by which, in disguise, the Prince and his friends went to and returned from their nocturnal rambles'. For the avoidance of doubt, John Erredge, the author, went further. For him, George's subterranean shaft was in the nature of a tunnel of love, an intimate conduit, practically a sexual organ in and of itself. He believed that George had recourse to it in pursuit of 'fun and frolic'. (It was also a convenient escape route in the event of discovery during one of his 'numerous peccadilloes'.) It was said that the fun-loving Prince, feeling at a loose end in his apartments, had merely to drop through a trapdoor, just like the ones installed at Edge Hill by his commoner coeval, and, by means of an 'intricate staircase', gain the tunnel. Once there, he was only minutes away from presenting the crown jewels before the appreciative gaze of an accommodating courtesan. George especially liked a roll in the hay with his regularly covered favourite, Mrs Fitzherbert. Had he tunnelled his way to her home in Brighton's Old Steine? Put it this way: it lay within comfortable drilling range of the royal bedchamber.

What was the truth about George and his underground proclivities? As the English have done for generations, I consulted the French for lessons in love; specifically, for instruction as to what the Prince really did with his passage. 'I came to Brighton to read history,' Adrien Joly told me over his shoulder. 'I married an English girl so now I can't leave!' Moving deftly beneath the low, humpbacked ceiling as he talked, Adrien was a spare figure, *distingué*, wearing a green sweater and a scarf indoors; though strictly speaking, we were no longer indoors so much as below doors. Originally from Lyons, Adrien, the Pavilion's curator, found himself working amid the faded tangerine wallpaper and the fantastical chinoiserie of Georgian Sussex. He assured me that it was a welcome distraction from meetings and paperwork to be plunging into the bowels of the building – better say, its *loins*.

We had left Adrien's draughty office, stepped over a bowing velvet rope, and down a tiled staircase – Victorian, alas, rather than original. We had inspected a squat, rusty – but once, it was easy to imagine, roaring – range. We had embarked on what Adrien assured me was two hundred feet of tunnel running the length of the building. 'George would use this to go and see his mistresses,' he said. I fancied he was rolling the phrase around his tongue, though I don't mean to imply anything about his Gallic inflection. On second thoughts, of course I do! How could I not? Adrien's very voice seemed to shrug, to convey by its tone the amused disdain in which he held the scurrilous stories about the former master of the house. 'I'm a Cartesian, I'm afraid,' he told me. It was not a phrase that George's tunnel had ever rung to before, I suspected. Adrien shot me his melting, stubbly smile, 'I'm not sure I'm the right man to be helping you.'

One of his former colleagues hadn't taken kindly to a journalist who attempted to use the Freedom of Information Act to confirm stories about a secret route to Mrs Fitzherbert's; this had the Lyonnais baffled. As sceptical as he was, this true son of the Enlightenment had no fear of honest enquiry, of reason. And so it was that he came to lay out for me his own thoughtful analysis of the princely tunnels. 'For me, what you have to imagine here is a *motorway* of servants,' he said. And so we did . . .

As much as George is celebrated as a swordsman, he was first and foremost a trencherman – he had form with tine as well as prong. John Nash's Pavilion, with its cupolas and minarets, recreates Kublai Khan's retreat in the minds of some beholders, a stately pleasure dome indeed. But in the right light, and to a susceptible onlooker, it resembles nothing so much as a groaning board, elaborately set, with its fluting condiments and its chafing dishes. George indulged his two favourite fleshly appetites at Brighton; indeed, they were inextricably commingled. Rejection of the royal favours was sealed not only by exclusion from George's duvet but by exile from his table: such was the fate of poor Mrs Fitzherbert, in the finish.

Perhaps the tunnel which Adrien and I were exploring was connected with George's carnal recreations; we would come to that. But there was no doubt that it was intrinsic to his great love affair with food. In the rooms above our heads, as many as seventy dishes would once have been served at dinner, depending on the prestige of the company and their number. To pique their gastric juices, the Prince and his companions sat down to lip-smacking soups, followed by a choice of fish: salt cod, carp, salmon or haddock. Four *removes*, or succulent sweetmeats, were next to go under the belt, succeeded by twelve *entrées*, dishes of flesh and fowl. Room was found for a further round of pâtés, an *assiette volante*, to say nothing of a sideboard buckling under joints and other cuts of beef, venison, mutton, game, cold meats and pies.

So much for the first course. Now for something that a man could really sink his teeth into: four roasts, from a selection including chicken, partridge, wild duck, rabbit, grouse and veal. These were chased down George's not so little red lane by trifle or brioches. The *entremets* or side dishes comprised both savoury and sweet *amuses bouches*: jellies flavoured with fruits, flowers or wine; fruit tarts; ice creams; meringues; rice dishes; and crème puddings made to traditional English recipes. In 1819, one light supper for eighteen – it was practically a TV dinner – consisted of a first course of '3 Soups, 3 Fish, 4 Removes, 12 Entrées, Assiette Volante, Side Board' followed by '4 Roasts, 4 Removes, 12 Entremets'.

In the ice houses of Brighton, they chipped away at their subterranean bergs around the clock to furnish the sorbets and *glaces* of the Pavilion, to pack the coolers where the wine glasses chilled, to make the princely drinks tinkle prettily. In the course of a single sitting, George was capable of seeing off by himself 'at least three bottles of wine, besides punch made with maraschino with lumps of solid ice in it, and a sort of spicy *liqueur* which he takes in great quantity', according to the disbelieving journal of the courtier Lord Glenbervie.

Nor could these liverish blow-outs be taken on a tray. On the contrary, the great dining table was furnished with not one but three cloths. First, it was covered with a damask, velvet or green cloth, and this in turn was overlaid with two crisp tablecloths, one of which was removed before the dessert course. A mill in Lisburn was proud to supply the Pavilion with Irish linen-damask tablecloths finished with elaborate designs and borders. The wine glasses, rimed over from their chilling cabinets, were brought to the table on silver-gilt trays. When the cheese was served, it was washed down with porter or ale, served in fresh glasses to replace the wine goblets.

There was an inherent contradiction, you might feel, between the proprieties of court life and its excesses, between the starched cloth and the fly-popping carousing. A French visitor was appalled to see the finger-bowl etiquette on display. Diners swigged from these bowls and spat out the contents. They then drained them to their brackish lees, rinsing their mouths out with these cocktails of gargle – often inserting a probing pinkie, like a swizzle stick, for good measure.

At this point the ladies retired, and things started to go downhill. Bottles endlessly circled the table. George was given to proposing one toast after another, urging the company to charge their glasses with a cry of 'A bumper!' At least one can say of him that he did not follow the country-house custom of the day by providing chamber pots on the sideboard. 'It is common practice to relieve oneself while the rest are drinking,' swooned one French visitor on a visit to England in the 1780s, 'one has no kind of concealment and the practice strikes me as most indecent.' George, as fastidious about his toilet as he was wanton at table, supplied more than thirty water closets at the Pavilion.

For all the doings of himself and his guests, George somehow got by with a domestic staff of barely 180. To him it was unimaginable that the liveried lower orders might crash through his salons and soirées with their brimming methuselahs and teetering platters of stuffed swan. So the Prince simply swept them out of sight: this was what Adrien meant by his 'motorway of servants'. The French curator was not one for the Great Man view of history, much preferring the vernacular narrative of life below stairs, a phrase never realised more literally than at Brighton. The corridor where we were standing had once been an autobahn of sous-chefs and pot-boys, a highway of help, running from north to south. It climbed ingeniously over the visitors' entrance to the Long Gallery: George's guests had processed through this, entirely oblivious of the retainers and flunkies bustling back and forth directly overhead in their concealed thoroughfare. Another flight of stairs plunged the workers straight back down to the basement, again bypassing the nobs on the ground floor altogether.

Adrien showed me storerooms which led off the main drag: they had once held foodstuffs and fuel. There were doors with faded legends, just discernible beneath more recent paint jobs. WOODSTORE, said one; COALSTORE, another. There were boilers below stairs, to nourish Nash's much admired underfloor heating. We took a detour through a side passage, and here we found the stone foundations of an eighteenth-century farmhouse which had stood on this spot before the Pavilion. 'George bought it at a time when there was nothing but cliffs between this part of the town and the sea,' said Adrien. The Prince was the great pioneer and patron of Brighton, making the place fashionable in a way that its sister resorts could only dream of: 'Bugger Bognor', a later royal murmured on his deathbed, for ever marking down another watering-hole on the Sussex riviera as somewhere missable, somewhere less than life-affirming.

From the main tunnel under the Pavilion, we found a dog-leg into a second underground passage. Surely this was the amatory conduit over which John Erredge and others had frothed so lubriciously. Was this not the secret way to Mrs Fitzherbert's, in the days, and indeed nights, when the going was good and the game was still worth the candle? In the early 1960s, something in the nature of a passage was indeed uncovered in a basement north of her old gaff, running under the pavement of Steine Lane. 'One might stand up with room to spare', according to one description. The Prince's friend was known to keep a nice drop to drink on hand in case favoured callers dropped by. She had an ale cellar, a beer cellar, another for wine in casks and yet another to hold wine in bottles. Had George surfaced among the barrels and the racks, perhaps selecting a nightcap before joining Mrs Fitzherbert in her bed? On the other hand, perhaps his tunnel had led him to another's arms entirely?

Adrien and I crocodiled our way towards the answer, beneath sparkling water droplets hanging from corroded iron plates in the ceiling. We jinked through a chicane of scaffolding: the Pavilion had the builders in. This tunnel was constructed in 1821, so it was getting on for two hundred years old and in need of running repairs, perhaps to the large black utility pipes that ran along one wall. A casement above us on our left was one of six circular laylights set into the lawn to provide light. The passage ran towards Marlborough Row, and it was at this address that a certain Lady Conyngham had once kept house, perhaps at Number 8 (now Northgate House). George was sweet on her, though the nature of the attraction eluded others. 'Lady Conyngham was an avaricious, interfering nepotist,' writes Jessica Rutherford in *A Prince's Passion*. 'She scandalised society by publicly wearing her "gifts", which were considered to be the property of the Crown.' One European princess said that George's ladyfriend had 'not an idea in her head; not a word to say for herself; nothing but a hand to accept presents and diamonds with and an enormous balcony to wear them on'.

Here, perhaps, we discern a glimmer of an insight into Lady C's appeal. At any rate, the King, as George had by now become, was known to have paid housecalls on Marlborough Row. Had he got there by subterranean means?

Adrien, for one, was not persuaded. By the time this tunnel was built, he told me, George was pushing sixty, and decades of manful grazing and sluicing had taken their toll. A pair of the royal breeches preserved for posterity in the collections of the Pavilion measures fifty-two inches around the waist; bearing in mind that His Highness would have been lashed into a corset before being shoe-horned into his trousers, his true girth was getting on for a cuddly sixty inches. The royal avoirdupois was the butt of many jokes. Lord Folkestone told his fellow MP Thomas Creevey that the princely embonpoint, left to its own devices, 'reaches his knees'. In his diary, Lord Glenbervie imagined George and another of his mistresses, the well-upholstered Lady Hertford, sitting on couches on opposite sides of a withdrawing-room: all at once, their stays failed, relaxing their iron grip, and 'the elastic protuberance of their confined stomachs set loose would immediately make contact across the room'.

According to Adrien, George tipped – *cracked* – the scales at twenty-three stone. He couldn't have dropped through a trapdoor, even if such a romantic means of egress had ever come to light. 'His private chambers had to be installed on the ground floor of the Pavilion because he was too heavy to climb stairs.' By the 1820s he was stricken by gout and dropsy, and was regularly bled by his physicians for his ailments. His exercise regimen was confined to walks in the gardens of the Pavilion and occasional undemanding trots in the covered riding school. Indeed, it seems the tunnel was dug in the first place to connect George's reinforced living quarters with the school and the stables, 'providing much desired privacy and protection from inclement weather', said Rutherford. In George's day, the passage had emerged on to a flight of steps leading up to Church Street. 'This tunnel . . . was probably the source of apocryphal stories of various secret tunnels in Brighton, used by the Prince for his nightly trysts.' In fact, George seems to have kept no secrets from Brighton, that shameless and unshockable town, and his paramours were known to all. His houseguests had seen him making his way out of the south gate of his estate and walking 'a few yards of the common street' to call on Lady Conyngham. Why bother, then, with sweaty subterfuges?

Adrien and I had now reached the end of the tunnel. It culminated in a locked white door. On the face of it, this was a reverse. But *au contraire*, it was a fitting finale to the mystery of the Pavilion and its tunnels. There was no royal boudoir behind this pearly portal, but a cockpit of fantasy and bravado, all the same. The royal who'd made the town the flamboyant resort it remains to this day enjoyed a theatrical connection even from beyond the grave. George's secret passage terminated within sniffing distance of the roaring crowd, in earshot of the greasepaint. Adrien and I were underneath Brighton's Pavilion Theatre: on the other side of the door were the actors' dressing-rooms. Well bugger me, then; and yes, bugger Bognor!

13

THE SALT OF THE EARTH

In a book that I remember consulting as a boy, the inner workings of the human body were revealed to be the full-time job of minute blokes in dungarees. Here, the teamsters of Muscle & Sinew were winching a hand into place; over there, the tattooed longshoremen of the large intestine were opening a cargo bay beneath a plummeting chop and a slew of greens. The smart guys, the ones making the big money, were all in the walnut boardroom. Arguably, this was an unduly premature introduction for a young shaver to the mechanistic ways of the modern world, with its *mise en scène* of drone-like subservience. But I rather cared for it, for its *inclusiveness*, as we might say now: a sense of everyone in his place and a place for everyone. In moments of childish distress, I would even imagine myself gratefully delegating my problems to one of these hidden hands, these tireless and trusty Mini-Mes. Please don't let me butter-finger this catch! Who will cap this gusher of a nosebleed? Send for the tiny roustabouts!

As I grew older, I realised that there were one or two shortcuts and oversimplifications, anatomically speaking, in the plates I had pored over. But they came back to me with the force of prophecy recently as I was investigating other machinations that are generally hidden from us – in short, as I was discovering what made the subterranean state tick. I learnt the business of men and women who toil unsung in the internal organs of the body politic. Some of them, to be sure, engage in the maintenance of prosaic if necessary functions, but their clandestine coevals include those bent on the most urgent and sensitive work of government imaginable – nothing less than the defence of the realm.

Where does the post come from? The stuff that still lands on the doormat, as opposed to arriving on line, is taken from the postman's satchel, of course, but how does it get there?

You're in the heart of one of our big cities – let's say it's Birmingham. You're in a shopping mall. You're walking past a coffee concession, then past Nando's, the name to trust for broiled fowl – when all at once you peel off from the milling throng, step through a nondescript service door, and follow a corridor until you reach a lift. It's a vanishing-cabinet, in which to make good your disappearance. On the control panel, the floors descend in order from '7' to '3' – and then there's nothing until 'B': '2' and '1' are missed out altogether. You select 'B', and quite soon you're pacing another corridor far below the mall. You're distracted by the unaccountable sight of a faded mural featuring a dolphin . . . You find yourself in a dimly lit tunnel. It's wide and the headroom more than generous. This would be big enough to drive through, you reflect. There's a cool, dry, earthy odour. You almost stumble into cardboard boxes, the detritus of rough sleepers. A series of alcoves are set back from the main drag, like family vaults in a catacomb. In one, you make out a sheaf of bank statements, miscellaneous mugshots, a passport. In another, there's a heap of portable typewriters and their cases, and you hear the chatter of keys, the ping of the carriage return, though the machines themselves remain undisturbed.

If you didn't already know it, you might be beginning to suspect by now that you're inside an art installation. It's called *Tunnel Vision* – 'do you really know what lurks beneath the pavement?'

What, if any, is the hoped-for resonance in the mind of the spectator? The tableau of the still Remingtons, with their ghostly, jabbering soundtrack, might reference the city's newspapers, the *Birmingham Post & Mail*, based somewhere overhead, and the vanished trades of the hot-metal age, now as irrecoverable as thatching and coopering. If it's not the *Post & Mail* we're meant to be thinking about, then surely it's the post and the mail, for we're in a disused tunnel that once provided an underground connection between Birmingham's chief sorting office and the city's main railway station. 'Just think how much information has passed through this space over the years?' muse the conceptual artists. 'How much ink and how much paper?' It's no disrespect to their compositions, both spatial and sonic, to say that the real draw is the tunnel itself. It's part of a network of passages and service shafts beneath the city, hidden, seldom visited and indeed largely forgotten. A man beside me in the gloom says to a girl with a nose-ring, 'It's like Swiss cheese down here.'

The Royal Mail tunnel is one of the longest of the buried pathways of the city, at getting on for a half a mile. It was once a single track road thrummingly occupied by electric buggies, with room on either side for a narrowish pavement. An overhead sign adjures, 'Drive With Caution'. Down here, in this overlooked quarter of canal town, the posties were like gondoliers, threading through the Stygian service tunnel with letters and parcels from their underground headquarters (above it now is a showpiece retail outlet, the Mail Box) to Platform 2 at Birmingham New Street (and vice versa). Plastic spills are still to be found on this roadway: they were used for securing mailbags before their journey to London aboard the fast train.

*

I'm a long way into a different tunnel in another city when I first hear the rumble. I stop what I'm doing; I'm fixed to the spot. I strain to hear the muffled clatter through a baffle of brickwork. Whatever it is, it's coming closer.

Historically speaking, there are judicious reasons for listening as though your life depended on it: a man died where I am now, knocked over and killed by careering wagons, by a runaway train. The unfortunate casualty, William Coulson, was in the wrong place at the wrong time. He was inspecting the tunnel. The word went round that it was out of bounds for the day; somehow, the message failed to reach the boys who were sending the wagons down. They had no idea that Coulson was below them when they slipped the brakes and set the dreadful wheels in motion. Admittedly, that was back in June 1852, and the chances of another man being run over in the tunnel are a good deal slimmer today, what with no wagons having rolled for a hundred and fifty years. But my companion Phil and I hear the infernal thunder of the bogies, all the same – they're almost upon us now! 'The sounds are magnified in this long cave,' as John le Carré writes in *The Naive and Sentimental Lover*. 'History, geology, not to speak of countless set-texts from medieval faculties at Oxford, all deepen and intensify the underground experience. Minotaurs, hermits, martyrs, miners, incarcerated since their first constructions, howl and clank their chains, for this is underground, where old men scratch for knowledge, gold, and death.' Phil's torch is suddenly trained on his chin, turning it yellow, as if it wasn't a sturdy flashlight in his hand at all but a buttercup from a childish game. 'Maybe it's a ghost train,' he whispers.

This is exactly what he tells the school parties he leads through the tunnel, milking the moment for all its child-frightening worth, before letting the nippers in on the secret that it's really the Metro, the underground railway, chugging through the rock and clay on the far side of the Victorian brickwork. It's one of the perquisites of subterranean exploration that you experience the familiar in an entirely extraordinary and perhaps disorientating context. There's also the ambiguous privilege that most will have no idea that you are in fact experiencing it in this way. From this day forward, you will appreciate the displacement of a train as few others will – seismically, you might almost say. On the other hand, one or two of your friends may tell you – airily and wrongly; *so* wrongly – that it's an insight they can live without. In all, Phil Thirkell and I encounter three or four trains in this way. In our confined roost, we are bats orienting ourselves by our wing-tips, tracking the Metro with our specially adapted sonar. Aside from the strains of trains, the only accompaniment to our journey is the sound of my hard-hat ricocheting off the roof: it makes a kind of *boing*, followed by a horrible scraping noise.

Phil and I are under his hometown of Newcastle upon Tyne. It's the home of coal as well, of course, and we are in a seam that runs directly underneath the city centre for a distance of two miles. This vein would never have been hacked out if it hadn't been for the black stuff, but it's not a face in its own right, it's not a pit. No deposits were shovelled out where we're standing. Instead, the Victoria Tunnel was dug as a means of transporting the city's emblematic export from the collieries to the River Tyne and so to market, without clogging the streets overhead with columns of mucky wagons. The tunnel was a great coal hole, then, part of the tracery of invisible infrastructure that has kept England in business.

Phil and I are pacing out this former chute of nutty slack at a time when the credit crunch is beginning to bite. That's fitting, because financial irregularities are what finished the tunnel off, not any issue with Newcastle's signature mineral itself: this isn't a seam that's been worked out. It belonged to the Northumberland & District Banking Company, which got into difficulties in 1857 and ceased trading. The tunnel closed after an operational life of just eighteen years, having been a full two years in the making. And if its chequered record, its dodgy tick-history, is thoroughly *à la mode*, so too is the self-effacing civic-mindedness of men and women like Phil, who are restoring the tunnel and preserving it for themselves and their neighbours. This curving column has the unaccountable property of one of Einstein's wormholes: you can tumble down it the way you came, in the direction of your history.

Phil has picked me up early, on an overcast winter's morning. It's Sunday and nobody is stirring: the fog on the Tyne is indeed all ours. In his BMW, I note his tache, blue eyes and genial aspect. For a Geordie in January, he is impressively tanned: as a retired man, he may have the time and means to enjoy trips to the sun. The most striking thing about Phil, perhaps, is his lustrous pony-tail. Physically speaking, my compact companion is well adapted to the tunnelling environment.

We pull up by a stretch of the Ouse, a tributary of Newcastle's great river, which is as squelchy as its name would lead you to expect. This slurping creek, with its keeled-over dinghies and beached skiffs, is overlooked by industrial units and building sites. One of the latter, soon to be an outpost of a hotel chain, is active on the Sabbath. Behind hoardings, the swinging arm of a crane is counterbalanced by a mighty pile that has been driven into the earth: over this great peg concrete rings have been horse-shoed on top of each other. Figures in fluorescent bibs are glimpsed on the scaffolding whenever the skein parts. Directly beneath these works is the entrance to the Victoria Tunnel.

Phil unlocks a door in a wall and we enter a flat-roofed brick adit. This is to the main drag what the Ouse is to the Tyne, a side-channel, a feeder. It was a comparatively late addition, an access route installed during the Second World War as part of a canny scheme, as they might say in these parts, to convert the wagonway into a municipal air-raid shelter. 'It was big enough for nine thousand people,' Phil assures me. 'You can see where they fixed the bunk beds to the walls.'

In a moment, we are in the tunnel proper. It measures seven and a half feet high by six feet three inches wide. It is a hybrid of twentieth-century improvements and additions – blast walls intended to limit the impact of bomb shockwaves, electricity cables sprouting from the brickwork – together with the original Victorian features. Like Bazalgette's sewers beneath London, the tunnel was built in a resilient oval shape – 'You imagine trying to crush an egg in your hand,' says Phil – and boasts a double-brick arched roof. We view an example of this stress-bearing feature. In the tunnel's sinuous innards, the arch is a sclerotic joint. Even I, a layman, can tell from this most cursory of physicals that there are complications with this important pressure-point: there are goitres of calcified limestone, stands of sweating brick. The experience of roaming the tunnel is indeed analogous to some fantastical circuit of the human body. It's like accessing the POV of a microscopic camera during keyhole surgery . . .

Taking coals to Newcastle is axiomatically the last word in farcical, mortifying ventures. However, there's another, less intuitive truth about the mining industry in these parts, and the tunnel is like a shortcut that returns us to it: the local burghers felt that even the lucrative business of sending their wares to the fireplaces and furnaces of the world was squalid and disreputable. Taking coals *from* Newcastle wasn't all it was cracked up to be either, in the rarefied opinion of these worthies, and they preferred to sweep it under the carpet; or rather, the carriageway.

The splendidly styled Spital Tongues Colliery was opened in 1835 to exploit reserves of coal at the heart of the city, beneath the Newcastle Town Moor, Nuns Moor and Castle Leazes districts. At first, the output was taken to the Tyne on carts. However, this was not only expensive but also unpopular with the city council. A surface wagonway was proposed, but the freemen of Newcastle who controlled the Town Moor – as they do to this day – blackballed this noisome scheme.

The nabobs of the North East were merely articulating wider misgivings about the new-fangled industrial process and its baleful spoor. At almost exactly the same time as they were turning their noses up at wagon-trains of coal, a similar revulsion at the muck that famously accompanies brass was observable on the great estates of the Duke of Devonshire in Derbyshire. Or rather, it wasn't observable. His lordship had wanted to build a great conservatory at Chatsworth, complete with steam boilers to ensure that his glassy parlour was habitable in all weathers, and one of the remarkable features of the finished article would be its tremendous discretion as to the source of the heating. Joseph Paxton, the distinguished botanist and engineer who would later build the Crystal Palace for the Great Exhibition, had accepted the ducal commission, and hidden everything out of sight: the eight boilers, the crater-sized coal hole, even the flue. A tall brick chimney, to ventilate the smoke, was lost among the oak and fir of Stand Wood.

It took three hundred tons of coal to heat the conservatory in winter. Chatsworth's supplies were delivered by rail to the halt of Rowley, three miles away, and fetched to the estate in horse-drawn carts along a lane which was invisible from the toff-loud gardens. At the bottom of the coal hole, men filled sturdy trolleys with the fuel, and dragged them along a narrow-gauge railway line through a tunnel to the secret boilers themselves. The conservatory was demolished in 1920, and bit by bit the coal hole and tunnel were filled in. But they were rediscovered and dug out again just half a dozen years ago. Discerning visitors to this most gracious of country piles can climb down into the fern-festooned coal pit and pace out the seventy-seven steps of the candle-flickering passageway, stepping over brief stretches of abandoned railway. It's cool and noiseless, even on a May Bank Holiday.

Passing Metro trains notwithstanding, the same can be said of the Victoria Tunnel, the rather more substantial undertaking under Newcastle. It was capable of shifting a season's worth of coke for the Chatsworth boilers in a single wagon-train: each 'gig' – low and oblong – could hold a Newcastle chaldron, or 2693 kilos, and there were up to thirty-two such gigs linked together to form a train: as many as three of these would leave the colliery every hour.

The tunnel was very likely assembled in sections: shafts were sunk to the required depth and then a stretch of the way would be dug out, before the whole process was repeated. At its deepest, the tunnel lies eighty-five feet below the chill northern streets and their hardy T-shirted denizens. Just like the Geordies of today, when their work was done the tunnellers gathered in the Bigg Market to celebrate. Two hundred men were 'regaled with a substantial supper and strong ale' at the Unicorn pub in 1842. The first wagons through the tunnel on opening day, 7 April, took half an hour to reach the river. There were four gigs of coal; another four held a band of musicians and local dignitaries: curiosity, and the financial clout of old King Coal, had got the better of the fastidious Tyneside establishment.

The Spital Tongues pit stood 222 feet above sea level, above the distant quayside. The tunnel described the gentlest of arcs from the one to the other, with an average gradient of 1 in 90. Gravity did all the work, propelling the wagons of coal down the hollowed hill to the wharves. They were attached by rope to a steam engine at the pit, and this hauled the empty wagons back up again.

I hear my buddy Phil say, 'One of our builders mentioned a crucifix down here.' I wonder what occult or sinister story I'm about to hear. My companion is studying a section of wall at knee height. There's a patch of damp-looking concrete, and what appears to be a smeared inscription on it. Phil says that the Friends of the Tunnel have been unable to make it out, though it appears to say 'Honour' near the top, and two or three lines below that is 'Stewart'. Is it some kind of laudatory roll? But who exactly is being laurelled? Who was Stewart? Only the wretched Coulson perished in the Victoria Tunnel when it was serving its original purpose, and there are no known blitz fatalities. 'It's only a theory, but the plaque might record those who died above ground in the bombing,' says Phil. To the right of this little tablet is a panel of about the same size showing in relief a small, soggy, crucified Christ.

Phil points out that the ceiling of the tunnel is streaked with soot. I run a hand over it. My dabs come back black with coal grime that was deposited here the best part of two hundred years ago and has remained undisturbed ever since, notwithstanding the bombing of the shipyards on the Tyne: the original soot scattered by wagoner Coulson and his muckers is what's on my filthy pinkies.

Urban explorers – people who enjoy going where they aren't strictly supposed to – have been into the stretch of tunnel that we're walking, and have recounted their exploits on line. 'They've got some pretty good photos,' Phil concedes. Spray-painted letters materialise out of the gloom on a brick partition in front of me. I spell them out, 'C . . . H . . . R—'

'Aye, that was a little shit called Chris who came down here and wrote his name everywhere,' says Phil.

The Victoria Tunnel passes right under the city, beneath some of its best-known landmarks. The word 'Tongues' in the name of the pit that the tunnel was formerly attached to stands for 'pieces of land at the margin', and the tunnel has marginal connotations, too: marginal in the modern, balance-sheet meaning of the word, but also in its simple capacity as a boundary, a marker. The tunnel cuts across the centre like the lifeline on a palm, and yet it is almost entirely unknown. When former US president Jimmy Carter visited Newcastle, city officials were as aghast as his secret service detail to find the tunnel on old plans of the city, and ordered all entrances and manhole covers sealed up for the duration of his stay.

Phil takes me on 'a drive of the tunnel', an overground tour. We are tracing out its profile on the surface of its heedless hometown. At a set of lights, Phil points to an aluminium-clad warehouse, 'Johnson's Decorating Centre', and tells me that the wagonway passes beneath it. I like the fact that there's a wholesale outlet for grout and sugar soap above ground, and a neglected Victorian passage directly below. It's not that one – the warehouse – is appreciably more prosaic than the other – I'm not sure that it is – it's just the sense of a hidden continuum: as well as sharing a horizontal plane with other warehouse units, the Decorating Centre is also on a vertical plane, where it abuts a secret tunnel. Emergency wartime entrances to the tunnel, other than the one that Phil and I took by the Ouse, are also located close to St Thomas's Church, and hard by a branch of Optical Express.

Phil drives down the city's central motorway. The tunnel passes beneath it, he says; in fact, it's a kind of subterranean shadow of the footbridge that we're just shooting the rapids of . . . We turn left, passing the fogbound Town Moor where the coal was dug out by the miners of Spital Tongues. There's the Spital House pub on the left, and opposite that, the spot where the tunnel once began, the old colliery, now a tower block called Mill House. 'There's nothing that you can identify with the tunnel here now,' says Phil.

But not far away, on Claremont Road, he pulls over again with a mischievous – even daring – air. Time is tight, he's due home to pick his wife up and take her out for Sunday lunch, so this is in the nature of a spree, a lark, that has to be smuggled under the radar. Phil goes to the boot of the Beamer and from under a rug produces a large metal ring, with a boss or nipple standing proud in the place where a giant might have had a precious stone mounted for his giantess. It's a key of some kind, I gather, of the sort that might turn a very ancient lock; a turnkey might wear it on his belt, the key to an important cell. I follow

Phil across the road and on to a grass verge. There is a line of lime trees, some early crocuses. Phil walks over to a drain – no, a manhole cover – inserts Shrek's engagement ring into a groove and pulls, leaning back as if he was taking part in a tug-of-war. From under the surface comes the sound of a mechanism moving: Phil almost falls backwards with the brute physics of the thing. The hatch flies off, revealing a set of steps, like stirrups mounted horizontally, that descend a short brick pipe and return us to the lost Victoria Tunnel.

Even subterranean systems that you and I use everyday, that we physically inhabit more or less unthinkingly, require maintenance, the attention of fitters and cleaners, gaffers and inspectors: underground crew. In an interstice between land and water, I feel the downdraft of a huge fan on my skin. It's sucking in the refreshing, ozone-rich air off a river, which is some distance overhead. From the tip of one blade at twelve o'clock, to another at six, the fan is perhaps four times taller than a man. It could be a stage set from *Metropolis*. Having said that, it could also pass for the propeller of a liner, of the sort frequently seen on the river in the past, or even of a battleship. Its fins turn slowly at first, but can gather pace with astonishing acceleration. The fan is said to be so finely balanced, calibrated to such hair-trigger tolerances, that even when the engines that drive it are switched off it will still revolve by itself; all it takes is the merest sigh of wind. This is a matter of concern for the engineers who service the fan – they could easily lose a hand, or an arm.

There are many road tunnels in England, a good few beneath rivers, but none surpasses the Mersey Tunnel, which was until quite recently the longest underwater tunnel ever built anywhere. It runs for two miles and 230 yards, and is wide enough to accommodate four lanes of traffic. In search of the Wormhole Caves, I'd already crossed the Mersey by rail, so to speak, and I liked the idea of fording the same waters again, only this time by road. Like the train journey, the trip through the Mersey Tunnel was one that I'd made many times before, on visits to family in Wallasey. In my memory, the drive from one riverbank to the other was a kind of relay from one pool of bright light to the next, travelling into the centre of the glow cast by each strip light in the ceiling, then exiting it, then entering the field of the next filament, and so on. This impression was reinforced by the distinctive tiger-stripe livery of the other vehicles. There was what appeared to be a pavement or gangway set hard against the wall of the underpass, but if pedestrians weren't actually banned from the Mersey Tunnel, they were certainly discouraged from it. I don't recall ever seeing anyone walking inside it. If I'd ever thought about it, I might have realised that the gangway was a serviceway provided for the staff who kept the tunnel running smoothly, as well as for the mechanics and medics and mop-up men who came running when it didn't.

Such are my souvenirs of time spent on the Mersey blacktop; now I'm seeing it as few have seen it – from off to one side, from below. I'm seeing it from the perspective of the gang on the gangway, in fact, and acquiring a knowledge of it that I'd never dreamed of when my experience of the tunnel was a more sedentary one. The ventilation, the ozone, the threat to overalled limbs – none of this gives pause to the drivers who are barrelling home from work only a few short yards from me. They don't consider the contractors and operators who are their partners in the ongoing venture of negotiating a riverbed on four wheels, of making a road tunnel work – of getting through it. In short, they have no thought for their secret sharers.

You could say there's an excuse for their indifference in that this feat of engineering, though monumental, is a monument lying on its side – and largely below water, at that. But not even this will wash. On the shores of the Mersey, and in plain view for miles around, towering ventilation shafts, its great gills, breathe for the tunnel; it is these shafts that admit the estuarine air, drawn in and diced by the vast propellers beneath. These stacks are listed buildings, fine, or at least large, examples of the Art Deco movement, thought by many observers to reflect the interest in all things Egyptian that was aroused by the opening of the Tutankhamun tomb at the same time as the towers were being raised. There are half a dozen of them in all; one, at Taylor Street in Liverpool, is now closed but still being cannibalised for parts. But the one I'm in – indeed, halfway down – is on the Pier Head, next to the triptych of buildings that dominates Liverpool's waterfront: the Port of Liverpool Building, the offices of the Cunard shipping line, and the Liver Building itself.

My companions are two charming ladies, Alison and Vicky, who work at the tunnel and are the guides for the tour I'm taking. I ask them, 'Forgive this idiot question, but what would happen if there wasn't ventilation like this?' It turns out it isn't such a dumb remark, after all. Breathability was an afterthought; the towers were added late, following dramatic events at the then newly opened Holland Tunnel in New York City. The drivers of the Big Apple would enter their hometown tunnel perfectly alert and perky, but even before they emerged barely half a mile later it was observed with alarm that they were becoming woozy, dropping off, nervelessly driving towards one another. The cause of this discomfiting phenomenon was traced to carbon monoxide fumes which built up in the tunnel because there was no provision for dispersing the cars' waste gases.

The Mersey Tunnel as a whole was a bit of an afterthought, too, inasmuch as it took the people of Merseyside many years to get around to it. The first serious scheme was put forward in 1825, but it would be another century before there was anything to show for it. In that time, the economic case for the route became irresistible. In the early decades of the nineteenth century, the population of Birkenhead, on the far shore, was a modest 310. In those days, the demand for cross-river traffic was met by the famous ferry. This service had been inaugurated by monks on the Wirral side. Defoe was helped from the boat to dry land in the arms of a strapping stevedore, and Dickens liked to take the ferry 'for the air'. There were no floating landing-stages on the river at the time, so as a general rule ferries docked at high tide, to prevent itinerant scribblers from going in fear of their shoe leather.

By the 1920s, however, there were an astonishing thirty-five million passengers a year crossing the Mersey, notwithstanding the rival merits of the railway below the water, which transported a further ten million travellers. There was talk of building a bridge but the wide estuary demanded a daunting span: for many years, the traveller had to go upriver as far as Warrington if he wanted to cross in this fashion. Planners in Liverpool proposed a suspension bridge, but this was vetoed on the grounds of its staggering price tag, £10,550,000, and because of fears that river traffic might inadvertently ram its piers.

When the road tunnel was first mooted, it was rejected as a hazard to the foundations of Liverpool buildings. Moreover, the city fathers weren't persuaded that such a link would be of as much benefit to them as it would to the smugglers and other reprobates who lived on the side of the water where my family came from. The folly of this attitude came home to them, however, when trains began running under the river. These services suited the commuters of Wirral just fine, but were of limited use in dispatching the goods which arrived daily in Liverpool's docks. It was in the 1920s that the road tunnel under the gunmetal waters was finally green-lighted. It was to be called Queensway, in honour of Queen Mary, the spouse of King George V. Sir Basil Mott, a distinguished tunneller who had worked on the London Underground, was retained as principal architect. But who was going to pay for the thing? By the time it was finished, it would cost more than £6 million – more than £7 million, if you threw in the purchase of land and the cost of borrowing to fund the construction. The government offered about a third of the total, on condition that Queensway was toll-free, but that meant defraying the rest of the expense through the rates, and Liverpudlians didn't like the sound of that. In January 1925 Chancellor Winston Churchill stumped up £2.5 million and allowed tolls for the first twenty years of the tunnel's life. More than eighty years later, however, drivers still fumble for £1.40 at the toll booths, where the coins are automatically counted, sucked away underground, and bagged.

Queensway isn't perfectly straight – it bends. This had proved to be the solution to the problem of tunnelling without disturbing the piles on which Liverpool's great edifices rested. On either bank of the river men sank shafts two hundred feet deep, and drove the tunnel through the rock. By modern tunnelling standards, Queensway is not outstandingly deep: its lowest point is 170 feet below the river's high-water level. When you drive – or stand – in the tunnel today, there are twenty feet of rock over your head, and river clay on top of that. The dig threw up 1,200,000 tons of stone and this was used to make the Otterspool Promenade, on the Liverpool side, as well as the King's Promenade beside the Wormhole Caves in New Brighton.

At Easter 1934, shortly before it was opened, eighty thousand Merseysiders walked through the spanking new tunnel. Queensway was a great source of civic pride. My friend Gerry told me that tunnel stats used to be published in the *Liverpool Echo*. That organ of record noted that eight million vehicles traversed the underwater road in 1953; by 1968, it was nineteen million.

As all Liverpudlians know, there's not one Mersey road tunnel, in fact, but two: the demand on Queensway produced severe congestion on the roads around it at peak times, and it was decided to commission a second bore, at a cost of £7.5 million. This alternative route ran from just north of the original tunnel on the Liverpool side, before emerging across the water at Seacombe, Wallasey. It was called Kingsway, and it was declared open in 1965 – by HM the Queen, her grandfather, the King, having done the honours at Queensway.

Someone in our party wonders when – if – the debt on the tunnels will be cleared. Well, explain Alison and Vicky, Queensway had almost paid for itself by the late 1960s. But then it was 'mortgaged' to pay for its little brother: you couldn't have one tunnel with a toll and one without, because the free one would be jammed and the other deserted. But the tunnels could be debt-free by the distant year 2042: while the running costs come to £15 million a year, the turnover is £25 million.

Vicky – very Scouse, big-hearted – could play mid-career Cilla Black in a telly biopic. She tells us about a room off the ventilation shaft, 'a secret room'. The pharaonic bulk of the shaft has deceived us into the delusion that we are on dry land, whereas the truth is that we are on the cusp of a great river. This goes to the heart of the Sphinx-like riddle of the secret room. From this chamber, it is possible to look straight through the foundations of the adjacent building into Liverpool's original docks, says Vicky, to wharves that are more than three hundred years old. 'But you can't go in it for safety reasons,' she adds, bringing us back down to earth – or not, in our riverine case.

A fat bloke in our party tells our guide that she's a 'temptress'.

'That's what they call me in the office,' says Vicky. She is in fact happily married to a policeman, who claims to have encountered a ghostly motorcyclist in the tunnel. This is what happened. Vicky's husband pulled a driver over. The man started to get out of his car but the policeman could hear the sound of an approaching motorbike so he told him to stay where he was. The roar of the bike drew nearer – and passed the stationary car and Vicky's husband, but of the bike and its rider there was nary a sight. The tunnel is also haunted by 'Gilly', a former caretaker of one of the great buildings on the Pier Head, who took exception to the excavations; as well as by 'Leaky', a one-time tunnel employee, who used to reside in a hostel but eventually took to living down in Queensway itself. Shortly after he died, he was seen in the tunnel again, as in more hale times.

You might imagine that the cars run along the floor of Queensway. But we're now making our way underneath the roadway, under the tyre-streaked tarmacadam itself, to a second, lower thoroughfare, a void left by the designers in the expectation that trams might run through it, to complement the columns of cars overhead. But the rail and ferry people, already vexed about losing custom to the road tunnel, drew the line at trolley cars in Queensway as well, so this space has only ever been used as a service area. Alison and Vicky are going to show our tour group the most recent additions to Queensway: built at considerable outlay, but in the hope that they might never be needed.

There's an empty wheelbarrow down here, and sturdy stone boxes that house the cables carrying electricity to Birkenhead: the cables are in oil, like fish, and sealed in masonry. There are outlines in white paint or chalk – one looks like the silhouette of a stiff – which are the work of surveyors who have been examining the base of the tunnel. They've been scoring it not for roadworthiness, at this subaquatic spot, but for seaworthiness. In this part of Queensway, it's less like the bottom of a roadway and more like the hull of a ship, though at the depth we find ourselves, not even a lugworm could expect to make much progress.

Whereas, higher up, the threshed air off the river was pleasantly revivifying, several fathoms further underground it is now tinglingly cold. Alison tells me that the fans are spinning at 26 miles an hour: enough, on the road above, to send drivers crashing into one another, or into the tunnel walls, like the groggy guinea-pigs who were the early adopters of the Holland Tunnel. The engineers have mitigated the impact of the gale by directing it on to rows of curved baffles, 'bananas', under the highway. These absorb most of the force of the windrush; pinprick holes above our heads then channel the now-pacified air to the carriageway. They work like the keys of a wind instrument.

Officially the tunnel is dry; it's claimed that the only water that enters is borne in on the tyres of its customers during inclement weather. But there is standing water where we are. The surface of the curved walls is mouldy with old distemper: this is the spot, or it's very like it, where the navvies who built the tunnel were photographed, fixed for ever in scenes of toil and spoil. At the height of the works, seventeen hundred men laboured beneath the water, clearing the route with handpicks and explosives. Before the job was done, nineteen of them lost their lives, in most cases the victims of electrocution. On the Liverpool shore, two tunnellers died in a roof collapse. Accident investigators were nonplussed when they established that the cause of the fall was unstable excavations dating back to Oliver Cromwell's siege of Liverpool Castle. The going was easier on Kingsway because the diggers had the advantage of better kit, huge mechanical moles which could punch through two hundred feet of substrata in a week.

But the riverbed remains dangerous, a place where people were never intended to be. And the particular hazards of road tunnels were grimly demonstrated by an inferno in the Mont Blanc pass in 1999, which cost thirty-nine lives. In the aftermath of the Alpine disaster, the Mersey Tunnel people installed refuges, which work on the same principle as climbers' huts. They are places in which to take cover when external conditions are inhospitable to life.

'We hope they're the biggest waste of money ever,' says Vicky. She's standing in the harsh neon light of one of the shelters. This brilliant shed, as well as half a dozen more like it, is where drivers would be directed to come in the event of a conflagration or other emergency under the river. They would be alerted by flashing signs, public-address announcements, and by the police interrupting and overriding any radio broadcast that they might be listening to. Inside the survival cabin, there's a monitor on which instructions would be relayed to the stranded motorists. Mounted above it is a little television camera, to let the control room see into the refuge: it functions like a telly entryphone. There's a toilet in the shelter and cartons of bottled water.

Vicky hopes that they will never again have to use the refuges; they already have, on at least one occasion. About four months before our tour, a car caught fire. It ran on mixed fuels: not just petrol but LPG – 'Like the vehicles the terrorists tried to ram into Glasgow airport, and left on the streets of London,' Vicky added. The risk from these fuels combusting in the tunnel persuaded staff to launch their emergency procedures and open the refuges.

At the end of the tour, Alison takes me to one side to say that her colleague Richard, an engineer, would be happy to show me the secret room, after all – that's if I want to. I don't demur.

In this mysterious cell, made of brick, there's a good deal of refuse on the ground – the reason visitors aren't allowed in. In fact, the secret room is as derelict-looking as the rest of the Mersey Tunnel complex is spick. There are neat holes, perhaps two feet square, cut into the wall opposite the door. They look like stripped-out dumb waiters. It's just as Vicky promised: the holes afford a view through the foundations of the ventilation shaft building that we're in, right through the piles of the adjacent building, the Port of Liverpool Building, one of the 'Three Graces' of the Pier Head; and so onwards, to the very wall of the original port, made of sandstone and dating from the eighteenth century. I thrust my head into the chasm and strain to make out the damp stone, the waterlogged timbers, the Mersey-marinaded piers. My neck is telescoped to its full extent. There's a boat trapped in there too, according to Richard, between the shaft and the old wharf. In vain I peer into the air pocket for rigging, for tattered sailcloth or barnacled plate. I hear Richard behind me saying that he's never ventured through the dumb waiter and into the adjoining chamber: 'It's full of water.'

I retract the spyglass of my spine; I'm back in the room. 'How deep is it?'

'Maybe twenty-five feet,' he says. He picks up a piece of broken brick and hands it to me. I lob it through the aperture into the dark – and I'm rewarded, a full beat later, by a deep and satisfying plop.

14

THE SECRET STATE

Dover was famously hymned by Dame Vera Lynn for the atypical blueness of its avian life and its magnificent escarpments. Here, you and I are concerned with what lies under these natural monuments as opposed to what twits and swoops over them, for this portion of the Kentish coast hides an unmatched miscellany of subterfuges and secret weapons.

From Norman times until the Cold War and beyond, the forgiving chalk has first furnished, then concealed, so many tunnels, caponiers, casemates, citadels, ravelins and redoubts – entire subterranean streets – that no gazetteer could find room for them all. These excavations were carried out in the name of national security, the defence of the realm: nowhere else but Dover has been so thoroughly undermined in the paradoxical cause of bolstering it, of shoring it up. The underground emplacements and embrasures were completed and then manned by those now known only to God, and perhaps the Ministry of Defence. These nameless men and women trained unblinking eyes on the ambiguous water margin of the Channel, that great moat around our island – the final fosse, the last ditch – but also the tide that bore all our enemies towards us.

The threat is different now – it might come from the air, from cyberspace, from the rucksacked dupe in the next seat – but for some, Dover remains on the frontline, an embattled outpost in timeless English scrapes with Europe, with foreigners at large.

The continent is separated from us by a mint-green sea today. It washes into the ferry port at the foot of the cliffs. The white hulls of the cross-Channel boats are an echo of the flinty flanks celebrated in dear Vera's song, and the carbon rising from their stacks recalls the ack-ack fire of the wartime batteries. Meanwhile, the supposed menace of the outsider is represented, up here on the heights, by a signpost to 'Dover Immigration Removal Centre'.

I'm walking through a tree-darkened defile in the shadow of a fort called the Drop Redoubt, one of two on the Western Heights. This brick-built Beau Geste went up at the turn of the nineteenth century to keep Napoleon at bay. There is a buzz of flies, and uncanny votive offerings of black plastic bags – full of pitbull poo, I'll wager – dangle from the lower branches of this canopy, like the cuddly toys awaiting the Lot's wife treatment under the sedimentary spring of Old Mother Shipton's Cave in Knaresborough.

The Western Heights are just around the bay from the slopes dominated by Dover Castle. In their day, they were 'the largest and strongest fortification in the country'. A sizeable contingent of the British Army was garrisoned here, thanks to a dubious strategy that anticipated old Boney landing somewhere between Hythe and Rye – whereupon our boys would break cover in Dover, sneak up on him and take him from the rear. William Cobbett, who had some experience of military installations from recces he'd made in Canada, was less than convinced. Writing up a visit to the Heights in his *Rural Rides*, he noted that a 'couple of square miles or more were hollowed out like honeycomb . . .

that either madness the most humiliating, or profligacy the most scandalous must have been at work here for years'. The barracks were not quite finished, but Cobbett reckoned that enough bricks had already been buried in the hill to build cottages for every working man in Kent and Sussex.

I've come here to sashay down what may very well be the greatest staircase in England; indeed, I expect to enjoy myself so much that I may very well sashay up it as well, all 140 steps of it. I doubt whether any stately home, grand hotel or Ruritanian chancellery can hold a candle – better say, stair-rod – to the Grand Shaft, a marvellously dotty but thoroughly effective set of three concentric staircases, which twist down through the Heights all the way to the delightfully dubbed Snargate Street below. This sunken tower has been compared by at least one historian to the finest flowerings of Sir Christopher Wren himself, 'at once combining the gracefulness of the stupendous vestige of architectural skill ... with the greatest simplicity and general accommodation'. And yet this stairway to heaven languishes all but unknown inside a hill in Kent, and is only accessible to the public on the rosiest of red-letter days.

One on top of another, the coils of steps descend around a vertical, circular, brick-faced light well, open at the crown. The Grand Shaft is like one of those frown-making paintings in which the artist has pulled a stroke of perspective on the viewer, except that in this case, the viewer steps through the frame and inhabits the conundrum. Like the ventilation towers on the Mersey, the Grand Shaft was bolted on at the last minute. The British Army had been marched to the top of the hill, ready to surprise the French where they were least expecting it, when the penny dropped with their officers that they would have to be marched down again first. Brigadier-General Twiss, who hatched the idea of the shaft, pointed out that it was more than a mile and a half on horseback from the garrison to the town, and that all the footpaths were 'so steep and chalky that a number of accidents will unavoidably happen during the wet weather and especially after floods'. He was voted £3947 7s from the war chest for his flights of fancy, and brought them in at £700 under budget in 1807. They served the twelve hundred men of the Grand Shaft barracks, which could still be seen until as late as the 1960s. On the debit side, the stairway was sunk through the middle of the parade ground, somewhat compromising its utility for drill practice.

If it's a Gordian problem to untangle the multiple staircase as you descend it, to decode the DNA of this double – *triple* – helix, you can at least grasp the conceit behind it: it meant that Twiss's boys could dismount the mountain three times as fast as they would on a single stairway. After the fear of invasion dwindled, the shaft became a tourist attraction, a vertical civvy street. The three lanes of traffic introduced by the military became institutionalised, with each staircase reserved for a separate class of tripper: 'Officers and their Ladies', 'Sergeants and their Wives' and 'Soldiers and their Women'. In 1812 a man called Leith won a bet by riding his horse from Snargate Street to the Western Heights taking the most direct route possible, and without putting so much as a hoof on unflagged chalk.

You might think that the furtive defences of the Western Heights made them the antithesis of Dover's much better-known castle; they are, after all, withdrawn into the sheltering stone whereas the castle rises defiantly from it. But you cannot spend any time within the proud piecrust of the castle's Norman battlements without realising that it, too, rests on a great cobbler of a cliff face, as calculatedly aerated as the Heights themselves. There are medieval silos, created by the engineers of Henry II. There is a fine caponier, excavated to enable the watch to reach vulnerable parts of the castle's outer defences without coming under fire themselves. This was added after the besieging forces of Prince Louis of France, later King Louis VIII, deployed miners to dig under the castle moat in 1216, rocking the foundations of a gate-tower to the point where it fell over.

As in the case of the Western Heights across the way, further tunnels were dug out beneath the castle as underground quarters for soldiers during the Napoleonic Wars. Seven casemates were linked near the cliff face by another, which led to a well and latrines. There were fireplaces, and ventilation was provided by adits drilled down from the castle grounds to the buried barracks below. As many as two thousand men were quartered safe out here. These digs had the virtue of being almost impervious to bombardment from any invading French ships or artillery pieces. But bedding down in the castle scarcely meant living like a king. There was limited light, meagre warmth and always the drear drizzle of hussar sweat, falling as condensation from the chalky ceilings in the unchanging microclimate of the bunkhouse.

It was in these same castle catacombs in the summer of 1940 that the evacuation of 400,000 troops from Dunkirk was improvised in less than a week. You can see where the strangely neglected hero of the hour, Vice-Admiral Bertram Ramsay, ran the plangently English exercise of Operation Dynamo. In a long underground chamber, the Admiralty Casemate, there's a video projection on to a far wall in which Ramsay's shade is seen pottering about his rooms, which were once here and included the rare and luxurious feature of a balcony. There is Ramsay's real bed as well as a hologram of a window. The admiral died in a plane crash in France, which may explain why he never enjoyed the golden reputation of other wartime generals and planners.

I'm with a tour party which is entering an underground operating theatre deep under the castle. We gather around the slab and listen to the voice-over of a surgeon, who has a downed airman under the knife. In the Artillery Ops Room, the old headsets with their rigging of brown webbing might be surgical appliances themselves. There's a chance to see a hotline installed for the exclusive use of the PM. Churchill's blower is a Daliesque contraption with a black body and a red receiver. It has a row of large knobs along the bottom which give this life-and-death comms equipment the appearance of a toaster. The suites frequented by Winnie and his chiefs-of-staff were made possible by more tunnelling: three specialist army companies dug to the west of the old Napoleonic shafts, to hollow out the 'annexe' system. The invasion of France was at hand, and Dover Castle was one of three possible operational headquarters, along with Devonport and Portsmouth. When Normandy was chosen as the beachhead of the liberation, Portsmouth became the focal point, which was probably just as well as the tunnelling crew had seriously pranged at Dover, triggering rock falls beneath the castle.

But it would be wrong to think that Dover's drilling days were done. In 1942 yet another grid of tunnels, codenamed Dumpy, was sunk fifty feet below the once pungent dorms of the Napoleonic casemates. It was with the war in Europe in mind that the order was given to initiate these ultimate tunnels, this deep-most bunker; but which war in Europe, exactly? By the time the work was done, the strategic planners already had an eye on a new and even more deadly threat, over the horizon from the soon to be vanquished enemy. Our party learn about Dumpy from our tour guide, Zack, albeit with his constricting coda that it's off limits. I write in caps in my notebook 'CAN I SEE RAMSAY'S BALCONY . . . DUMPY?'

Alas, the admiral's balcony has long since been sealed up. As for Dumpy, Zack speaks to his duty manager, Dan, and as a special favour, and because Dan's a bit of a tunnel nut himself, he agrees to take me down to the secret citadel . . .

Dan and I begin by retracing some of the steps that I took on the legit, the public, tour, until we reach a door – it's more of a hatch, really, of the sort you might expect to find in a Whitehall ministry or the hull of a nuclear sub, barring unauthorised access to warheads or a ticking particle accelerator. This portal opens on to a staircase, every bit as beguiling, in its way, as the Grand Shaft on the far side of the port. The stairway is roofed in thick metal hoops and falls steeply away from us. What we find at the foot of it is a vast subterranean office complex. It could almost be Ricky Gervais's stationery firm from *The Office*, but for the instructive differences that it's inside a cliff, and entirely empty.

Dan and I walk through room after room, each painted an institutional marigold and subconsciously inspired, if that's the word, by the minimalist lines of the Nissen hut. All the contents are gone, unless they were never here in the first place: desks, chairs, filing cabinets, the parts and stores of office life. But no, this place has seen action. In 1958, the Home Office acquired Dumpy from the Admiralty and turned it into one of ten Regional Seats of Government (RSGs) around the UK. This was during the Cold War, when the gravest external danger to the country appeared to be the red peril of the Soviet Union. In the event of Armageddon, amidst all the devastation and carnage, the RSGs would be the last holdouts of the Civil Service – thank God! – divvying up any remaining resources and seeing a measure of law and order. It was in the unlikely confines of Dumpy that our response to the Cuban missile crisis was strategised and war-gamed in 1962 by men with lots of frogging and piping on their jackets. (Don't say, 'What response?')

'It's the size of a football pitch down here,' says Dan. I'm glad to be walking through the bare, butterscotchy rooms – this bureaucrat's vision of nuclear winter – in the resourceful company of a man with not one but two industrial-strength yellow torches clipped to his waistband. We pass through a curiously shaped door, which is straight where it's hinged, but curved where the handle is. This admits us to another unlived-in, unacknowledged, *anti*-room, which gives the impression of a bigger room having been subdivided. It's Dan's opinion that 'the powers that be' had intended to cleave asunder all or most of the chambers that we are walking through, presumably to provide living-space for tens or scores of key workers. One room, bigger than the others, could comfortably be rendered into four. Two-thirds of the way down there's a partition, a kind of trellis, something a jerrybuilding landlord or botching handyman might have knocked up as a façade for shelves or lockers. Strip lights are suspended from the ceiling, giving the whole the air of a deserted classroom.

At least the ablution blocks are fitted with orange toilet cubicles, and a row of washbasins. 'Are they still plumbed in?'

Dan shakes his head. But I try a tap, all the same. It's an odd sensation, in its own modest way, to turn on a faucet – a shiny, stainless steel one, at that – and see nothing come out of it. It's like taking a step and missing your footing, or essaying a tee shot and failing to connect with the ball. 'I find these amazing,' said Dan, meaning the unsullied sanitaryware. 'The fact that they had all this down here and they never used any of it.'

The government installed the latest communications equipment and generators deep below the castle. There had been reservoirs of fuel and water. Dan and I put the air-conditioning on, as much as anything to prove that it still works, that this isn't all a dream – a curiously inert, medicated sort of dream. Dan throws a switch in the darkness of one of the indoor Nissens and a fan groans into life. Presently, playful fingers of air are toying with the hem of my shorts, *à la* Monroe.

It was in the signal year of 1984 that the Home Office abandoned Dumpy for good and took all its stuff away – perhaps it was a mandarin's idea of a joke. The rooms and passages that Dan and I are roaming, directly underneath one of the country's most popular tourist attractions, have been all but untouched for more than twenty years. I've been assuming that the preposterous 'Dumpy' is an acronym, but now I wonder if it isn't straightforwardly adjectival, referring to the deserted, the dumped, bunker. Perhaps there's an allusion to a 'dumpee', one who has been dumped. Who was the genius, after all, who thought it would be a good idea to situate a nuclear bunker in porous, breathable chalk – the real reason, surely, why the top brass and the permanent secretaries turned off the lights and tiptoed away?

Dan would like to open Dumpy to the public. The problem is that there aren't sufficient fire escapes. And once that was put right, the next thing would be paying for all the interactivity that's *de rigueur* these days, in order to grip youngsters' imaginations.

We return to the point where we left the Second World War tour, but instead of climbing a staircase we take the lift. It's no ordinary lift. It was fitted by the big boys from London. Dan knows what to do: he has the clearance, he has the codes. The lift duly arrives, and it sighs us up and out again rather higher in the cliff face, through a suitably inconspicuous door, close to the counter where the tour groups are mustered. But as if making a note for future reference, I register before we leave Dumpy that there's a sign above the button that calls the lift. And what this makes clear is that the button alone won't save you, baby! The sign spells out to people who've escaped the regular tour, or somehow fallen by the wayside, that their only hope of returning to civilisation is to break the glass panel, as in the case of fire. But this panel doesn't contain an alarm switch, or even an axe. It contains a key. To have any hope of summoning the lift, what you have to do is place the key in a keyhole beside the lift doors: this and this alone removes an invisible lock from the call-button, putting it under your control at last. In other words, the lift that springs the lost and lonely civilian from Dumpy can only be abracadabraed with a secret key hidden halfway down the cliffside.

I may be one of the few outsiders to have plumbed Dumpy: if anyone else has done it, odds on he or she is an urban adventurer, like 'Chris' who tagged the Victoria Tunnel in Newcastle to the chagrin of my friend Phil Thirkell. Chris and his ilk are habitués of the infernal regions, insinuating themselves into often tortuous or unlawful places below ground, before returning to document their trips on the Internet. Indeed, this often seems to be the *raison d'être* of their sorties – to post pictures or videos on line, accompanied by their laconic, even terse, captions. They are creatures of nickname and chat room, of text speak, of smileys and their opposites, the gurning, frowning scowleys. Urban adventurers are the free climbers of the hidden realm, bent on bagging the unknown Monroes of the upside-down world.

For my penultimate sally into the secret state, I joined forces with an urban sherpa from the West Country, a man who must go by the Conradian moniker of N. N took me to a classified hideaway even more substantial than Dumpy, a place set aside not just for the men in scrambled egg but for the royal family themselves. You've been there yourself, very likely, without suspecting a thing – why would you? This is a compound inside a bunker inside a quarry, the whole adroitly concealed behind the unexceptionable frontage of a railway bridge.

It takes a fast train going at a good clip a full minute to clear the Box Tunnel on the main line from London to Bristol, built by Isambard Kingdom Brunel and the longest rail tunnel in Europe in its day. The tunnel hides the entrance to 'Burlington', a name perhaps chosen to evoke in the sheltering shut-away royals within, fond memories of St James's and its elegant purlieus. The quarrymen who extracted Bath stone the colour of set honey to open up this great concealed space could have had no idea that it would one day become a refuge for their sovereign and her ministers, that it would contain ten kilometres of roadways – even its own pub and restful murals limned by a noted artist.

Nor is Burlington an outpost all to itself. Straddling the border of Wiltshire and Somerset, the meadows and hedgerows of this corner of the English countryside are blowsy and drowsy in high summer, and yet they positively crackle with the high-tech militaria of deep-cover, utterly deniable, installations.

N tells me that he'll be wearing a 'cream top' and combat trousers. I'll bet you will, I think. I drive down a vertiginous street in Bristol and catch sight of him – of someone who answers to his description but who, decisively, has the look in his eye of someone waiting to be recognised, identified. We go to a coffee shop. I order a macchiato. N plumps for a milkshake.

His top is beige rather than cream, if this is going to be a historical document worthy of the name. He is, I'm relieved to note, an amiable fellow of average height or less. He has longish, blondish hair which falls in a curtain-parting. I say I'm relieved because I was expecting, or bracing myself for, a class warrior, an eco-guerrilla, a Swampy – not that I have anything against anyone who fits that bill, per se, but that I doubt my ability to keep up with, to run with, that crowd.

N is not out to cause trouble. He has something in common with urban explorers, he concedes, but dissociates himself from their habit of going where they're not wanted, of effectively breaking into derelict properties for a nosey. He produces a sheaf of research from his rucksack. He believes that his meticulously sourced and thorough website will bear him out as bona fide if he's ever stopped by the authorities. (If they do apprehend him, they'll probably find that they are in receipt of several of his – I'm sure courteously written – Freedom of Information Act requests.)

We take the M4 heading east and turn off towards Corsham, not far from Bath. We drive up a country lane through a confetti of pollen, and pull up by a five-bar gate. N slips into a pair of unexpectedly dainty boots. I'm wearing a T-shirt in stripes of pink and grey, as well as the absurd, throwback footwear I was once persuaded to spend quite a lot of money on in an old-fashioned cobbler's. It's a kind of NCO's shoe, complete with

Blakey-loud heel, which can trace its uncompromising styling to the exacting test-bed that is the South African veldt.

As so often, it's not what one fears will go wrong that does in fact go wrong. I'm worrying about the shame, the self-reproach, and indeed the criminal record of an arrest. N and I are mooching about near MoD property – and I don't even know the half of it yet. I'm unaware that we are practically within laserscope range of a government tracking centre which is in constant touch with our fleet of nuclear subs; as well as of a green building doing its best to be nondescript, where the military monitors live links and broadband traffic from Iraq and Afghanistan. It's a good job that I've gone with the salmon-and-sardine top – unbelievably, the most presentable thing that I have with me, but also the kind of look that a terrorist is least likely to affect. But who knows, now, after the attacks by *doctors* that are all over the papers?

But as to the underground ramble itself, the physical experience, I'm unconcerned, reassured that N seems biddable and isn't looking to be a hero.

Big mistake.

We bear off the road and into a copse. Very soon we are at our destination: Ridge Quarry. Its presence is given away only by a kind of concrete hood, or perhaps it's a shed, protruding from the undergrowth. If that seems vague, it's because my mind is full of what bars my way into the quarry: a stack of large, moss-covered stone slabs.

I'm in need of spending a penny and think that I'll do this before N and I go in. This is a good idea, though an even better one might have been to watch N, the accomplished urban rambler, negotiate the blocks guarding the entrance, a formidable barrier. By the time I've returned from the wringing thicket, he's already inside and peering at me from over the top of the stones. I square up to them, to the task: it's the Letterbox of Alum Pot all over again.

I've sagely made sure that nothing will fall out of my pockets. As an additional precaution, I pass N my rucksack. Now I'm ready to make my entrance; or, to put it another way, I can't put it off any longer. I go in feet first, as if descending a ladder on board ship – and I see that there is a set of steps awaiting me on the other side, in fact, so this seems sound enough, good practice.

No, no! Argh! That's torn it! Unfortunately, it seems that my legs and hips are as much of me as I'm able to fit through the gap. N is very good: not looking at his watch, not tittering. On the contrary, he is patient, tactful, pointing out that he is no slip of a thing himself. If *he* can do it, so can I. He says he thinks they've made the entrance smaller, tighter, since he was last here. Is this just to make me feel better about being stuck? This of course raises the question: who are *they*? And why haven't they sealed the quarry up altogether, for that matter?

'Would you rather go somewhere else?' asks N. Then, 'Of course . . .' or 'The thing is . . .' or 'The thing to remember is . . .' all of this prefacing the substantive point that '. . . you've got to get out again.' A good point well made, and many thanks, N, for flagging it up. Indeed, I can think of little else, once I finally enter the quarry, and then for the hour or more that we spend inside it, other than how the fuck I'm going to get out at the end of it.

But I do get in – I won't say elegantly, I won't use a word like 'textbook'. But in I suddenly, thankfully, am. ('If you can get in, you can get out,' N reassuringly glosses.) I think I made it by just squeezing, shoving – forcing – myself through the abrading, unforgiving slot.

Taking hold of a handrail, I follow N gingerly into the blackness, still twitching with the adrenaline of negotiating the aperture into the quarry, also querying if I've done myself an injury; but mostly, as I say, wondering how I will later extricate myself, if at all.

As its name indicates, Ridge Quarry was worked for its stone long before it and its environs were reimagined as a hard-shell refuge for the royals. From the end of the nineteenth century onwards, it was hacked out by men like Frank 'Tanky' Elms, who described the life underground:

> Quarrying was one of the most skilful, arduous, least rewarding jobs, requiring great stamina and patience. There was never a rougher, tougher, harder-swearing and harder-working gang of men than the real quarrymen . . . I wouldn't think there was any harder, more soul-destroying job on this earth. I have often thought that if law-breakers had to do a term underground quarrying in the old-fashioned method, very few would want to go back again.

These men smoked short-stemmed clay pipes, 'nose-warmers', and played practical jokes on each other, such as laying detonators under trolleys. ('It went off like a cannon. Father's hat fell off and swear words just rolled out.') They also developed formidable skills as masons. Cutting a block of stone entailed making horizontal and vertical incisions in the seam with picks, before inserting staves behind the desired lump in order to lever it out. Men known as choppers had the job of bedding the stone; that is, hacking off all the rough edges to leave a flat-faced block for the men on the surface to cut up as required. Tanky Elms said:

> When I think of the pickers swinging their long-handled picks with head and shoulders rubbing against the ceiling, with the accuracy of Ian Botham playing a stroke against the fastest bowler in the world, it was remarkable. The choppers swung axes as heavy as twelve pounds to bed a stone, some up to twelve foot long and six foot wide, finishing with a bed almost as level as a billiard table for a mere pittance of a living. These men have never received the recognition or living they truly deserved.

Our torches disclose graffiti and sculpture, or at least inventive whittling, from the quarry's history. A grudging valediction – 'Some get a clock, others nothing' – catches the bolshie tone of Elms himself. There's a cartoon of a man and a woman, and a lengthy freehand passage expressing thanks, apparently on behalf of a bridegroom, to his various supporters including his 'best man'. Perhaps it's only here, underground, that one can still catch a sense of how the trade of quarrying was for so long ingrained in the locality.

In the evenings, says Elms, the quarrymen used to go to the pub, to play dominoes or a game known as 'Tippit'. 'As they died off so they would move nearer to the door. When I go there now I am the only one there, so I sit in the end seat nearest the door; I'm bound to be the next to go.'

The dark and stony place where men like Elms laboured attracted the interest of the highest in the land. The government had known since the Great War about the hazards of aerial bombardment of munitions plants. In January 1916 a Zeppelin had inched along the path of the River Trent, hoping to locate and destroy a factory making high explosives. A rumour went around that the munitions minister, Lord Chetwynd, happened to be touring the factory when he came across three German spies grimly heliographing the dirigible. He lost no time in drawing his revolver and shooting them dead. Getting wind of this aggrandising yarn, his lordship arranged for a sexton to dig three graves on a nearby hillside and fill them with rocks: his reputation was made. Chetwynd's successors were similarly alive to the political capital to be gained by stockpiling weapons securely, so in 1936 they paid £47,000 for Ridge and neighbouring quarries in order to convert them into arms dumps. Munitions were winched down the staircase which N and I had descended.

We also come across a pile of pitch-black pit props and other debris, which was the site of a lift shaft until it was clumsily filled in during peacetime. At the height of the Second World War, more than 300,000 tons of explosives were tucked away a hundred feet under the fields and woods of Corsham. They were arrayed in 125 acres of bomb-proof tunnels, well away from the Luftwaffe-strafed docks of Bristol. At Ridge alone, where two shifts of stackers worked round the clock, the quarry was capable of disappearing no less than four hundred tons of bombs a day. On the eve of the invasion of Europe, which had provoked furious if cack-handed tunnelling beneath Dover Castle, the arsenal at Ridge weighed in at more than 31,000 tons.

You would imagine that a prerequisite of the good husbandry of weapons systems is a sound, level floor, and Ridge still fulfils the brief more than sixty years on – not so other local quarries, according to N, where he finds himself climbing over obstacles. That said, he has had his unnerving moments even here. In one corner, the clearance overhead is noticeably tighter than it was where we entered, and in this low-ceilinged area there's the noise of rushing water, the stone under foot is slippery, and icy droplets fall insistently on your head. When the quarrymen worked in this part of Ridge, they were wet through within half an hour. Tanky Elms and his oppos would often have to eat in such conditions, producing their food not from totemic snap tins but 'flask-baskets'. 'These were a tradition with the quarrymen. They were straw baskets bound with a sort of hessian and with two handles. You put a rope or a strap on it and hung it over your shoulder and carried your food in it. You had to put your food right up on the [stone] pillars and make sure the rats didn't get at it. They would climb a straight face, but if the face was perpendicular or overhanging they couldn't climb it – there were hundreds of rats down there.'

There's no sign of rats today – there's nothing for them to eat – but Ridge still has the power to unnerve. N tells me that he once came here by himself to take photographs for his website. He set up his camera, primed his slave flashes – in short, he was good to go – 'But I was kind of freaked out by it, by the noise of the water. It gets on your nerves after a while. I had to get out.'

Ah yes: getting out. If entering the quarry was bad, exiting it is worse. As before, N goes first. There's something about his physique – above ground, he is all wrong: short, rotund, almost womanly without being remotely feminine. But underground, it all works, somehow, he's in his element. I squeeze out like a truckle of Wensleydale through a grater; I'll be lobbing dollops of liniment towards the smarting small of my back for days to come, until I'm almost as dextrous as one of Tanky Elms's pickers.

We go on to the railway track, where the trains clatter through to Bristol. We're approaching the part of this great former quarry complex where the Windsors would have been – the Queen Motherlode, if you will. N and I are near the tunnel where, if all else failed, the royals would alight from their warranted rolling-stock in the sidings, and enter the secret bastion of Burlington. Like Ridge, it was a weapons strongroom during the war, though it was also big enough, at some 240 acres, to be an underground factory for military aircraft engines, into the bargain. Like Dumpy, it was refitted as a Cold War shelter, for Prime Minister Macmillan and four thousand of his closest aides and officials, as well as the Queen and her nearest and dearest. It was equipped with what was then the largest telephone exchange in the country, and a BBC studio from where the premier could address his crisped and smoking domain. A network of underground power stations supplied a hundred thousand lights, which lit the way to a pub, the Rose and Crown, modelled on the Red Lion, the favourite Whitehall boozer of the political classes.

Unlike the Regional Seat of Government that I had promenaded under the Dover clifftops, Burlington was done out with all the accoutrements and appurtenances of the 1950s workplace, including glass ashtrays, loo brushes and government-issue tea sets. Hundreds of swivel-chairs were delivered in 1959 but never taken out of their dust sheets. There were portraits of the Queen and Princess Margaret, as well as sporting scenes in the canteen painted by the artist Olga Lehmann, who went on to design costumes for films including *The Guns of Navarone*. Burlington has been compared by one military historian to a set from *The Avengers*. Its shelf life narrowly exceeded Dumpy's: the clue is in the old telephone directories, which date from 1989, the year the Berlin Wall came down. The same Rolls-Royce minds that had come to the conclusion at Dover that nuclear radiation and chalk-based accommodation didn't mix, had also realised that not even the royal train was capable of evacuating the first family to Bath in the time allowed by a four-minute warning.

The last hush-hush documents were removed from Burlington in 1995, though it was another decade before it was finally declassified and its existence acknowledged. In 2005 it was tentatively put up for sale – offers in the region of £5 million – though any buyer was also required to take on a cashiered army base above ground. But with no end in sight to the war on terror – not to mention the onset of a property crash – it's no great surprise to find that there are no 'For Sale' boards outside Burlington now.

There's another remarkable subterranean structure nearby, part of the same great Corsham ramification. It's a tunnel, a mile and a quarter in length, which rises from beside the railway line to high in the overlooking hill, a place called Monkton Farley. Like Ridge and Burlington, it was an old quarry, adapted in the Second World War to a new role as a magazine. And where N and I are standing there was once a railway station. Trains laden with munitions disgorged their loads on to pallets which were then cranked deep into the hillside on a production line, an electrified conveyor belt, itself the successor to an equally unlikely aerial ropeway. All you'd notice now from a passing train, if anything, is a rusting iron roof, which you might mistake for the wreck of a ruined barn. But this corrugated awning still conceals a set of points where the wagons debouched their deadly payload. 'Somewhere in England, Monday,' begins a piece in the *Daily Express* of 23 November 1943. '. . . A lonely-looking policeman is at this very moment stamping his cold feet on a bleak railway siding . . . behind him slopes a tunnel to the preposterous underworld built as a series of permanent ammunition depots, the biggest of their kind, each a lavish Temple to Mars.'

From the old station, N and I descend a step or two to the necessary offices and loos, all pungently derelict, and thence to the foothills of the tunnel itself, which was fashioned using the cut 'n' cover method (to an aficionado of the subterranean, cut 'n' cover is the new rock 'n' roll). The tunnel bears evidence of fitful habitation: day-glo doodlings, tea-lights, a graffito that says 'Don't Look Back' and a copy of the *Daily Star* from just two days ago. 'People sometimes have raves in here,' says N, with what may be a note of disappointment.

The old conveyor belt used to be thirty inches across, rattling through the bobbins at a lick of 75 feet per minute, according to the pathologically detailed *Secret Underground Cities* by Nick McCamley. The author, who has made his home nearby, is a hero and mentor to N, while his book is one of the essential texts of English subterranea: it's the *Canterbury Tales* of the scene, you might say, the *Beowulf*. 'Men were stationed at intervals along the conveyor belt charged with the unutterably boring task of keeping watch over the thousands of ammunition boxes as they trundled past in the cold miserable gloom, checking that none slipped off or jammed.'

The mighty elastic band is no more – long since removed, looted, withered, perished. But several of its serried trestles remain. They radiate away into the dark, concrete-lined hillside like the most gruelling indoor hurdling track ever devised. Even on a hot, sunny day, the tunnel is cool and dark. It's as much as seven feet wide, and tall enough for a man to stand up in. We climb to the very top, to the old Monkton Farley quarry. This is where the munitions were clanked into bays for safe-keeping. Blocks have been cemented over the entrance of the quarry, but someone, perhaps a raver, has worked one or two of them loose enough to admit a draught – it's really quite a gust. After this chamber was no longer needed by the armed forces, it was briefly home to an unlikely museum run by none other than Nick McCamley himself, though it has since been replaced by a data storage operation. Now retired, McCamley continues to write, and sells his highly fancied bird photographs online.

As any honest troglodyte will tell you, half the fun of going underground is coming up to the surface again; and perhaps vice versa. After my earlier ordeal at Ridge, Monkton Farley is one quarry I'm determined to walk away from. Emerging from the mile-long tunnel, I gambol beside the railway line once more, and confirm to myself that it's warm. It's bright. I take a renewed pleasure in the butterflies alighting on the rampant trackside weeds, and even feel well disposed to the hairy-arsed horsefly that is tattooing my arm.

Just like the old *Yellow Pages* left on the desks at Burlington, the subterranean isn't only there for the nasty things in life. Indeed, as well as warehousing weapons and even royals below ground, you can also store the very essence of life itself, in this unimprovably secure and changeless environment. 'Environment' is the operative word for the pioneering Millennium Seedbank project, a nursery of the netherworld which I found secreted under a substantial slice of Sussex. Like an insatiable gardener, forever snaffling and scrounging sprigs and clippings, this initiative intends to gather into its commodious bosom a specimen of every pip and kernel on earth, in what I'm bound to call a hedge against global warming. At first sight, it could hardly be further removed from the reinforcements of Dover and the Bath stone bunkers, and yet if the coming conflicts on earth are over basic resources, as predicted, then the seedbank could find itself on the frontline. It already has a quality of embattlement about it, because it's a kind of ark. It follows that Roger Smith, who helped to set it up, is its Noah.

Certainly, Roger has an authoritative, if not authoritarian, manner, as well as a well-developed antediluvian streak. When I invite him to peek over the horizon of the years, for instance, he retorts, 'If I could see the future, I'd be in the City of London, being carried on a gold palanquin by as many Nubian slaves as you care to mention.' But until that golden dawn, Roger will continue to put in an appearance at Wakehurst, in the grounds of the titular stately home where his seedbank has accumulated no less that 96 per cent of native UK plant species – and counting. In its voracious sights are the fruits of the tropical drylands, where a fifth of the world's population live. In extreme dry conditions – in a drought – plants don't grow, of course. 'And the idea is, we'll have the building blocks to rebuild whatever can be rebuilt.' Roger adds a pithy word of caution. 'Desertification is non-linear; in other words, you can't always put things back the way they were. We fool around with the world not knowing how bits work or how to put it all back again.'

The seedbank's upper storey is above ground and under glass. I follow Roger beneath this cloche to a reception room, where plants arrive from the four corners of the globe. 'The sun never sets on the Millennium Seedbank project.'

The samples turn up in what look like laundry bags; but then this *is* a kind of laundry – or drying-room, anyway. Plants die fifty times more slowly in a dry room than in ambient conditions. The largest seeds that can be preserved are the issue of palm trees. 'We can't dry conkers, for instance, I'm afraid.' Trees are the dominant vegetation on earth – Roger throws an arboreal shape, demonstrating surprising gracefulness for a big man – and a single tree can produce thousands if not millions of seeds. But the wonder of it is that it will reproduce itself if just one of them grows.

The bank is administered by Kew Gardens and has partners in many countries who are 'trained furiously' to harvest and then dispatch seeds. Timing is all important. 'What was it Mr Birds Eye used to say?' muses Roger, as if trying to recall the tutorials of an influential don – 'Up to the moment when the pod went pop?' All this international reaping and trafficking is covered by rules laid down at the Earth summit in Rio de Janeiro in 1992. 'We are not bio-pirates. The fact that I may have a parrot on my shoulder and a wooden leg is merely a form of dress that I appreciate,' says Roger, his arms folded, and clad in fact in a suede jacket and lilac sweater over a black shirt.

'What's the most striking thing you've found?'

'What do I want to say?' ponders Roger, in a characteristic trope. 'No one has ever set out to catalogue all the plants in the world before. We don't get enough people on the ground doing the police-style fingertip search to be sure we've found everything. But our people in Crete have come across some plants that are not normally found there . . .' He makes these Cretan blooms sound like the Giant Rat of Sumatra, a story for which the world is not yet ready. 'Now,' he says, 'I think you'll enjoy the splendour of the humid room.'

As at Dover and Corsham, Adolf Hitler was the unlikely midwife of invention where the country's reserves of plant life were concerned, seventy years ago. One of the great campaigns of wartime was the restocking of the British Isles, and that went for vital vegetable goodness as well as for steel and shells. 'All the vitamin C that we were used to was going to the bottom of the briny because of German U-boats,' said Roger. It's a footnote to the life of the late Magnus Pyke, the windmill-armed telly boffin, that he was responsible for creating rose-hip syrup to plug the gap in the national diet. The rose hips were collected by schoolchildren, and sent off by the WI to Kew, where they were put through a mangle by Dr Pike and friends.

Dramatic events like these raised awareness of the need to safeguard our horticultural heritage. The seedbank's first home was within the stately pile of Wakehurst itself. It started life in the chapel of the big house. 'All available security measures taken advantage of,' says Roger, as dry as the drying-room itself, where young women are consulting an impressive spectrometer to assess the viability of some husks.

Wakehurst had been one of Britain's wartime 'roll-over centres', which were conceived on the same dubious premise as the sting-in-the-tail strategy of the Western Heights garrison in Dover during the Napoleonic wars. The idea was that if the Nazis came ashore in Sussex, the Wakehurst complement – 'mostly rude hockey gels, gels recruited at Fortnum & Mason' – would lie low in tunnels until the enemy had passed over their heads, so to speak, then spring up and club them with their sticks while their backs were turned. This place had a subterranean past, then, even before it became a kind of sperm bank for our menopausal planet.

Roger's seeds live down a spiral staircase, in a vault on the other side of a formidable door. He counsels me against over-excitement. 'What do I want to say? It's not a very visual sport. It's not Ricky Hatton.'

All the same, it's not what I'm expecting. What I'm expecting is a heat-holding hamam, a throttling trellis of variegated abandon, corn as high as an elephant's eye. I'm expecting a cross between an illicit cannabis farm and a screeching bayou. Instead there is a central lock-up or back room, prowled by Roger's gene jockeys, while off this, portholes afford a view into the strongrooms of the bank itself: a quantity of well-ordered shelving can be made out. This is no teeming tropic, far from it. The four safes are kept at a temperature of minus 20 degrees centigrade.

Roger steers me towards one of his giant freezer cabinets. His fingers encircle the handle. 'I have to tell you, this is a place with a high heart-attack risk.' In the breath-catching cold, we study the pill boxes that hold Roger's desiccated nuts and seeds. 'The packaging industry would say, "Go with argon! Weld in stainless steel!" But the seeds wouldn't like it.'

I said a moment ago that the specimens live here, but they don't, not really. They reside in a chilly limbo from which they can be resuscitated after two hundred years or more – or at least, that's the plan. 'Every ten years, we take out a batch and test them,' says Roger. Small wonder that this cryogenic garden centre calls to mind the unacknowledged warren at the heart of the Rockwell experiment.

The genes of fish swimming in the Arctic have been used in the cultivation of oilseed rape, so that it can be grown in more northerly climes. Roger smiles, 'The truth is, whether we like it or not, we're on a ride somewhere.'

The reason the seeds are stored underground is because it's easier to keep them at a constant temperature. The cold rooms rest on a pontoon of breeze-blocks which act as a layer of insulation, to stop the concrete floor below from freezing, which in turn could lead to cracks opening up in the ground.

'What would you do in the event of a major emergency, some big catastrophe?'

'If they have a nuclear unhappiness in France?' muses Roger. 'We will read about it and stop the air circulating.'

There are more than 24,000 species at Wakehurst, with a target of 30,000 within another two years: that's 10 per cent of the world's plant population. 'There's space down here for thirty-seven buses,' says Roger (buses, like football pitches and swimming pools, having been adopted at some point by an unknown international committee as universally accepted units of area). The Millennium Seedbank costs £7 million a year to run, with some of the money coming from the Millennium Fund. At the time of writing, it has assured funds until 2009 only. 'Nobody's ever looked at the variety of seeds that we're looking at. Everybody's saying that we must do something about global warming,' says Roger. 'Well, we're doing something about it.'

I tell him that I fear for him, that one day an ungrateful fly-trap or triffid will turn on its daddy. 'People will say, "It's what he would have wanted."'

'No, they won't,' says Roger. 'They'll say "He was a stubborn old bugger."'

15

CLEAN SLATE

For the following account of mining in the Lake District and the Forest of Dean, I thought I'd begin by hanging off the side of a mountain, in driving wind and freezing, brittle rain. A thousand feet below me is a slate-grey pass once known as 'the worst road in England'. In a matter of minutes, a clear November sky has turned the same colour as the pass. Even more impressively, it has also filled it. In the dwindling visibility, I'm focusing intently on the fingers of my left hand, as they fumble with the jaws of a karabiner. A brace of these clasps is the only thing holding me on to Fleetwith Pike, apart from the fingers of my right hand. I'm intent on these groping digits of mine because it's better than the alternative, which is to be intent on the drop. The karabiners are wonderful, but also treacherous. They attach me to a rope, but not if they fail to close properly, and not when they stubbornly refuse to respond to my oafish caresses. Why won't this bloody thing snap down and in on itself, like it's supposed to? At the full extent of my reach, I strain to release the catch. It's snagged somehow. My numbing fingers are as deft and nimble as links of sausage. I can feel the strength ebb from my other hand, the one that's holding on to the mountain.

What do I think I'm doing? At first sight, the answer's the one in plain view. I'm climbing. Or climbing *badly*, with no evidence of any gift for the pursuit, if you want to make a point of it. The less intuitive answer is that I'm working. I'm mining, to be precise. Yes, I'm suspended in millions of square feet of bleak Lake District air – not much chance of claustrophobia out here, though vertigo is another matter – and yet I'm doing what hundreds if not thousands of miners have done in these parts. Incredibly, this was how they got to work, before doing their shifts in the mines that produced Cumbria's much prized slate – there's a reason for the singular hue of the grey rock hereabouts. And though I might feel beads of sweat running icy-cold from beneath my hard-hat, the fact of the matter is that I've got it easy. The real miners used to be lowered down the side of the mountain in wicker baskets, to begin hacking away at the rock in order to excavate the adits, tunnels that would eventually give them access to valuable seams. 'This is where men have lost their lives, some blown off the crag face by the ferocious winds that sweep through the valley, some felled by rock falls inside the mountain while they worked by candlelight, and some crushed by huge clogs [blocks of slate] slipping out of the winch chains or rolling the wrong way,' writes Celia Weir Taylor in *The Brilliant Darkness*, an account of local slate mining. 'We will never know how many lives have been taken by Fleetwith Pike as it has tried jealously to keep hold of its beautiful green slate.'

You would know little of the exploits of these men, risking everything in the mining equivalents of dumb waiters, if you only drove through the pass below, as the trippers do. You could miss the evidence that still survives to document the ant-hill activity of the slate miners. You could be forgiven for thinking that the bare mountain, having cast off its puny interlopers, had been restored to a state of pristine wildness – or indeed, for failing to guess that the miners had ever been there at all. Certainly, you'd do well to surmise that the helicopter that thwocked through the pass below me just before the weather closed in was linked to the mine's bold revival.

As I've been climbing, I've passed the rusty pylon of an aerial ropeway that once winched parts to the mine, and in turn, lowered slate down the mountainside to be dressed and sold. I've seen metal bars, like drill bits, standing proud from a rockface and rising up the mountainside at an angle of sixty degrees: these are the stair-rods of a slate staircase, one of many on these slopes, built by the men of the Lakes so that they could reach established adits without going in for in the hair-raising outdoor pursuit of miner-in-a-basket. I'm traversing a wide, bare rock in the sleety twilight, and I'm about to swing out on a rope for fifty feet or so across a high ravine, always assuming, of course, that I can crack the combination of my unbiddable karabiners. I'm climbing the *via ferrata*, the iron road improvised for generations by the miners of Honister Pass to get them to and from work.

You might think that a wind-whistling mountainside was an unlikely spot to reflect on the subterranean. But when I haul myself up by a handhold left by slate-cutters scores of years ago, I can't help but give a silent vote of thanks to these shadowy pioneers. If the precipitate edges of the *via ferrata* don't help you to put yourself into the flailing hobnails of a miner, then nothing will.

Lives have been lived underground in England, by people who are still walking around the place and able to tell the tale. These are not the troglodytes of Wolverley or the cave dwellers of 'Gibraltar', but huge men with hands like grappling-hooks. These giants are robust and active into what others consider to be old age. Like the life they have led, they can appear hard and forbidding, but when the light falls on a hitherto unsuspected facet of them, you are struck by something wholly unexpected: they scintillate – on the face of it, an unlikely claim to make of old boys who have spent a lifetime down mines; but then I am talking, I suppose, of rough diamonds.

This is not a paean to horny-handed sons of toil, or a lament for a vanished mining industry – the proud banners, the snap tins, the unabashed manliness of the pithead baths. We've all heard those before, stirring and necessary as they doubtless are. No, I merely hope to grub up a little stake of pay-dirt on the remarkable lives of men who have spent every working day in underground England. The reader will forgive, I hope, my ransacking of the thesaurus for terms meaning 'extraction', because it seems as though the English mining story itself has to be uncovered and brought out into the open. So swiftly and thoroughly has this once staple industry been effaced from the culture, from the national conversation, that one might plausibly say that mining has gone underground.

At Honister, the extraordinary figure of 'Uncle' John Taylor awaits us, a man blinded in one eye as a teenager by a bomb, a no-nonsense Lakelander with a perhaps unexpected taste for champagne and American cars. On the bluff and unassuming face of it, John, now seventy-four, is that thoroughly sympathetic figure, the gentle giant – part Tommy Cooper, part Desperate Dan. You can imagine him blue-chinned and tucking into cow pie. But along with his easy laugh came an equal readiness to offer violence until well into his senior years. He had an almost Sicilian propensity to switch from cordiality to brute force and back again in the blink of that one good eye. John is a man out of myth, you feel, awe-inspiring and still a law unto himself, the Cyclops of Honister Pass.

But first to the story of the equally formidable Robin 'Robbie' Morgan, seventy-three years old himself. Had it not been for an accident of geography, Big John and Robbie might have found themselves working alongside each other. One man was from the Lakes, the other from 250 miles away in the Forest of Dean in Gloucestershire, but both have their roots in jet-hard mining stock. In Robbie's case, his family was also strangely susceptible to spiritual vibrations. His father, a miner before him, had the gift of moving inanimate objects without touching them. Les Morgan would levitate heavy wooden pub tables and send them hurtling across the snugs of the Forest of Dean. 'A barmaid once jumped on board, but the table kept moving,' said Robbie. If Robbie hadn't been sitting in front of me as he was telling the tale, if I hadn't already been with him into the tunnels of the mine he still works, I would never have believed him. But if such a down-to-earth man tells you a thing like this, he's doing nothing more than giving you the facts, uncanny as they may be. 'Finally, the old chap gave it up. It bothered him, you see. He couldn't even go out in the dark by himself in the end.'

And yet strangely enough – strangely enough to an outsider, anyway – the spooked Morgan Senior went on contentedly mining for as long as he was physically able. Perhaps it soothed him. But then mining – going down into the earth, lying in the wet and the blackness, and knocking coal down almost on top of yourself from just above your head – this is what the men of the Forest of Dean have been bred to. They don't dwell on the discomforts of such a life, even the horrors of it, as some might see them. In the Forest, it always held that you were either a miner or a tree-feller. In 1849 it was recorded that there were more men *under* the Forest than there were on the surface.

It's an enchanted plateau isolated between two rivers, and celebrated in a local motto: 'Happy is the eye betwixt the Severn and the Wye.' The Forest is not part of Wales – though many inhabitants, including Robbie Morgan, have Welsh names – but nor is it English in the same way as the Cotswolds, say, or the city of Bristol, neither of which are any distance away. Indeed, the people living on the fringes of the Forest are the first to make fun of its separateness, with the unwarranted, even actionable slur that it's the incest capital of the country. Certainly, this is a corner of the realm unto itself, where old traditions and superstitions persist. Here they understand that a man like Les Morgan could be perfectly at home underground and yet be seized by a fear of the dark.

There's a legend about an old woman who used to let the miners leave their tools and work clothes in her cottage when they clocked off at the end of their shift. She was one of several crones, reputed to have unearthly powers, who lived alone in the depths of the Dean and practised herbal medicine. The miners' favourite recreation was hare-coursing, but one furry quarry always eluded their dogs. This animal would break cover beneath a holly tree in a place called Edge Hills, run for a mile or two through the forest, then return to the tree and disappear. 'The Mystery of the Vanishing Hare soon became a sport amongst the miners, so much so that they had a wager on who would catch it first,' notes local folklorist Elaine Wright. They consulted a 'wiseman' who lived at the village of Cinderford, not far from where Robbie Morgan mines today. This seer loaned the miners his spayed bitch, advising them to hold her from the hare, and to set her free only when the long-eared fiend was about to dive back into the folds of its earth. They suited the coursing action to the words, and the wiseman's bitch duly snagged the hare, sinking her teeth hard into the creature's stomach.

Elaine Wright takes up the story, 'The hare squealed out in pain, but freed itself and vanished once again beneath the holly tree. The next morning, the miners left home for work as usual, talking about the previous day's sport and wondering whether they would be able to use the same ruse again, when they noticed that the old woman was not there to meet them as she usually did. They called to her several times and, as there was no answer, knocked on her door. There was still no sign of life so they forced the door open. The old woman was lying dead on the floor with what appeared to be a dog bite in her side.' The ruins of her cottage can still be seen, it's said, but it's now thought to be a spot best avoided at night. Perhaps the story of the leveret-lady of Edge Hills was at the back of the troubled mind of old man Morgan.

Historically, the Forest was a forbidding place, unwelcoming to outsiders. Even after the Romans had conquered the rest of England, the Dean held out against them. It took five years of hard scrapping during the mid-first century AD to subjugate the locals, a tribe known as the Silures, who had settled the Forest in about 450 BC. The Silures, led by Caractacus, ringed their bosky home with forts, the remains of which can still be made out at Washberry, Littledean, Lydney, Soudley, Symonds Yat and elsewhere. 'Now began an epic struggle,' writes Dean historian Mike Wilding, 'the desperate battle of a single tribe without armour against the iron discipline and stern valour of the greatest military power of the day.' The Roman leader, Aulus Plautius, died before the Forest capitulated, and so did his successor Ostorius, exhausted by the pitiless contest. 'Not until every Roman, both active and retired, had been brought into service, did this Silurian stronghold fall, with scarcely an able-bodied tribesman left in action. In the Scowles [cavities], which surround the Dean, worked the descendants of the followers of Caractacus for over three centuries, silent and resentfully supplying the Romans with iron. They followed the ore leads, eating them out of the rock until all that was left was these huge cavities, which continue down a maze of tunnels which honeycomb the Dean.'

In time, the people of the Forest also mounted a stout rearguard action against the invading Saxons, resisting what they saw as the unwelcome miscegenation that was part of the Saxon 'offer'. In stark contrast to the reputation they're unfairly saddled with these days, the Forest folk rejected interbreeding. They also insisted on the exclusivity of their mineral rights to the Dean, established perhaps as long ago as the time of the Celts. There's evidence for this in the Celtic-derived names associated with mining in the area: the word 'gale', for instance, meaning a birthright, a holding; and 'vern', a helpmate or apprentice.

Ancient Phoenician scrolls document commerce with the people
of the Forest, who are said to have bartered with iron bars. At all
events, they insisted that they were free to work the mines just as
their forefathers had done, whatever the Saxons thought on the
subject, and that no 'foreigner' could join them underground
except by their leave.

We discern here the roots of a great tradition of this Arcadian
nook: free mining. Under common law dating from feudal times,
and codified by Edward I (reigned 1272–1307), the men of the
Forest of Dean are free to mine their native coal and iron
provided certain archaic conditions are fulfilled. A miner must
have been born within the Hundred of St Briavels, which includes
most of the Forest: a 'hundred' was an area of the country
capable of raising five score men to take up arms on behalf of the
King. In his skirmishes with the Welsh and Scottish, Edward had
cause to be grateful to the foresters, who were well versed in
transferable skills including archery, stalking and engineering.
Moreover, it was to the parochial estates of St Briavels and their
resident miners that the well-advised monarch turned if he was
looking for explosives know-how.

Small wonder that Edward was happy to reward the men by
registering their privileges in the 'Book of Dennis', which was a
glossary of the miners' earlier 'Lawes [sic] and Privileges. The
'Dennis' of the title is thought to be a typo for 'denu', the Celtic
term for an area of wooded valleys. His Majesty acknowledged
that the miners' rights had existed 'tyme out of minde'. The rules
stated that a man had to work for 'a year and a day' in the mines
of the Forest to qualify as a free miner in his own right, and that
he had to register with the King's representative, the gaveller, who
granted mining rights and collected dues. The miners were
allowed to hold their own parliament, or Speech House, a
custom that survives to this day, those with a stake in the
resonantly named mines of the Dean – Favourite, Lydbrook Deep
Level, New Found Out – gathering every month to compare

notes and ventilate grievances at the present Speech House near Cinderford. Their sessions are listed in the local paper, *Forest Review*. As late as the nationalisation of coal in 1946, the rugged independence of miners in the Forest of Dean was recognised in a clause exempting their jealously defended gales from state ownership.

Such perquisites may have encouraged the people of the Forest to think of themselves as a breed apart. Certainly, they grew no more hospitable over time. Until well into the Middle Ages, occasional visitors would recount stories of the 'wild and barbarous' types encountered among the trees. Wilding writes, 'They went to such great extremes to keep out strangers that the Book of Dennis . . . forbade the entry of any wheeled vehicle into the Forest.'

There was perhaps a folk-memory of this in my own latterday entrée when I set out from Lydney, once a wooded bastion of the court of King Caractacus, but in the autumn of 2008 a more modest railway halt. Though I travelled by wheeled vehicle, in the shape of a Japanese car driven by a cabbie called John, it wasn't a taxi as the rest of the country would recognise one. After we had been going for several minutes, I realised with a pulse of horror that I couldn't see a meter. 'Oh, we don't have them in the Forest,' said John.

'No meters? You're like your own republic out here. Do you recognise Gordon Brown? The Queen?'

I was on more familiar territory, or thought I was, when I half caught something that John said over his shoulder. 'The place is being taken over . . . they're going around in packs' – surely a reference to England's notorious yob culture, penetrating even here, among the stands of lime planted long ago by Edward VII? But no – John was referring to wild boar! These swine had the run of the Forest. John himself had known them barrel out of the woods right in front of his bumper.

Through copses of trees hung with metallic leaves – they might have been by-products of the mineral trade hereabouts – I was on my way to see Robbie Morgan, the oldest free miner in the Forest of Dean, as unlikely and as thick-skinned a survivor in his own way as one of its tusked hogs. With its smoking chimneys, his long, single-storey shed sunk in a valley might have been a hill-billy's still. And there *was* something of the American boondocks about the place, in truth, what with all the baseball caps and facial hair in evidence: not only Robbie's own snowy sideburns, but also the tache of a younger miner, James, who called by to see him, and the wispy, almost Amish, goatee of another, Richard. That said, there was no moonshine in Robbie's shack, only tea and toast. It was a café and a muster point for Hopewell Mining Museum, the tourist attraction that he was running in tandem with his viable mine next door, the Phoenix. Here, his boots planted wide apart before a coal fire, he munched a thickly buttered round. At first, the coke-warmed room put me in mind of an old-fashioned clerkish office, or of a Sunday-best sitting room. But what it most closely resembled, I decided finally, was the waiting-room of a railway station on a branch line years ago.

'I don't have anything up top,' Robbie was telling me. He didn't pass the eleven-plus to go to grammar school so he became a miner, like his old man, first going down a mine at the age of thirteen. 'I used to get a bit scared . . .' He looked a huge man, much bigger than I am. And even after he had levered himself from his chair and I could see that he was no taller than me, six feet two or so – if anything, a little shorter, what with his slight stoop – the impression persisted. He had big, dirty hands. His checked shirt was slashed open, and wiry white hair peeked from under his dirty hard-hat.

At first, he was all business. He wanted me to know that he had a mine to maintain. He'd had it for fifteen years and he took care of it all by himself now, since the sudden death two years earlier of his son Neil, in his early fifties. 'He was working on the Friday, dead on the Tuesday.' But he was more expansive once we were underground, in his mine, the place he felt most at home. With two hundred feet of rock above our heads, he pointed out a seam of coal, dark and glossy as a thoroughbred's flank. It was made of rotted giant ferns, three hundred million years old, he said. 'In the Forest of Dean in those days, there were dragonflies two feet long.' He demonstrated as an angler might have done. The Phoenix has been worked since 1821. Though a pamphlet on local mines in Robbie's own museum lists it as surviving on a 'care and maintenance basis', he insisted that he was still mining.

And I didn't doubt it, either, as I followed the single-minded septuagenarian deeper into his gale. 'A lot of people today haven't seen a coal fire, never mind a coalmine,' he said, in the clammy gloom where he has spent his working life. He recounted fluctuations in the market for bijoux nuggets of coal, otherwise known as 'small'. As much as I was treading in his footsteps through the tunnels of the mine, I was also trying to negotiate the sometimes barely penetrable byways of his speech. There was the jargon, and then there was the mouthful-of-marbles accent. 'The last one I sin,' said Robbie, talking now about a rare red squirrel. He was fascinated by the zoology of the mining environment. 'I know of a frog falling seven hundred feet, down the deepest pit in the Forest,' he said, the beam of his lamp on me. 'He survived. Their bones is like rubber.'

The miners have to be almost as lithe as the local pondlife. The coalface in a Dean mine is narrow, and the men must work on their stomachs or their backs. The coal is surrounded by clay, and when it rains in the Forest this becomes waterlogged, and covers the miners in a grey film. The weight of the clay is supported on pit props made from Forest timber, although, as Robbie explained, 'The biggest problem we have isn't the roof coming down, it's the floor coming up.' This was due to the brute physics of mining: after the men removed the coal and mud, what was left rushed to fill the vacuum.

Once, men would have moved forward four feet or so every day in a mine like this, sometimes using gelignite to bring the rock down. Fathers worked alongside sons, the boys dragging carts ('hodding'), the men daubing their names or numbers on to the carts in lime to make sure they were paid for what they'd dug. A cart could weigh half a ton when full. There were wooden 'doors' in the mines, and boys as young as six opening and shutting them. This was to divert and regulate the flow of air, but also to admit horses trussed up in garish tack – masks, with candles burning at the crown. This headgear, designed to stop the horses from shying at the naked flames, helped them and their grooms to see in the gloom.

Suddenly in the open air once more, I reeled before the light-saturated noon, which had an overwhelming candlepower of its own. Emerging with Robbie out of a tunnel and into the ancient woods, I wouldn't have been surprised to see a royal hunting party jangling past in pursuit of boar.

By now, Robbie was telling me about his family, about his Uncle Arch, aka 'Buller', a miner like all the Morgans, also a drinker and a fighter. Once, at the end of the night shift, after putting all the unused gelignite away safely in the explosives tin, Buller found that he still had a stick of it on him, so he slipped it into his satchel. He went to the pub and then to bed. At nine in the evening, before he went back to work, his wife cooked him a meal, and just as he was sitting down by the heater to eat it, she emptied all the rubbish from his satchel into its fiery maw. 'It wouldn't have been so bad, only he had a detonator in there as well,' said Robbie. 'There was a bloody great bang and the grille of the Rayburn blew off! Can you imagine it, a stick of gelignite going off in your living-room?' The grille flew across the room and embedded itself in the opposite wall, a shard of glowing shrapnel. Buller was saved only because he was sitting to one side of the heater rather than in front of it. When the neighbours asked about the explosion, his wife claimed that she had put a tin of peas on to boil without piercing the can. 'But I don't think they believed that when they saw the huge crack in the wall!'

Before he stopped going out of an evening, Robbie's dad Les liked getting into scraps with Buller. The two of them would go to the pub on a Sunday, their only day off, in the hope of picking a fight with the gypsies, who also drank there. 'Us kids would go along and watch. I can remember Buller and my Dad fighting each other in the corridor of the pub. It was very narrow and the pair of them filled it.'

Robbie might not have had 'much up top', according to him, but he didn't get into trouble like his dad, and he was keeping the Phoenix going on scrounged spare parts and his own nous. 'I spotted a big steam boiler – they were going to cut him up for scrap, so I had him.' He had turned an old oil tank into a shed for his tools. 'You've got to improvise,' he told me.

But this resourceful man didn't give me the brush-off I was expecting when I asked him if he was alive to otherworldly phenomena like the mysterious powers of his dad, Les the levitator, who worked such wonders through those slugger's hands of his. Robbie caught me off-guard with a ghost story. It concerned a know-all he had once worked with, and how one day he had hidden from this man, so he thought, in the Phoenix, in a tunnel first dug in the 1830s. 'I could hear him walking towards me and I was hiding behind a cart, waiting to jump out on him, I suppose. Then I heard him stop. Well, I waited for him to carry on towards me, I waited as long as I could, and then I thought, Sod this! So I stood up, expecting him to say something clever, and there was nobody there!' Robbie laughed. 'Can you imagine if anyone had seen me, trying to scare a ghost like that?'

Soon, the only free miners in the Forest will be ghosts, or so it seems. From 1838 to 2007, a total of 4358 names were registered by the gaveller, but in the last decade only twenty-one young men came forward to claim their birthright. Free miners have become as elusive as the vanishing hare that their great-great-grandfathers pursued. There were seven mines left in November 2007, of which only two were producing coal (the others were on 'care and maintenance' or under development). Robbie told me, 'This is very likely to die out as a tradition because they've closed all the hospitals in the Forest of Dean. Now only children born at home will qualify.' Mind you, he added, a midwife who had visited his mining museum in recent months told him that there were still fifty births a year in the Forest, so perhaps all was not lost.

He was going back underground now. 'Well, I might see you again one day,' he said, almost fondly. He set off a little stiffly towards the mouth of a tunnel, another entrance to Phoenix mine. There was the churning sound of a fan. Robbie thought of something. He looked back over his shoulder. 'Only don't leave it too long, will you, because I'm already shaking on!'

Like the slates he has cut – *rived* – all his long life, 'Uncle' John Taylor of Honister is made of the same adamantine stuff as Robbie Morgan. But perhaps because he has lived beneath the big Lakeland sky, or because of the adventures he has had, he is ebullient and outgoing where his fellow miner from the Forest of Dean is harder to tease out. Another man might not have come back as strong as John did from the bomb blast that he suffered as an eighteen-year-old. A dab hand with gunpowder in a slate mine in his day, John was quick to add that the explosion had nothing to do with his career underground. 'It was what they call "friendly fire" these days,' he said, and laughed his deep, booming laugh. It happened at Bagshot, Surrey, where John was on manoeuvres with the Royal Horse Guards. Military surgeons, or perhaps the passage of time, had made a good job of his missing right eye. It was as if his brow creased over the socket, and his cheekbone stood proud to shield it. Had his appearance developed like this, these past fifty years or so, as a way of compensating for his wound? His good eye – grey-green, the colour of slate – was warm but clear; it didn't miss a thing. Unblinking, you might say.

The battlefield explosion cost John his best friend, who had been right beside him. 'He was also called Taylor. They thought *I'd* been killed. They told our mam it was me.' At this multiple heartache of so long ago, John could only laugh. I can hardly recall a moment with him at Honister when he *wasn't* laughing. What in others might have seemed wearing, even idiotic, was in John's case a handy barometer of the big man's mood. Only once all that day did his craggy countenance cloud over and his laughter cease. It was as he was telling me in a terse whisper, quite unlike the sonorous voice I'd grown used to, about a fellow slate-river who had annoyed him. It seemed such a trifling thing, as he outlined it, but there was no doubting its effect on John, or the pile-drivingly effective means he had chosen to restore his equilibrium. Uncle John's laugh was like a canary in a coal mine, I concluded: when it stopped, it was time to make a run for it.

On Fleetwith Pike, at the bottom of the slope where I had at last freed my karabiners and swung out across the plunging ravine – thereby joining the miners' mile-high club – Uncle John put things into perspective for me when he said that he himself had been accustomed to circumnavigate the mountain while leisurely clutching his tuck box – his 'bait bag'. We were following the rusty narrow-gauge rails of the old slate carts leading into the mine. Inside, we stopped to admire the way the old timers had put the tunnel together, slotting the slate around themselves as deftly as if they were dry-stone walling.

Slate is made of volcanic ash, settled in water millions of years ago and then compressed, which is what gives it its distinctive fine-grained quality. Glaciation exposed three parallel slate veins on the sides of the Gatesgarthdale valley, including Honister, each lying at an angle of thirty degrees to the horizontal. The first people to make a living off the mountain picked up the slate where it lay amid rocky outcrops. There was an established trade by Norman times, when monastic buildings were often roofed in slate. Indeed, it's thought that the monks of Furness Abbey were the first men to mine the material underground at Honister, in the mid-seventeenth century.

A hundred years later, tunnels, or 'levels', leading to chambers deep within the crag had been excavated – indeed, quarrying on a large scale, all carried out by the fitful illumination of tallow candles, was under way by 1750. The miners lived where they worked, inside the great bluff of the Pike, or else in rude bothies on the raw fellside. The slate was carried by pack-ponies for fifteen miles or so across sheer and treacherous fells to the nearest port, at Whitehaven. The damaged, unusable slate and the accompanying clay was simply tipped down the side of the mountain, to fall hundreds of feet on to the scree below.

Transportation links improved with the coming of the railway to Keswick in 1864, and with a road from Buttermere to Seatoller for horses and carts. But the most rapid, albeit hair-raising, means of getting Honister's products to market was 'handsledging' down a rattling Cresta Run of slate from the quarry to the road, a descent of seventeen miles. The men of Honister were alpinists, then, too, not only climbing the mountain but also luging to the bottom, laden with the fruits of their labour. Celia Weir Taylor, who is John's younger sister, writes, 'The youngest and fittest men were chosen for the task – practising first with an empty sledge, running in front holding onto the two shafts straight down the hillside to the road. The sledge run would be bedded down with fine shillies [small stones or gravel], enabling not only a smooth ride for the slates but also allowing the men to dig their heels in for more control of the 260lbs of slates. The only braking system was to press down harder on the shafts.' The men's downhill record at Honister was set by Joseph Clark in 1891, when he tobogganed a staggering payload of 10,880 pounds of slate to the road in a single day.

Uncle John told me that a good miner could produce a hundred tons a month. 'We used to get a bonus of a shilling a ton after we'd taken out eighty,' he said. 'It were two shillings after a hundred; three after a hundred and twenty.'

'Was it competitive?'

'*Very* competitive. I know the first time we earned £3 a day, it was a record.' Once, at the pictures in Keswick, John and the boys had seen a newsreel explaining the making of champagne, and they decided to celebrate their achievement in bubbly. They drank the Borrowdale Hotel dry. 'All the people were saying, "Honister must have had a good month – they're all drunk again!"'

John had a taste for the good things in life. With his wages and bonuses, he bought himself the boss's car: a Buick belonging to Commander Hoare, the man who owned the mine. 'It used to do sixty in first gear!' The sprauncy ride drew glances in the Lakes, not all of them admiring. Once, in Keswick, a man took it upon himself to dawdle across the road in front of the Buick. Gravely, John told me how he was compelled to step out of the vehicle and offer physical violence to this nuisance.

There are no fewer than eleven miles of tunnels in the mountainside. There's a cavern called 'Rat Trap', and another known as 'Fiddlers', where John showed me how he used to ram gunpowder into a groove in the rock, to expose the slate. 'We used to set it off last thing at night, so that all the dust had cleared by the time we came back again in the morning. Up there,' he said, pointing to a shelf high in the cavern, a kind of minstrel gallery, 'that's where a man called Pond Pepper fell and broke his back.'

The most astonishing thing John showed me was a metal railway, streaming with water and rising up inside the crag at an angle of 30 degrees – though it looked even more vertiginous. Nine hundred feet long, it stretched above us into the blackness and reached to the very top of the Pike. Miners worked in side passages off this track, and the slate that they dug out was put into carts and winched down the water-plashing rails. It was all too easy to imagine a clog slipping out of a winch chain or rolling in the wrong direction, and taking a miner or two with it. In fact, it was incredible to think that this underground railway had ever been built, let alone that men had made their tortuous living from it every day. Here was another stunning sighting of England's great subterranean berg, the undreamt-of mass that lurks just beneath the surface of the everyday.

The mining tradition at Honister so nearly slid away altogether. Although slate from Honister has roofed the finest hotels in London and kept the rain off the Establishment at Buckingham Palace and Scotland Yard, the mine was undercut by cheaper competitors in Wales and overseas, and finally by manmade materials. When it closed in 1986, Uncle John's days of Buicks and bubbly appeared to be behind him. The mine at the heart of the lonely pass was abandoned for a decade or more, the carts' rails rusting, the remorseless Cumbrian weather finding its way into the tunnels, the roads on the mountain washed away. But then one day John's nephew Mark, restaurateur and helicopter pilot, was flying his grandfather over the pass when the old boy said how sad it was to see the mine in ruins, the place where generations of the family's menfolk had worked. This sparked in Mark, entrepreneur and wunderkind of the Taylor clan, an ambitious if not downright foolhardy scheme to bring Honister back to life again.

It was Mark's helicopter I had looked down on during my ascent of Fleetwith Pike, shuttling him to an appointment elsewhere in Lakeland. For some reason, the sight made me think of the film *Jurassic Park*. Perhaps it was the notion of an isolated community built – *rebuilt* – to the well-intentioned whim of one man, in surroundings that were less than hospitable. I had seen pictures of Mark and heard him interviewed. He was forty-two but looked younger. He reminded me of Jamie Oliver – his youth, his background in the hospitality trade, a certain blokey accessibility.

It was late afternoon, and I was thawing out over a bowl of soup at the mine, when Mark choppered back to Honister for a chat. He was wearing a grimy jacket zipped up to the chin, and a chunky pilot's watch. He could make more money elsewhere, he agreed, but he wanted to live in the Lakes, to develop something that would contribute to the area. After he bought Honister mine, he worked seven days a week at first, he said, sometimes putting in a twenty-four-hour 'shift' there. 'It was hell. Really, it was hell.' His hands swept the wooden table in broad arcs, palms down.

I mentioned my time with Uncle John, and Mark told me how the pair of them had nearly fallen out over the mine. Mark had taken him on with the warning that he couldn't afford to pay him. 'Pay me when you can,' said John. There had been so much debris to remove before mining could resume in earnest. Mark decided that the job called for a small underground train – 'I don't know how we got it up here with just a Land Rover.' The man who sold him the train warned that he would need to charge the battery up, but he would have to run it down first until it was flat, rather like a mobile phone. Uncle John, watching Mark drive the miniature train back and forth all day, lost patience with his new boss. 'If you keep riding up and down in your choo-choo train, I'm off,' he said. And with that, he was.

Mark said, 'We didn't see John again for days. When he finally reappeared, we went into the mine together to look at all the rubble.'

'Right, then,' said John heavily. 'I'll see you in six months.'

Mark calculated that the train could shift the spoil much faster than John's six months, which was based on his experience of digging out a mine by hand. Three days later, he invited his uncle back to Honister. The same chamber was now clear of debris. 'Choo choo train!' Mark said. And John immediately held out his hand. 'He could see I was right, and he's a big enough man to admit it.'

Now Honister was producing slate again – tiles, funerary headstones and dressed slabs for kitchens and bathrooms. Mark had installed new machinery, including a crusher that produced the granular slate that builders and gardeners demand. The stuff that the miners had once discarded down the mountainside was now where the money was. Honister was also drawing visitors, just as it had in Victorian times when top-hatted tourists would take the charabanc from the smart hotels of Keswick as far as Seatoller, and climb the rest of the way up a steep track, 'The worst road in the land'. Mark had plans to convert one underground chamber into an amphitheatre: the jazz saxophonist Snake Davis had already tested its acoustics. Mark thought he might have found an angle on the overcrowded mineral-water market. So many people had remarked on what a good brew they made at the mine, he thought he might enter Honister in a tea-making challenge. Practically all of Mark's family was employed at the mine: Uncle Bill, and Celia, Mark's Mum, as well as John, of course.

I thought of the story John had told me, the one that he recounted under his breath in a terse voice, and made him stop laughing. It involved another mine-worker, who was also something of a body-builder. 'He fancied himself,' said John derisively. There had been some sort of dispute over a clog – a matter of where it should go, perhaps, or who should shift it. I imagined that Uncle John's co-worker had no inkling of how this annoyed him, or what was about to happen. 'I dropped him,' said John matter-of-factly. He was fifty-seven years old at the time. All it took was one blow. I didn't doubt it: I wouldn't fancy taking John on *now*, a one-eyed man in his seventies. 'This lad was all into weight-lifting and eating the right stuff but he wasn't brought up hard,' said John. He laughed, the old Uncle John once more. 'Oh, it's been a grand life. A make-believe life.'

AFTERWORD

WORMHOLES REDUX

Out of a clear blue cosmos, a wormhole appeared: yes, the Wormhole Caves of Wallasey. They, and the white villa that stood on top of them, belonged to a pharmacist, and I thought it a kind of alchemy to find myself at last among these curious features of the upside-down empyrean. After I had been to see them with Gerry the Green Badge guide, and got no further than a padlocked wicket in a garden overlooking Liverpool bay, I had been in correspondence with the owner, Dr Cubbin, and this genial, bespectacled apothecary had turned the base metal of hope into the glimmering krugerrand of reality.

Which makes it all the more shaming to admit that by the time I approached the Wormhole at last, doubt had entered my mind, like sea water in a grotto: I was wondering if I had built up my hopes of the caves too high. After all, they were sandstone crannies under a house, as far as I was aware, perhaps no more roomy than the ones I had known in my grandmother's old place a few streets away on Victoria Road. I was going to look for those, too. I was wondering how much the strange, concertinaing effect of time – the wormhole of the years – might have altered the proportions of Nana's back kitchen. Long ago, it had been something to be lost in Ali Baba's spud-scented cave. What had become of it, under the auspices of the dance studio and the Chandleresque detective agency which had succeeded my family on the premises?

Hidden behind the sandstone promontories of Wallasey, otherwise known as the Red and Yellow Noses, the Wormhole Caves had once been linked to a smugglers' network, with entries from several points of the lawless shoreline. But these nooks had been sealed up. A cluster of caves adjoining Dr Cubbin's villa had taken a direct hit in the war from a German aircraft jettisoning its bombs on the way home; these too were inaccessible. In truth, I was expecting a utility room or a coal-bunker, a domestic grot like Nana's – though none the worse for that. I little imagined that I would shortly be saying to Dr Cubbin, with the full weight of the imperfect cavern connoisseurship at my command, 'These may be the finest caves in private hands in this country.' It was the sort of thing that was fun to say, and perhaps fun for the good doctor to hear; he chuckled indulgently, at any rate. But it was sincerely meant, for all that. In my travels I had plunged into the abyss of Gaping Gill – the Yorkshire canyon has rightly been compared to a cathedral, and I was like a rapidly defenestrating stained-glass-fitter; I had crawled to the heart of the Sphinx-like monument of Silbury Hill; but I never felt more like Indiana Jones than when the medicine man at last opened the padlock on the door beneath his brick amphitheatre, and led me down steps as crumbly as old teeth to the extraordinary mermaid's grotto forty feet or more beneath his house.

What was magically opening up around us was a high-ceilinged chamber with a whiff of the sea and a palpable tang of salt. It was utterly dark, apart from the beam of Dr Cubbin's torch. It was a scene out of *Moonfleet*, or perhaps the poem by George Wither reproduced in the pages of that yarn: 'The strange music of the waves/Beating on these hollow caves'. The Irish Sea had once boxed the old Red and Yellow Noses square on the hooter; the tide had slapped against the sandstone until the 1930s, when it was finally fended off by the King's Promenade, itself the product of the rock and clay thrown up by the Mersey Tunnel works. A golf course was laid between the prom and Dr Cubbin's house. Now the caves began behind a wall just off a fairway; they ran for some 250 yards, all the way under the good doctor's property to the railway line, the same one that had brought Gerry and me from Liverpool to see the caves in the first place.

Like a true Einsteinian wormhole, like the best subterranean passage, this was a conduit through time. At the rear of the system, men had scored faces into the sandstone: these recalled the grave, worshipful frieze left by the Knights Templar under the bookmaker's in Royston. Another gouged, all but indecipherable, grafitto was no more than a date, a year. It began '16 . . .'

The property overhead was originally built around 1835 as a summer residence by Peter Greenall, of the brewing dynasty Greenall Whitley. He would entertain to breakfast the commandant of Fort Perch Rock, a battery erected a mile or so down the shore as a bulwark against Napoleon. This officer would ride his mount along the beach and tie him up at the Noses; with a jangle of spurs, he would stomp through the cleft just where Dr Cubbin and I were standing, and ascend another cave system before throwing up a trapdoor in the family dining-room and addressing himself to the kedgeree. The commandant's caves became inaccessible after a direct hit on the courtyard, where a second stick of German bombs fell to earth.

'And here – here's the bed they used,' said Dr Cubbin.

'They?'

'The people who lived here, whoever they were.' Sure enough, my host's light picked out a sandstone ledge, long and wide enough for a man to lie on, in one chamber of the caves; and rudimentary shelves, carved out of the stone. The troglodytes to whom Dr Cubbin referred were temporary inhabitants, in all probability – men dodging Navy press-gangs, as well as runners of grog and baccy – though he made them sound like a mysterious, long-lost race, and it wasn't too difficult to imagine them that way when you were in their strange, salt-saturated habitat.

There were other denizens, too. 'We had a skull taken from here,' said Dr Cubbin. He had no idea how old it was but it had been in the Wormhole Caves for as long as he'd had them, for as long as the previous owner had been in possession, too. Youngsters broke into the tunnels; perhaps the same ones who left beer cans and knickers in the adjacent coppice, and laid their fires there. Maybe they had snatched the blanched noggin. Dr Cubbin had learnt, from the old boy who'd had the place before him, not to inquire too closely as to what else might have been dry-cured down here in the caves. Each bony find brought a visit from the coroner.

The naturalist Richard Mabey has written about Victorian entomologists who coined the word 'dusking' to describe their evening expeditions. 'They'd go out in the twilight with lanterns and sugar snares, hoping to lure the ghostly creatures into their nets. Hapless moths apart, I rather like the idea of dusking.' Well, hapless moths apart, I rather did, too. So much so that I was inclined to poach it, as if it were itself a collectable red admiral. The phrase seemed to capture something of the footloose business of butterfly-netting after history in the half-light of the subterranean. This was why I was here. The fascination of travelling the English underground lay in coming upon the unseen, the unexpected – the unimagined. This was the payoff for posting myself through the Letterbox in Alum Pot, for wriggling into priest-holes, for wedging myself in a nook of the secret complex at Corsham. Who would guess at the presence of such curios who only rambled over the dales, or motored through the Welsh Marches, or merely rode through Brunel's Box Tunnel on the rattler to Bristol? It was the fugitive nature of this hidden England that made it so appealing. Its attractions were out of sight, but not out of mind. Why did I want to see them, to bag them? Because they weren't there.

Dr Cubbin was a busy man – a pharmaceutist who commanded the lecture theatre as well as the dispensary; a leading Liverpool clubman; a father of three – and my entertaining tour of his home caught something of the man himself. I saw the grand piano, the ballroom, the winded bouncy castle. Exiting the cool, rock-lined wine cellar, we stepped into the shortest of corridors, little more than a pace and a half in length.

'Walls!' declared Dr Cubbin. I must have looked as baffled as I felt because he had to repeat himself before I caught his drift: it wasn't a corridor at all, it seemed, but a section through a monstrous wall, a fifty-two-inch thick buttress which perhaps helped to explain how the house that Greenall built was still standing over its massive pit. In an outhouse, Dr Cubbin showed me more home improvements. What lay behind these stout shorings-up, he demanded of me? The answer was yet another cave system. The former occupier, Norman Kingham, had had them sealed off. 'He was an architect, away from home a lot. He did it for his wife, to give her peace of mind.'

It seemed that a domestic who'd worked at the house a long time ago, perhaps in Greenall's day, had had a child, a daughter. 'The girl went into these caves one day and never came out,' said Dr Cubbin.

'You're a man of reason, doctor,' I protested. 'A son of the Enlightenment. You don't believe in that kind of thing!'

'I'm not sensitive to ghosts, no,' he said. 'But I've had builders at the house who won't be on their own on the lower floors.'

There were no ghosts to fear at Seacliff, Nana's old Wallasey home, or if there were, the builders whom I found there seemed to be taking these shades in their stride. Alan and Dave were having their lunch in the yard, a spot of salad at a trestle table. The outside loo, Uncle Stephen's sheds – these things had gone. Instead there were patio heaters, decking. I asked after the dance studio.

'They had pamper days,' said Alan in a clarifying tone. 'You know: massage, spa. The lad who ran it also had a detective agency.'

'Did he?' I was delighted to have this confirmed.

'Yeah, in the end he found there was just too much paperwork in the pamper-day thing so he packed it in, concentrated on the detecting.'

But not even that had proved worthwhile, and the hardboiled gumshoe of New Brighton had sold up to Alan and Dave. They'd sunk quite a bit of money into Seacliff and Hazeldene next door, as well as plenty of craftsmanship and care. I wandered through the ground floor of Hazeldene. I went into the sitting-room where Auntie Ethel had played sonatas and show tunes for the commercial travellers and the theatrical turns who stayed at the hotel, the repertory company of guests. Ethel's salon was now part of a two-bedroom apartment, awaiting making good. The rest of the place was already sold off, occupied, including my grandparents' old rooms on the lower ground floor. The stairs down to them weren't as steep as they had been; their home seemed smaller altogether.

'My sister and I were talking about the basement, about the scullery. We remember it as a kind of cave—'

'Yes,' said Dave, the taller of the entrepreneurial pair.

'That's right.' Alan said they'd found a big cave at the bottom of Hazeldene, too. 'A scullery, as you say, or a coal hole.'

'That's where I used to scoop out the ice cream for the desserts.'

Alan and Dave had filled the caves in; there wasn't really the call for them these days, they said. I was disappointed that I couldn't see them, but there was compensation in the story that

Alan and Dave told me about their open day. This was part of their marketing strategy for the apartments. They'd gathered from more than one visitor to the open day that the houses had been a home for distressed submariners in the 1920s, before Nana's time. These men had been traumatised by sinkings and scuttlings in the Great War. They were the original nervous wrecks, shivering and shaking on the seabed. I imagined them sitting in their roll-neck sweaters and caps in the rocky cool of Seacliff, as it would later become. Perhaps some kind of primitive aversion therapy had seen them installed underground, in an environment that was calculated to remind them of Fingal's Cave. Maybe the modish medical opinion of the day was that these sailors had a psychological version of the bends, and could only gradually be brought to the surface again.

I'd like to think that these jangled U-boaters came to appreciate the sheltering solidity of Nana's cave-house, just as her grandchildren did, and that they were transported from their troubles by its craggy consolations.

SELECT BIBLIOGRAPHY

Bacon, Jean and Stuart, *The Search for Dunwich: City Under the Sea* (n.p.: Segment Publications, 1979)

Bede (trans. Leo Shorley-Price and D. H. Farmer), *Ecclesiastical History of the English People* (London: Penguin, 2003) [*Historia ecclesiastica gentis Anglorum* completed 731]

Brue, Alexia, *Cathedrals of the Flesh: In Search of the Perfect Bath* (London: Bloomsbury, 2003)

Burnley, Kenneth, and Guy Huntington, *Images of Wirral: A Celebration in Words and Photographs of a Unique Peninsula* (Heswall: Silver Birch Press, 1991)

Camm, Dom Bede, *The Life of Saint John Wall, OFM* (Kidderminster: Harvington Hall, 1972)

Carver, Martin, *Sutton Hoo: Burial Ground of Kings?* (London: British Museum Press, 1998)

Chippindale, Christopher, *Stonehenge Complete* (London: Thames & Hudson, 1983)

Coad, J. G., *Hellfire Corner: Dover Castle's Secret Tunnels and the Dunkirk Evacuation* (London: English Heritage, 1993)

Comfort, Nicholas, *The Lost City of Dunwich* (Lavenham: Terence Dalton, 1994)

Crawford, Harriet (ed.), *Subterranean Britain: Aspects of Underground Archaeology* (London: John Baker, 1979)

David, Sister Mary (ed.), 'Living Stones, The Story of Malling Abbey' (Malling Abbey)

Defoe, Daniel, *A Tour Through the Whole Island of Great Britain* (London: Penguin 2005; first published 1724–27)

Durrant, Chris, *Basil Brown, Astronomer, Archaeologist, Enigma: A Biography* (London: National Trust, 2004)

Errand, Jeremy, *Secret Passages and Hiding-Places* (Newton Abbot: David & Charles, 1974)

Falkner, J. Meade, *Moonfleet* (London: Penguin, 2007; first published 1898)

Fernande, Marianne, and Jessica Rutherford, *A Prince's Passion: The Life of the Royal Pavilion* (Brighton: Brighton and Hove City Council, 2003)

Gemmell, A., and J. O. Myers, *Underground Adventure* (Castle Cary: Mendip, 1990)

Gillett, John E., *Of Caves and Caving: A Way of Life* (Lincoln, NE: Writers Club Press, 2002)

Hall, Sarah, *Haweswater* (London: Faber, 2002)

Hodgetts, Michael, *Life at Harvington 1250–2000* (Birmingham: Archdiocese of Birmingham Historical Commission, 2002)

Hughes, Pat, 'Hindlip Hall' (Desk Top Publishing)

Le Vay, Benedict, *Eccentric Britain: The Bradt Guide to Britain's Follies and Foibles* (Chalfont St Peter: Bradt, 2000)

Lesser, Wendy, *The Life Below Ground: A Study of the Subterranean in Literature and History* (London: Faber, 1987)

Lovelock, James, *Life and Death Underground* (London: G. Bell, 1963)

Mabey, Richard, *Nature Cure* (London: Pimlico, 2006)

Macfarlane, Robert, *The Wild Places* (London: Granta, 2007)

Major, Alan P., *Hidden Kent* (Newbury: Countryside Books, 1994)

Marshall, Des, and Donald Rust, *Selected Caves of Britain and Ireland* (Hinckley: Cordee, 1997)

McCamley, N. J., *Secret Underground Cities: An Account of Some of Britain's Subterranean Defence, Factory and Storage Sites in the Second World War* (Barnsley: Leo Cooper, 1998)

Moore, Jim, *Underground Liverpool* (Liverpool: Bluecoat Press, 1998)

Pennick, Nigel, *The Subterranean Kingdom: A Survey of Man-Made Structures Beneath the Earth* (Wellingborough: Turnstone Press, 1981)

Peverley, John, *Dover's Hidden Fortress: The History and Preservation of the Western Heights Fortifications* (Dover: Dover Society, 1996)

Preston, John, *The Dig* (London: Viking, 2007)

Richardson, Tim, *The Arcadian Friends: Inventing the English Landscape Garden* (London: Bantam, 2007)

Rook, Tony, *Roman Baths in Britain* (Princes Risborough: Shire Archaeology, 1992)

Roud, Steve, *The English Year: A Month-by-Month Guide to the Nation's Customs and Festivals, from May Day to Mischief Night* (London: Penguin, 2006)

Savage, Robert J. G., *Natural History of the Goldney Garden Grotto, Clifton, Bristol* (Bristol: University of Bristol, 1989)

Sebald, W. G. (trans. Michael Hulse), *The Rings of Saturn* (London: Vintage, 2002)

Taylor, Michael Ray, *Cave Passages: Roaming the Underground Wilderness* (London: Vintage, 1997)

Verne, Jules, *Journey to the Centre of the Earth* (London: Penguin, 2007; first published in English 1871)

Waltham, Tony, *Sandstone Caves of Nottingham* (Nottingham: East Midlands Geological Society, 1996)

Watson, Sally, *Secret Underground Bristol* (Bristol: Broadcast Books, 2002)

Wells, H. G., *The War of the Worlds* (London: Penguin, 2005; first published 1898)

Westwood, Jennifer, and Jacqueline Simpson, *The Lore of the Land: A Guide to England's Legends, from Spring-Heeled Jack to the Witches of Warboys* (London: Penguin, 2005)

Wolfe, David W., *Tales from the Underground* (New York: Perseus, 2001)

INDEX